DAREDEVIL

DAREDEVIL

DAREDEVIL: THE MOVIE

Writer-**Bruce Jones**
Penciler-**Manuel Garcia**
Inker-**Scott Hanna**
Colors-**Chris Sotomayor**
Letters-**Dave Sharpe with Cory Petit**
Based on the Screenplay by **Mark Steven Johnson**
Editor-**Andrew Lis**
Painted cover by **Brian Stelfreeze**

ULTIMATE DAREDEVIL & ELEKTRA #1

Writer-**Greg Rucka**
Penciler-**Salvador Larroca**
Inker-**Danny Miki**
Colors-**UDON Studios**
Letters-**Chris Eliopoulos**
Editor-**Jennifer Lee**
Cover by **Salvador Larroca**

DAREDEVIL #32

Writer-**Brian Michael Bendis**
Artist-**Alex Maleev**
Colors-**Matt Hollingsworth**
Letters-**Richard Starkings & Comicraft's Jason Levine**
Editor-**Stuart Moore**
Associate Managing Editor-**Kelly Lamy**
Managing Editor-**Nanci Dakesian**
Cover by **Alex Maleev**

SPIDER-MAN'S TANGLED WEB #4

Writer-**Greg Rucka**
Artist-**Eduardo Risso**
Colors-**Steve Buccellato**
Letters-**Richard Starkings & Comicraft's Wes Abbott**
Assistant Editor-**John Miesegaes**
Editor-**Axel Alonso**
Cover by **Eduardo Risso**

DAREDEVIL: THE MOVIE. Contains material originally published in magazine form as DAREDEVIL: MOVIE ADAPTATION, DAREDEVIL (Vol. 2) #32, ULTIMATE DAREDEVIL A[ ] ELEKTRA #1 and SPIDER-MAN'S TANGLED WEB #4. First printing 2003. ISBN# 0-7851-0959-5. Published by MARVEL COMICS, a division of MARVEL ENTERTAINMENT GRO[ ] INC. OFFICE OF PUBLICATION: 10 East 40th Street, New York, NY 10016. Copyright © 2001, 2002 and 2003 Marvel Characters, Inc. All rights reserved. DAREDEVIL: THE MOV[ ] Copyright © Fox and Regency Ent. (USA). All rights reserved. $12.99 per copy in the U.S. and $21.00 in Canada (GST #R127032852); Canadian Agreement #40668537. All ch[ ] acters featured in this issue and the distinctive names and likenesses thereof, and all related indicia are trademarks of Marvel Characters, Inc. No similarity between any of names, characters, persons, and/or institutions in this magazine with those of any living or dead person or institution is intended, and any such similarity which may exist is pu[ ] ly coincidental. **Printed in Canada.** STAN LEE, Chairman Emeritus. For information regarding advertising in Marvel Comics or on Marvel.com, please contact Russell Brow[ ] Executive Vice President, Consumer Products, Promotions and Media Sales at 212-576-8561 or rbrown@marvel.com

10 9 8 7 6 5 4 3 2 1

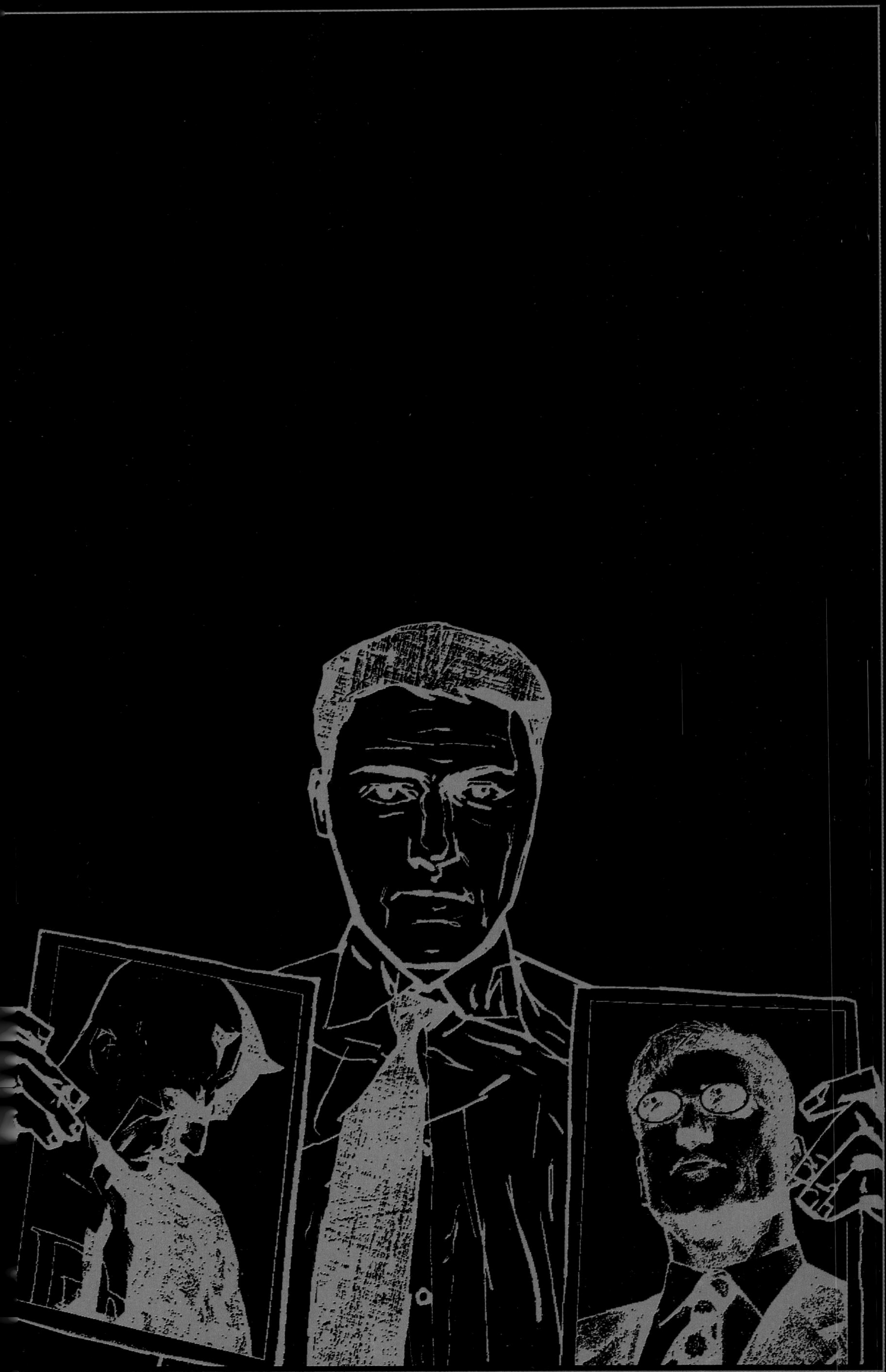

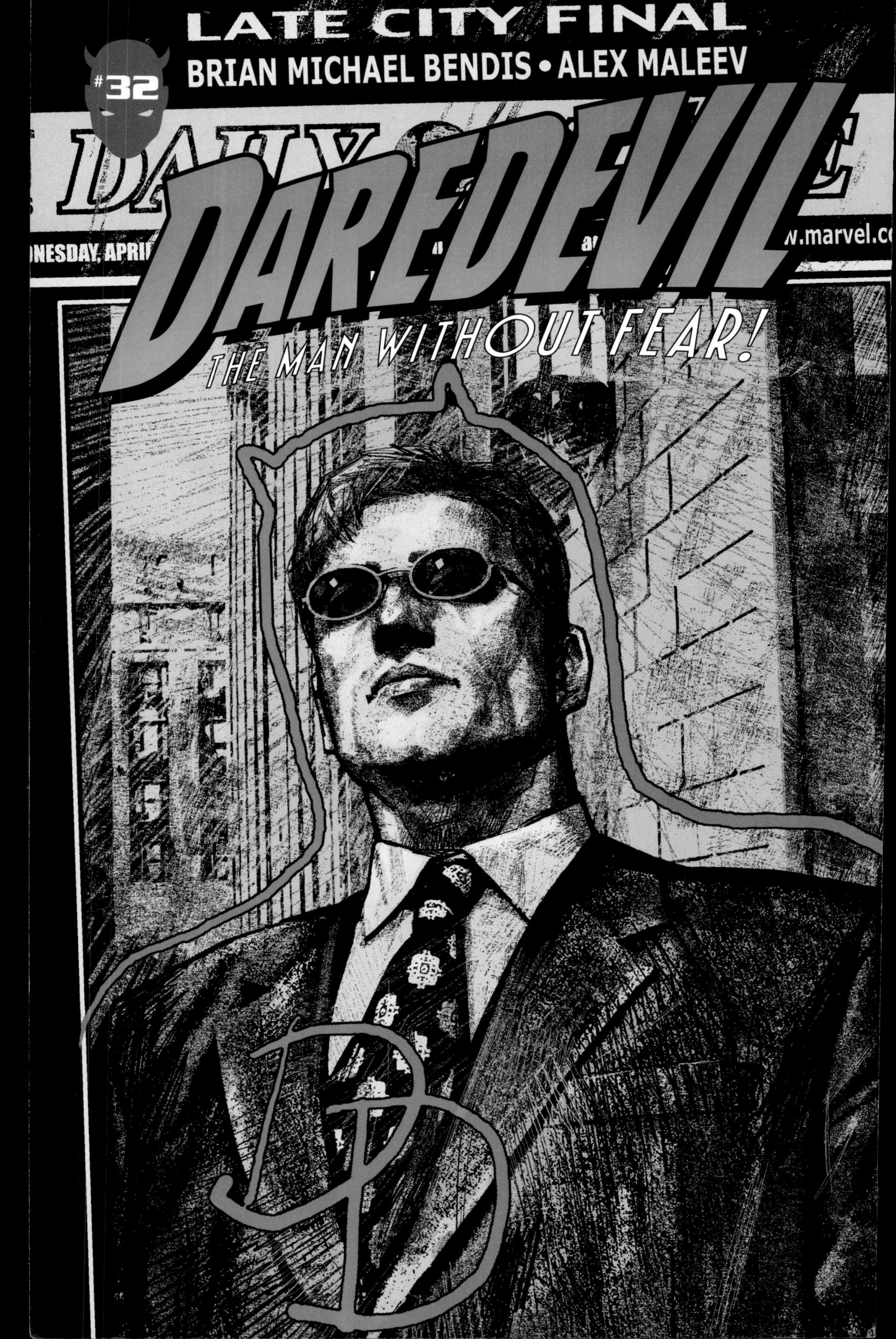
LATE CITY FINAL
#32
BRIAN MICHAEL BENDIS • ALEX MALEEV
DAREDEVIL
THE MAN WITHOUT FEAR!

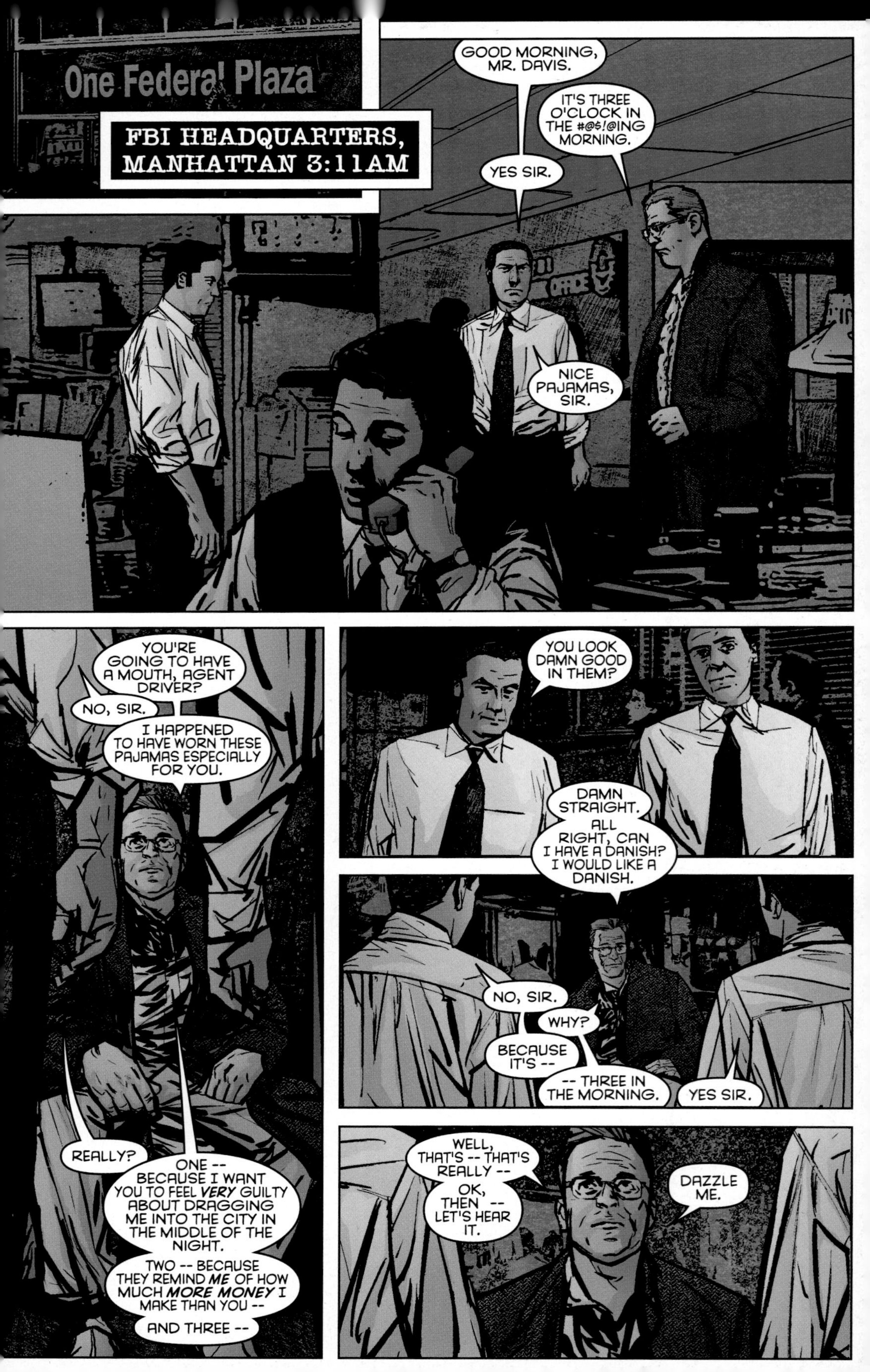
One Federal Plaza
FBI HEADQUARTERS, MANHATTAN 3:11AM
GOOD MORNING, MR. DAVIS.
IT'S THREE O'CLOCK IN THE #@$!@ING MORNING.
YES SIR.
NICE PAJAMAS, SIR.
YOU'RE GOING TO HAVE A MOUTH, AGENT DRIVER?
NO, SIR.
I HAPPENED TO HAVE WORN THESE PAJAMAS ESPECIALLY FOR YOU.
REALLY?
ONE -- BECAUSE I WANT YOU TO FEEL *VERY* GUILTY ABOUT DRAGGING ME INTO THE CITY IN THE MIDDLE OF THE NIGHT.
TWO -- BECAUSE THEY REMIND *ME* OF HOW MUCH *MORE MONEY* I MAKE THAN YOU --
AND THREE --
YOU LOOK DAMN GOOD IN THEM?
DAMN STRAIGHT.
ALL RIGHT, CAN I HAVE A DANISH? I WOULD LIKE A DANISH.
NO, SIR.
WHY?
BECAUSE IT'S --
-- THREE IN THE MORNING.
YES SIR.
WELL, THAT'S -- THAT'S REALLY --
OK, THEN -- LET'S HEAR IT.
DAZZLE ME.

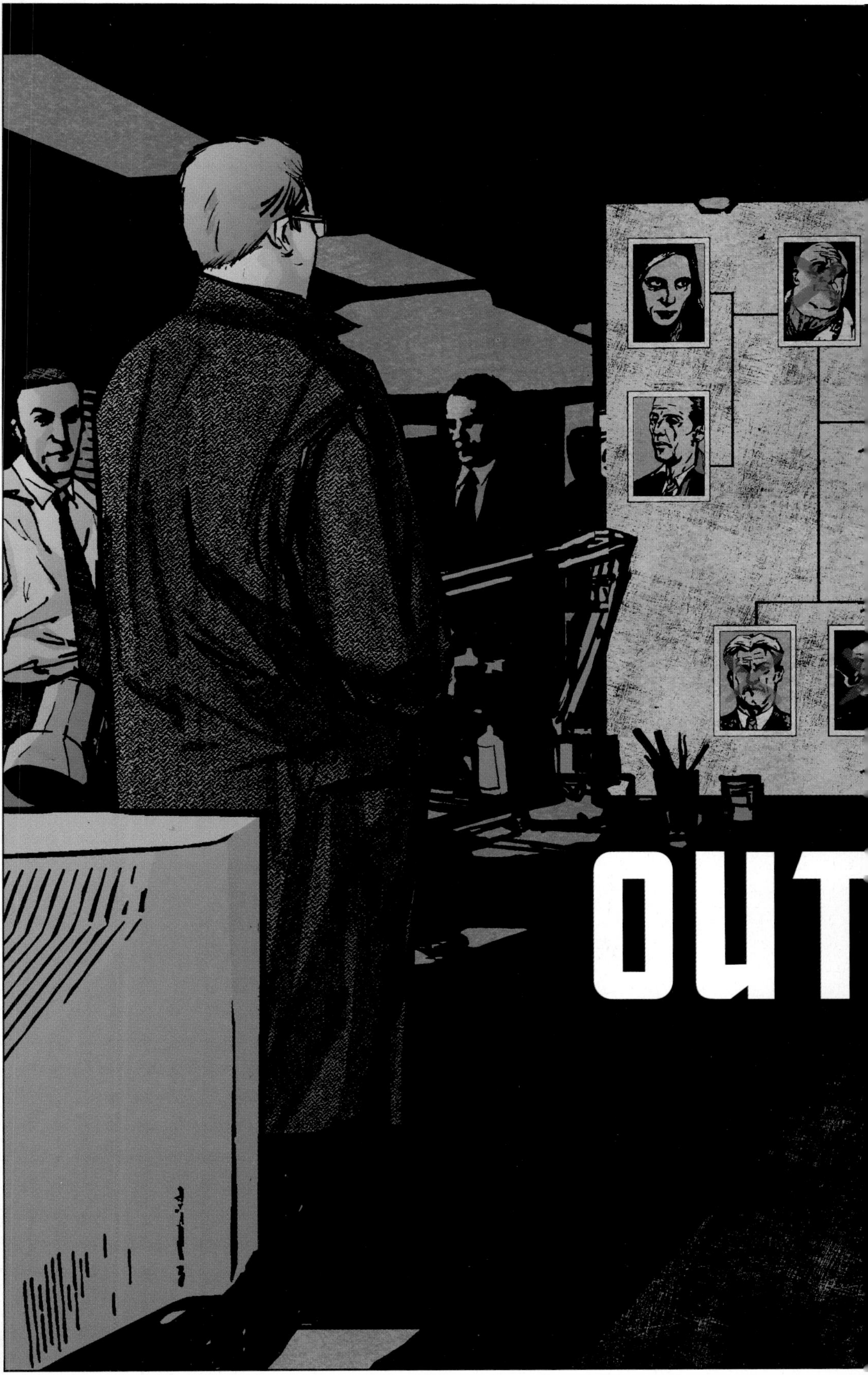
OUT

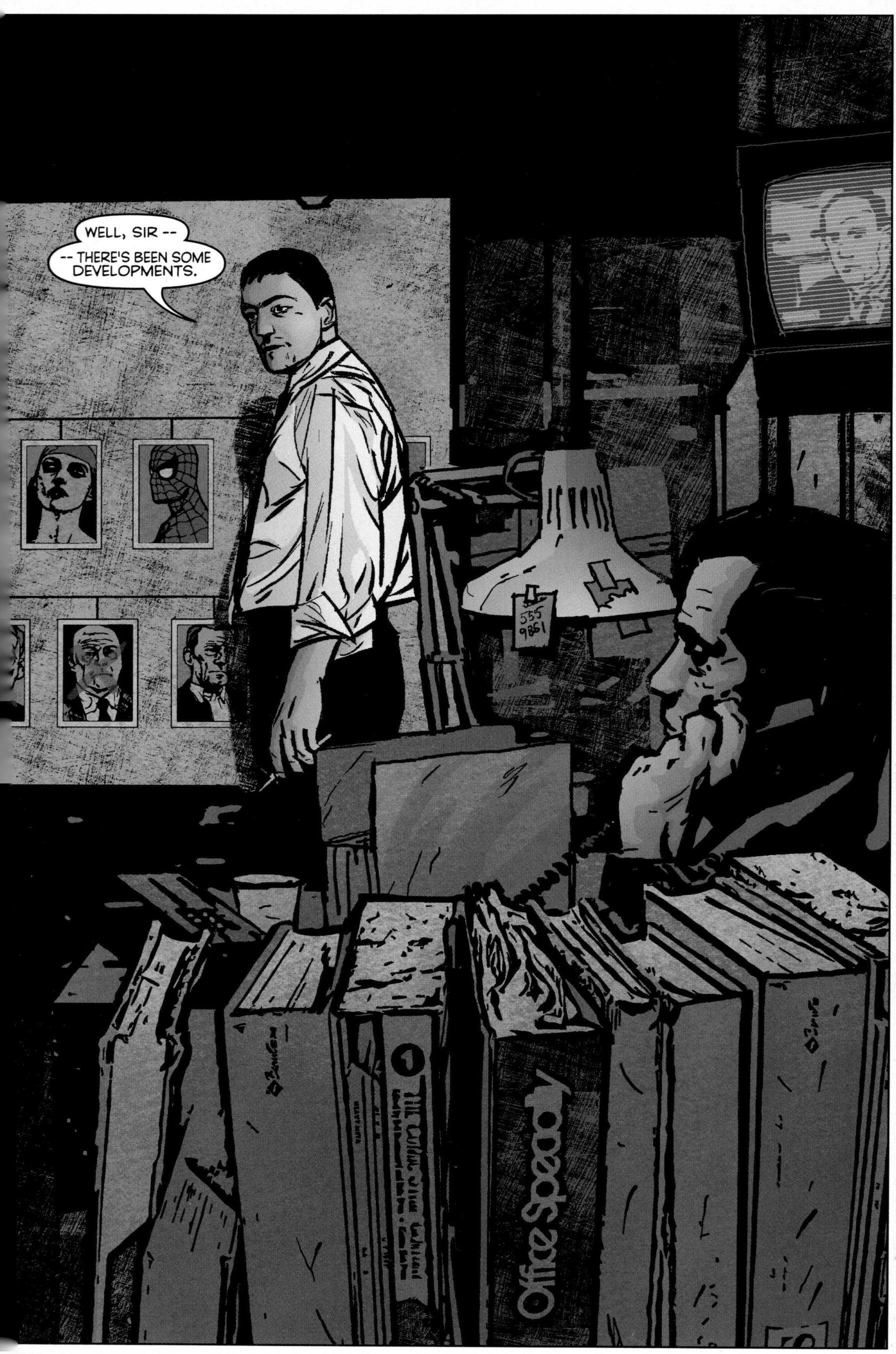
WELL, SIR --
-- THERE'S BEEN SOME DEVELOPMENTS.
555 9861

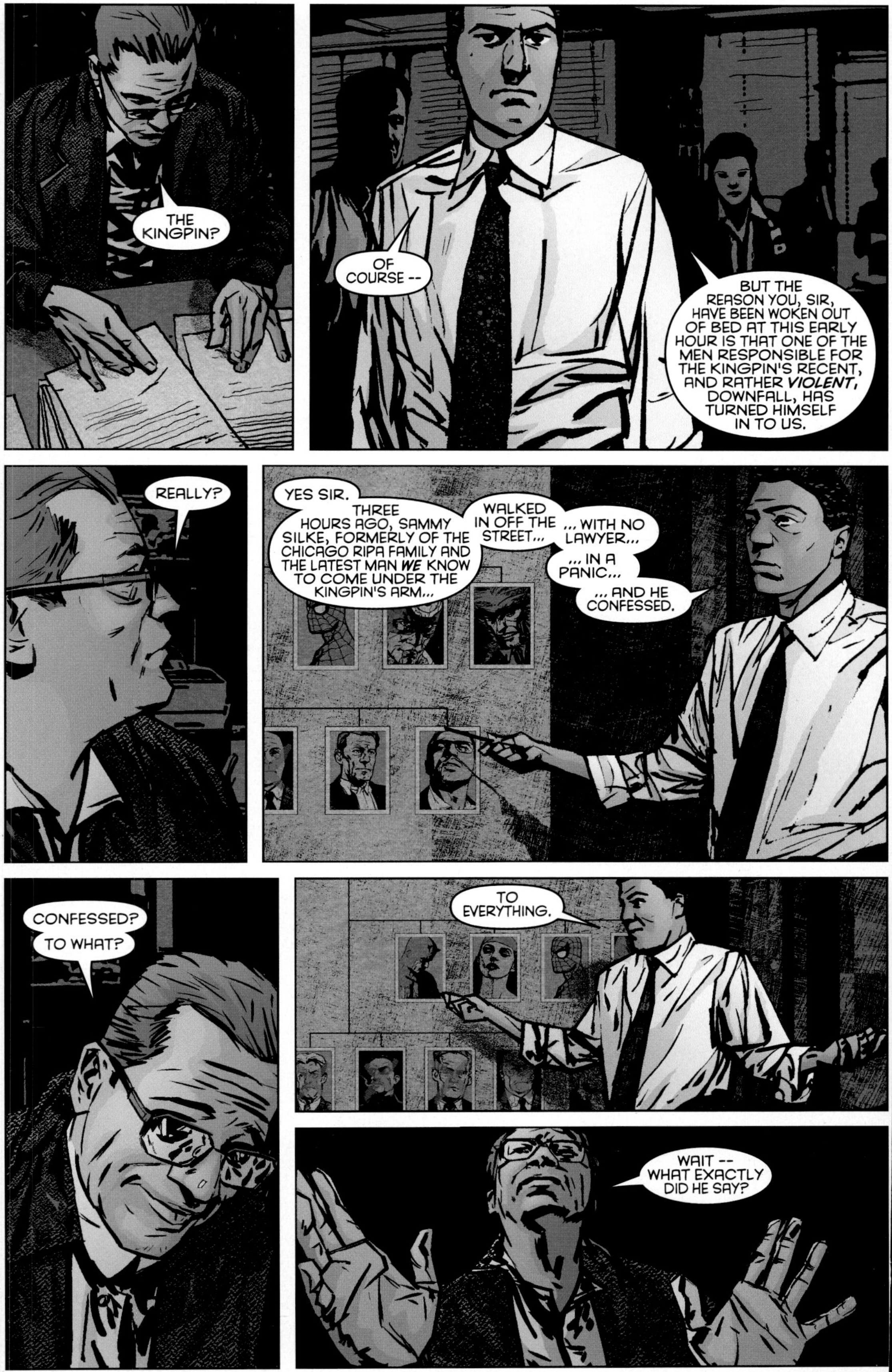
THE KINGPIN?
OF COURSE --
BUT THE REASON YOU, SIR, HAVE BEEN WOKEN OUT OF BED AT THIS EARLY HOUR IS THAT ONE OF THE MEN RESPONSIBLE FOR THE KINGPIN'S RECENT, AND RATHER VIOLENT, DOWNFALL, HAS TURNED HIMSELF IN TO US.
REALLY?
YES SIR. THREE HOURS AGO, SAMMY SILKE, FORMERLY OF THE CHICAGO RIPA FAMILY AND THE LATEST MAN WE KNOW TO COME UNDER THE KINGPIN'S ARM...
WALKED IN OFF THE STREET...
... WITH NO LAWYER...
... IN A PANIC...
... AND HE CONFESSED.
CONFESSED? TO WHAT?
TO EVERYTHING.
WAIT -- WHAT EXACTLY DID HE SAY?

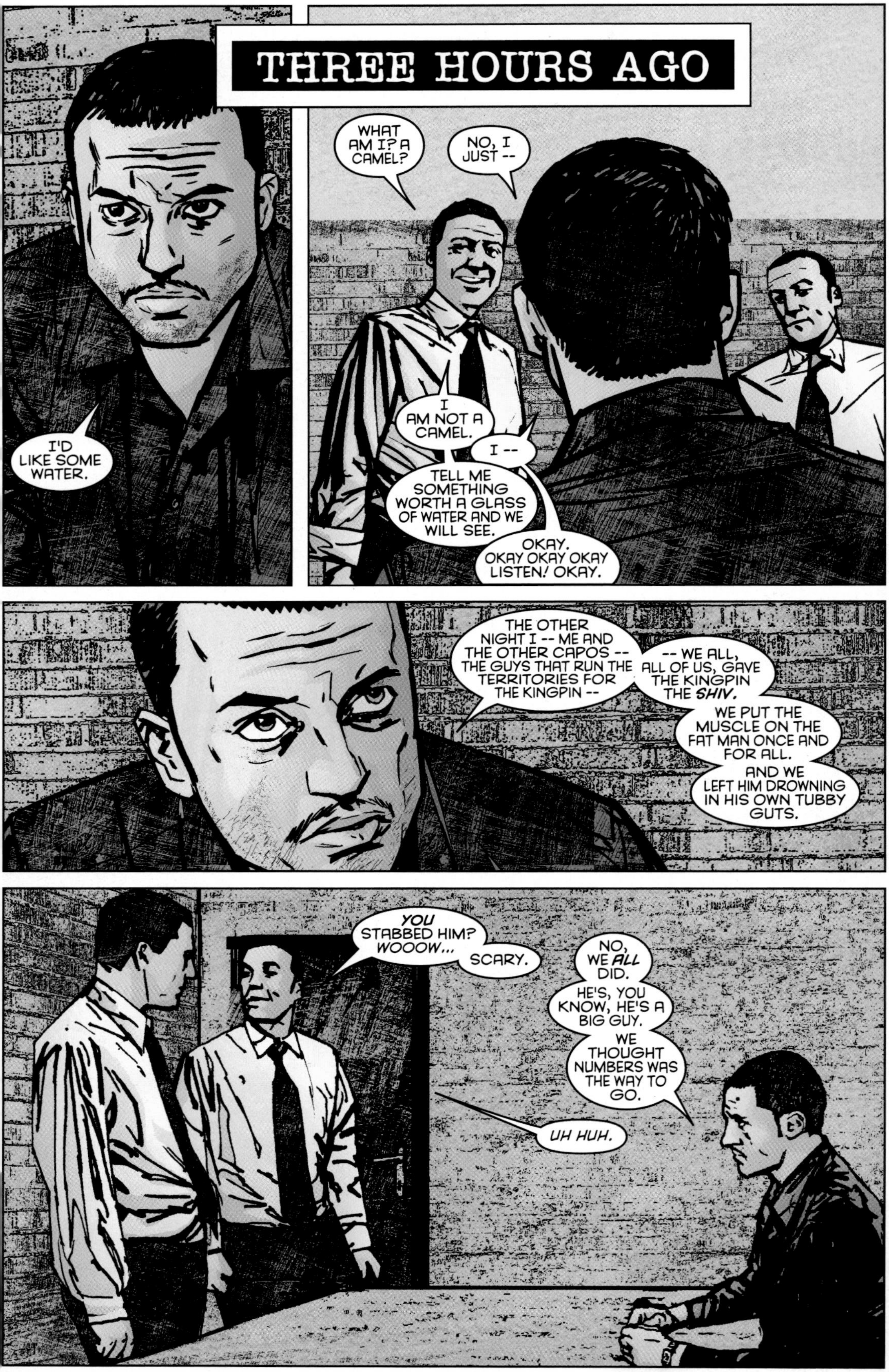
THREE HOURS AGO
I'D LIKE SOME WATER.
WHAT AM I? A CAMEL?
NO, I JUST --
I AM NOT A CAMEL.
I --
TELL ME SOMETHING WORTH A GLASS OF WATER AND WE WILL SEE.
OKAY. OKAY OKAY OKAY LISTEN! OKAY.
THE OTHER NIGHT I -- ME AND THE OTHER CAPOS -- THE GUYS THAT RUN THE TERRITORIES FOR THE KINGPIN --
-- WE ALL, ALL OF US, GAVE THE KINGPIN THE SHIV.
WE PUT THE MUSCLE ON THE FAT MAN ONCE AND FOR ALL.
AND WE LEFT HIM DROWNING IN HIS OWN TUBBY GUTS.
YOU STABBED HIM? WOOOW...
SCARY.
NO, WE ALL DID.
HE'S, YOU KNOW, HE'S A BIG GUY.
WE THOUGHT NUMBERS WAS THE WAY TO GO.
UH HUH.

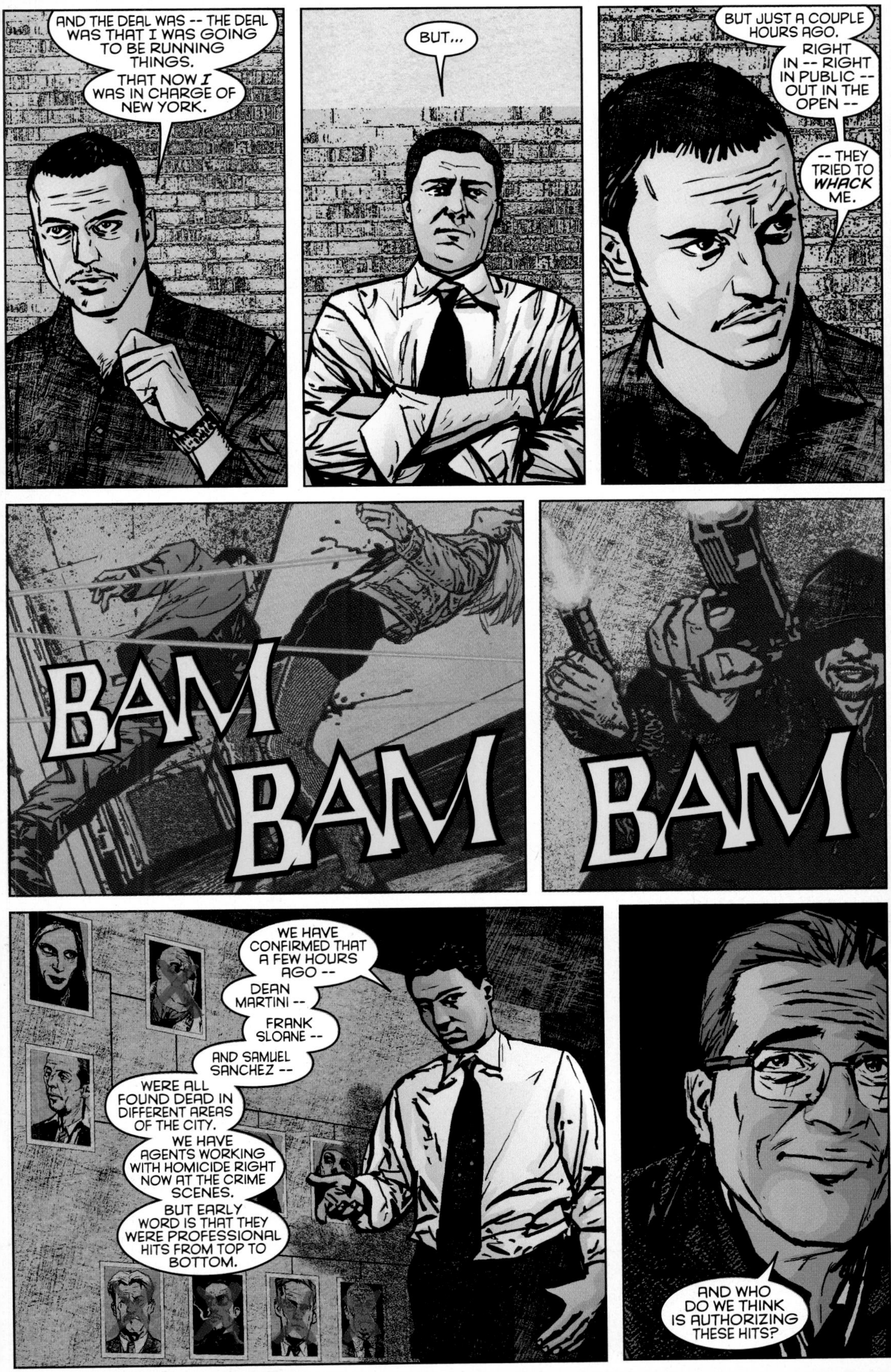
AND THE DEAL WAS -- THE DEAL WAS THAT I WAS GOING TO BE RUNNING THINGS.
THAT NOW I WAS IN CHARGE OF NEW YORK.
BUT...
BUT JUST A COUPLE HOURS AGO.
RIGHT IN -- RIGHT IN PUBLIC -- OUT IN THE OPEN --
-- THEY TRIED TO WHACK ME.
BAM
BAM
BAM
WE HAVE CONFIRMED THAT A FEW HOURS AGO --
DEAN MARTINI --
FRANK SLOANE --
AND SAMUEL SANCHEZ --
WERE ALL FOUND DEAD IN DIFFERENT AREAS OF THE CITY.
WE HAVE AGENTS WORKING WITH HOMICIDE RIGHT NOW AT THE CRIME SCENES.
BUT EARLY WORD IS THAT THEY WERE PROFESSIONAL HITS FROM TOP TO BOTTOM.
AND WHO DO WE THINK IS AUTHORIZING THESE HITS?

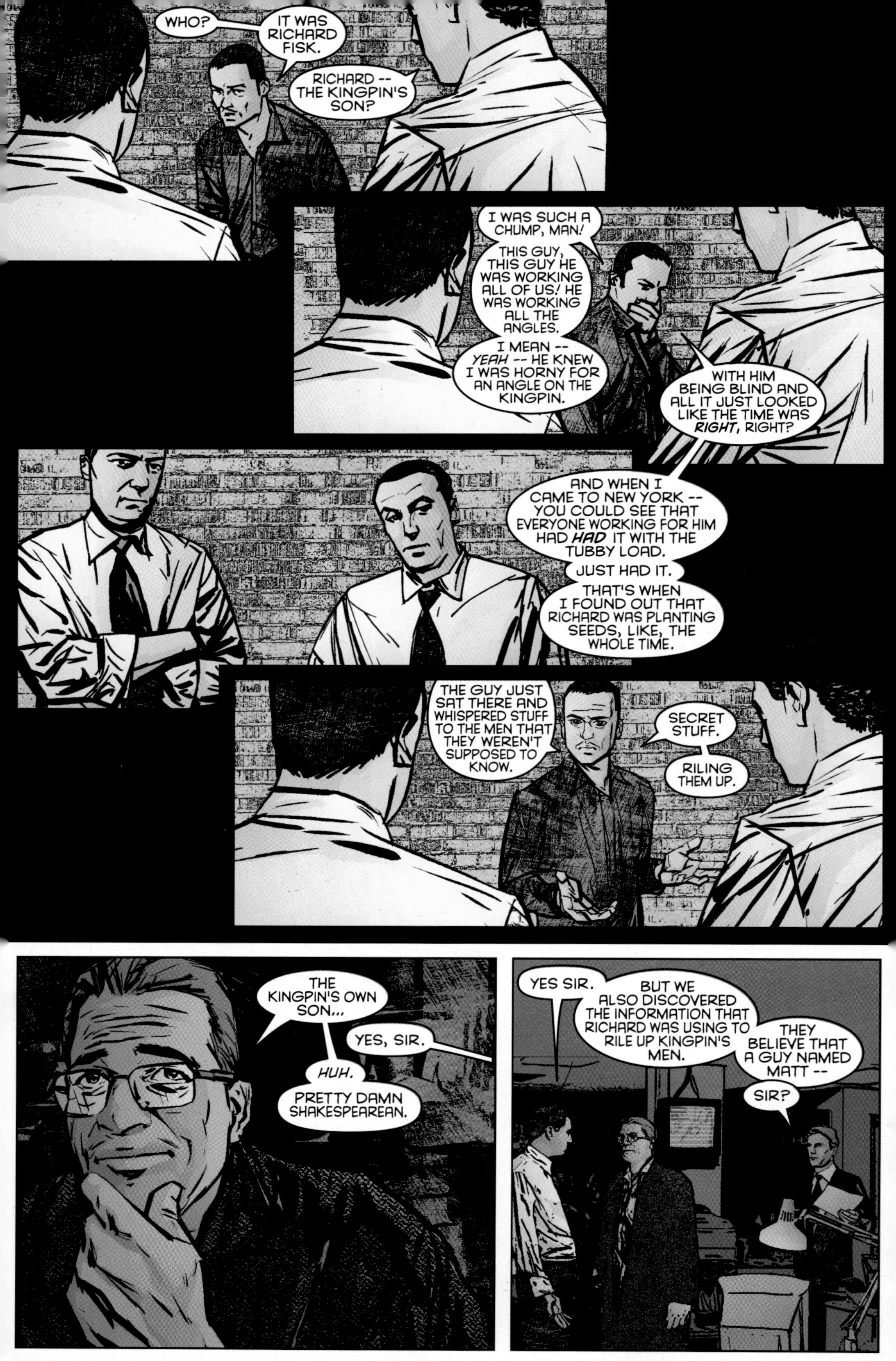
WHO?
IT WAS RICHARD FISK.
RICHARD -- THE KINGPIN'S SON?
I WAS SUCH A CHUMP, MAN!
THIS GUY, THIS GUY HE WAS WORKING ALL OF US! HE WAS WORKING ALL THE ANGLES.
I MEAN -- YEAH -- HE KNEW I WAS HORNY FOR AN ANGLE ON THE KINGPIN.
WITH HIM BEING BLIND AND ALL IT JUST LOOKED LIKE THE TIME WAS RIGHT, RIGHT?
AND WHEN I CAME TO NEW YORK -- YOU COULD SEE THAT EVERYONE WORKING FOR HIM HAD HAD IT WITH THE TUBBY LOAD.
JUST HAD IT.
THAT'S WHEN I FOUND OUT THAT RICHARD WAS PLANTING SEEDS, LIKE, THE WHOLE TIME.
THE GUY JUST SAT THERE AND WHISPERED STUFF TO THE MEN THAT THEY WEREN'T SUPPOSED TO KNOW.
SECRET STUFF.
RILING THEM UP.
THE KINGPIN'S OWN SON...
YES, SIR.
HUH.
PRETTY DAMN SHAKESPEAREAN.
YES SIR.
BUT WE ALSO DISCOVERED THE INFORMATION THAT RICHARD WAS USING TO RILE UP KINGPIN'S MEN.
THEY BELIEVE THAT A GUY NAMED MATT --
SIR?

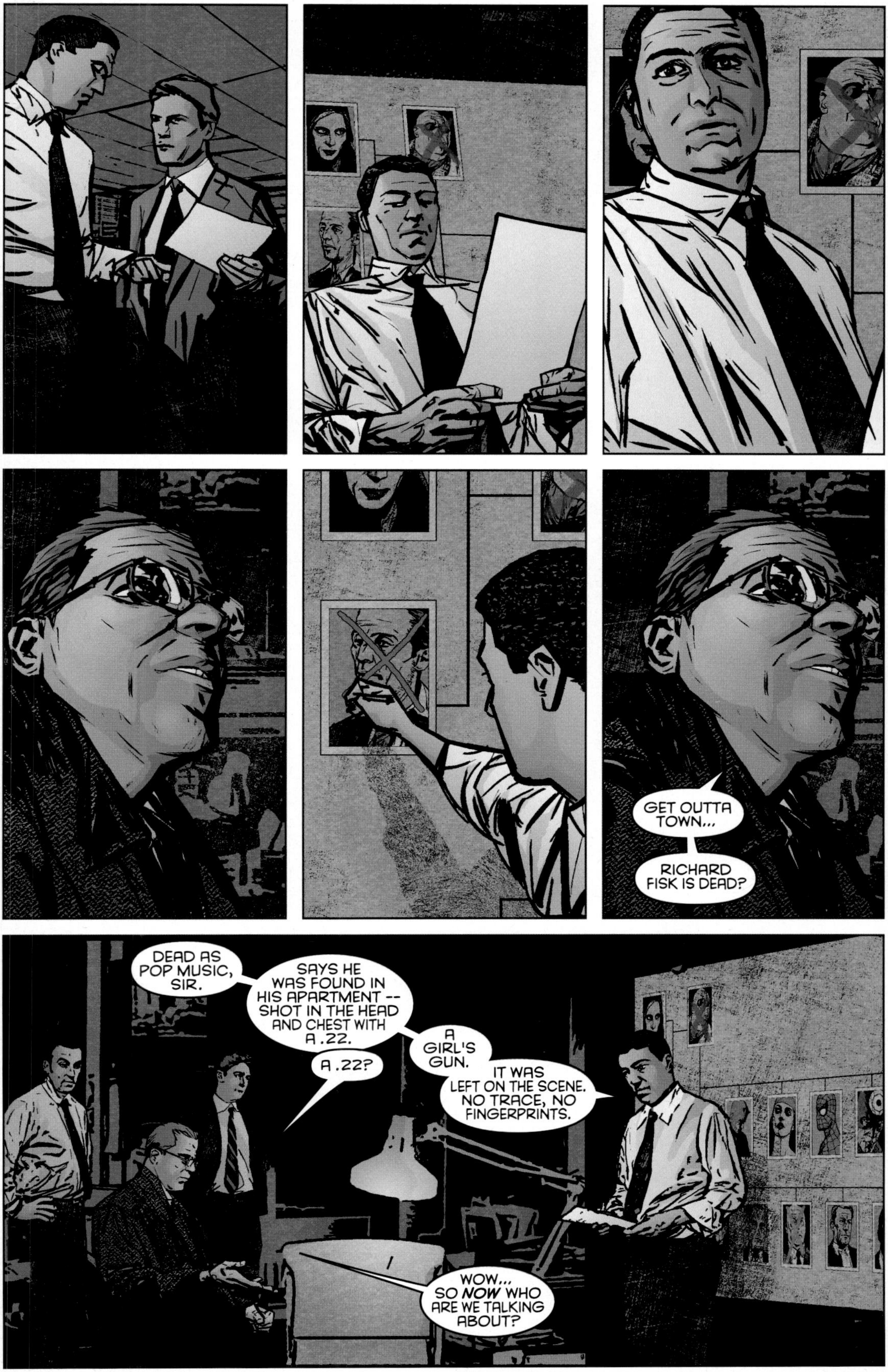
GET OUTTA TOWN...
RICHARD FISK IS DEAD?
DEAD AS POP MUSIC, SIR.
SAYS HE WAS FOUND IN HIS APARTMENT -- SHOT IN THE HEAD AND CHEST WITH A .22.
A .22?
A GIRL'S GUN.
IT WAS LEFT ON THE SCENE. NO TRACE, NO FINGERPRINTS.
WOW... SO NOW WHO ARE WE TALKING ABOUT?

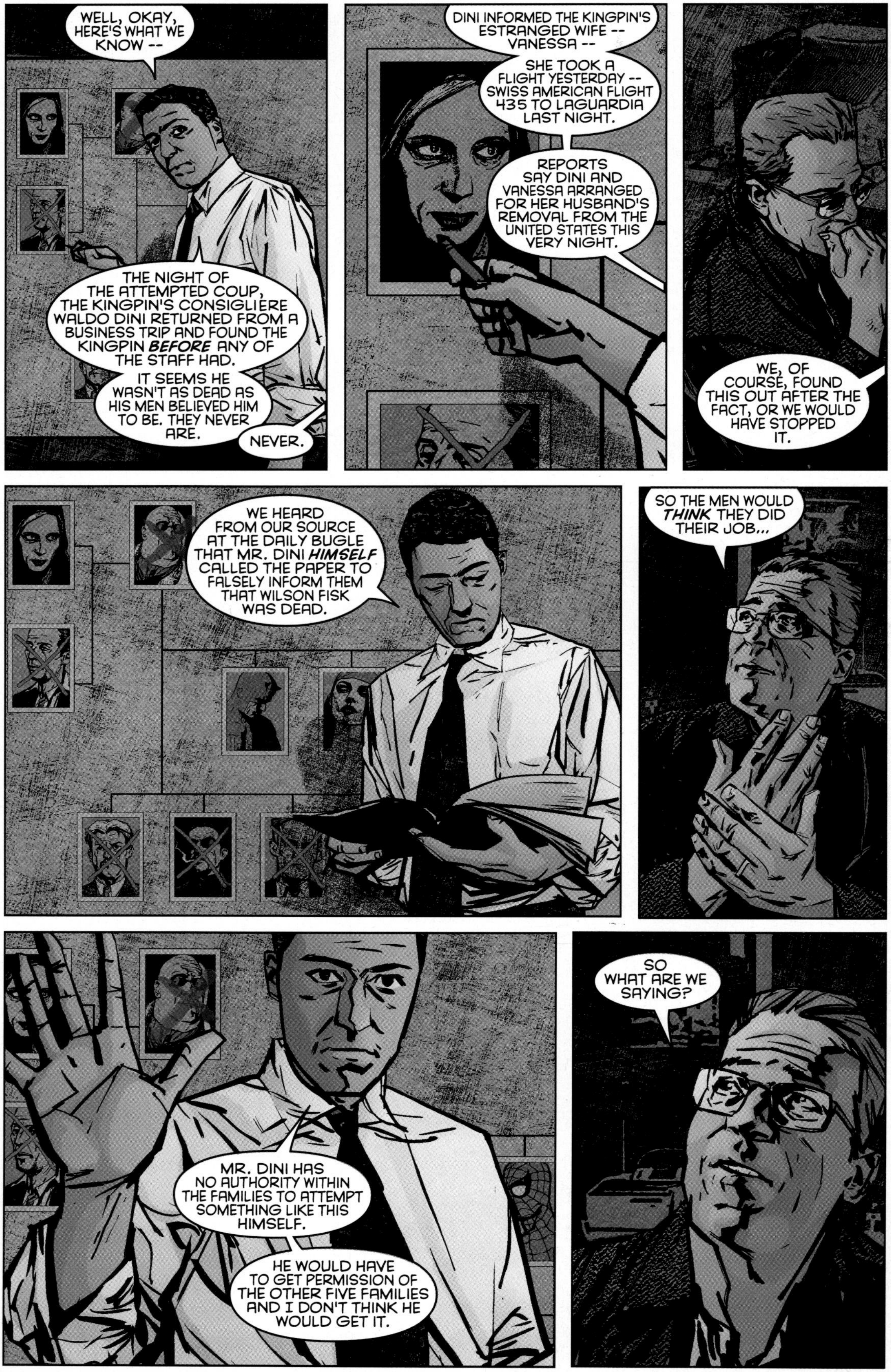
WELL, OKAY, HERE'S WHAT WE KNOW --
THE NIGHT OF THE ATTEMPTED COUP, THE KINGPIN'S CONSIGLIÈRE WALDO DINI RETURNED FROM A BUSINESS TRIP AND FOUND THE KINGPIN *BEFORE* ANY OF THE STAFF HAD.
IT SEEMS HE WASN'T AS DEAD AS HIS MEN BELIEVED HIM TO BE. THEY NEVER ARE.
NEVER.
DINI INFORMED THE KINGPIN'S ESTRANGED WIFE -- VANESSA --
SHE TOOK A FLIGHT YESTERDAY -- SWISS AMERICAN FLIGHT 435 TO LAGUARDIA LAST NIGHT.
REPORTS SAY DINI AND VANESSA ARRANGED FOR HER HUSBAND'S REMOVAL FROM THE UNITED STATES THIS VERY NIGHT.
WE, OF COURSE, FOUND THIS OUT AFTER THE FACT, OR WE WOULD HAVE STOPPED IT.
WE HEARD FROM OUR SOURCE AT THE DAILY BUGLE THAT MR. DINI *HIMSELF* CALLED THE PAPER TO FALSELY INFORM THEM THAT WILSON FISK WAS DEAD.
SO THE MEN WOULD *THINK* THEY DID THEIR JOB...
MR. DINI HAS NO AUTHORITY WITHIN THE FAMILIES TO ATTEMPT SOMETHING LIKE THIS HIMSELF.
HE WOULD HAVE TO GET PERMISSION OF THE OTHER FIVE FAMILIES AND I DON'T THINK HE WOULD GET IT.
SO WHAT ARE WE SAYING?

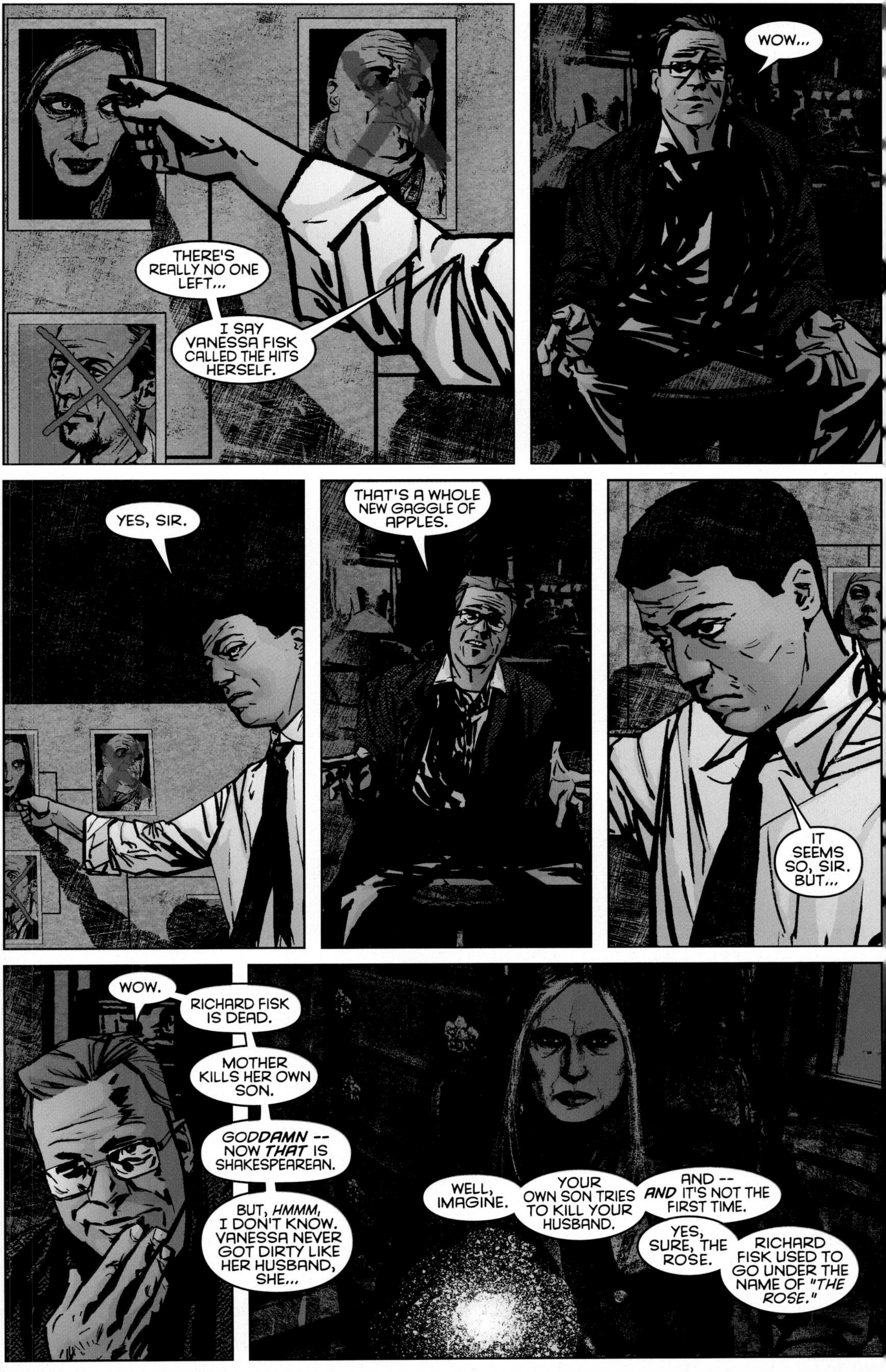
THERE'S REALLY NO ONE LEFT...
I SAY VANESSA FISK CALLED THE HITS HERSELF.
WOW...
YES, SIR.
THAT'S A WHOLE NEW GAGGLE OF APPLES.
IT SEEMS SO, SIR. BUT...
WOW.
RICHARD FISK IS DEAD.
MOTHER KILLS HER OWN SON.
GODDAMN -- NOW THAT IS SHAKESPEAREAN.
BUT, HMMM, I DON'T KNOW. VANESSA NEVER GOT DIRTY LIKE HER HUSBAND, SHE...
WELL, IMAGINE.
YOUR OWN SON TRIES TO KILL YOUR HUSBAND.
AND -- AND IT'S NOT THE FIRST TIME.
YES, SURE, THE ROSE.
RICHARD FISK USED TO GO UNDER THE NAME OF "THE ROSE."

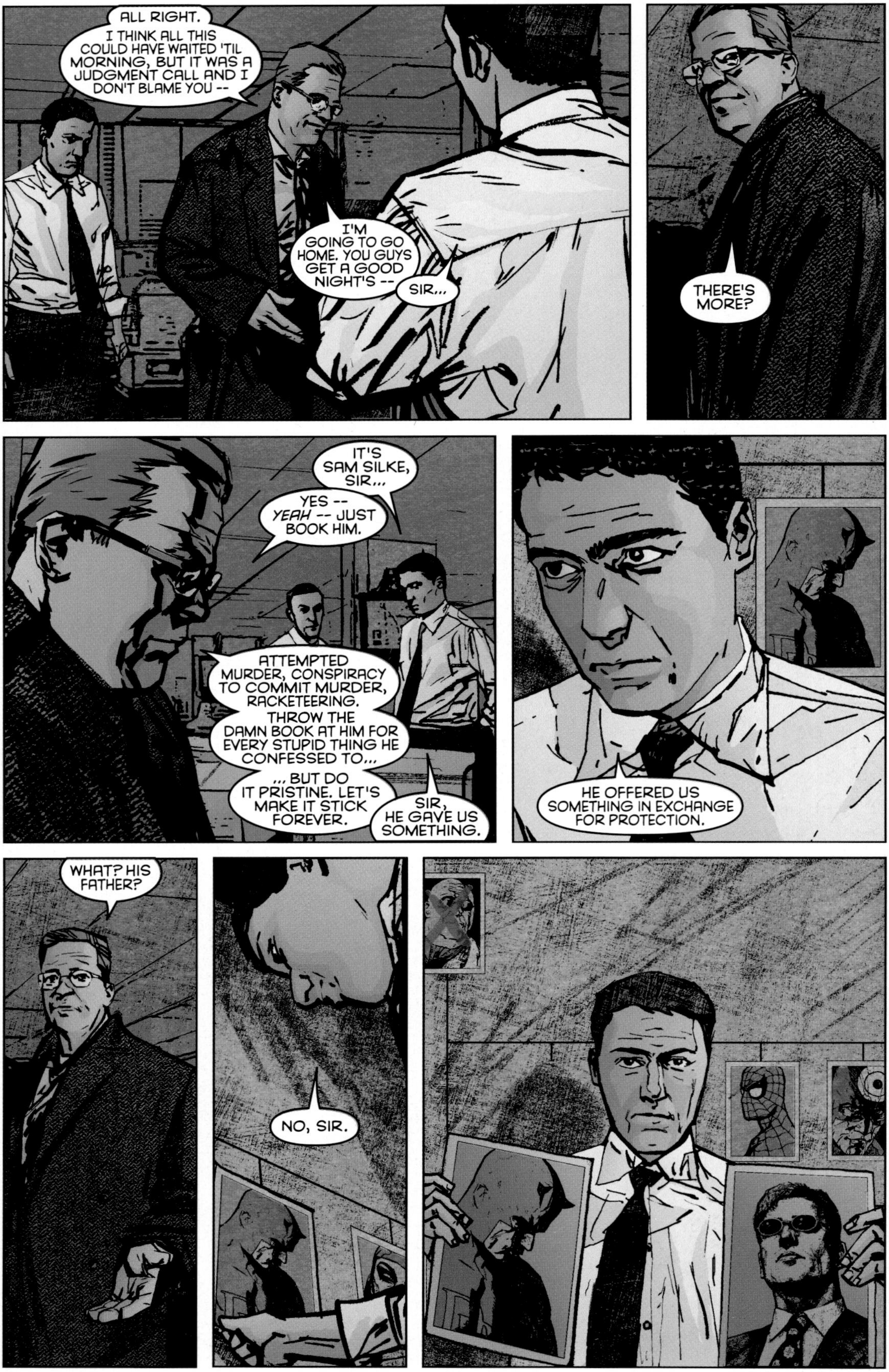
ALL RIGHT.
I THINK ALL THIS COULD HAVE WAITED 'TIL MORNING, BUT IT WAS A JUDGMENT CALL AND I DON'T BLAME YOU --
I'M GOING TO GO HOME. YOU GUYS GET A GOOD NIGHT'S --
SIR...
THERE'S MORE?
IT'S SAM SILKE, SIR...
YES -- *YEAH* -- JUST BOOK HIM.
ATTEMPTED MURDER, CONSPIRACY TO COMMIT MURDER, RACKETEERING.
THROW THE DAMN BOOK AT HIM FOR EVERY STUPID THING HE CONFESSED TO...
... BUT DO IT PRISTINE. LET'S MAKE IT STICK FOREVER.
SIR, HE GAVE US SOMETHING.
HE OFFERED US SOMETHING IN EXCHANGE FOR PROTECTION.
WHAT? HIS FATHER?
NO, SIR.

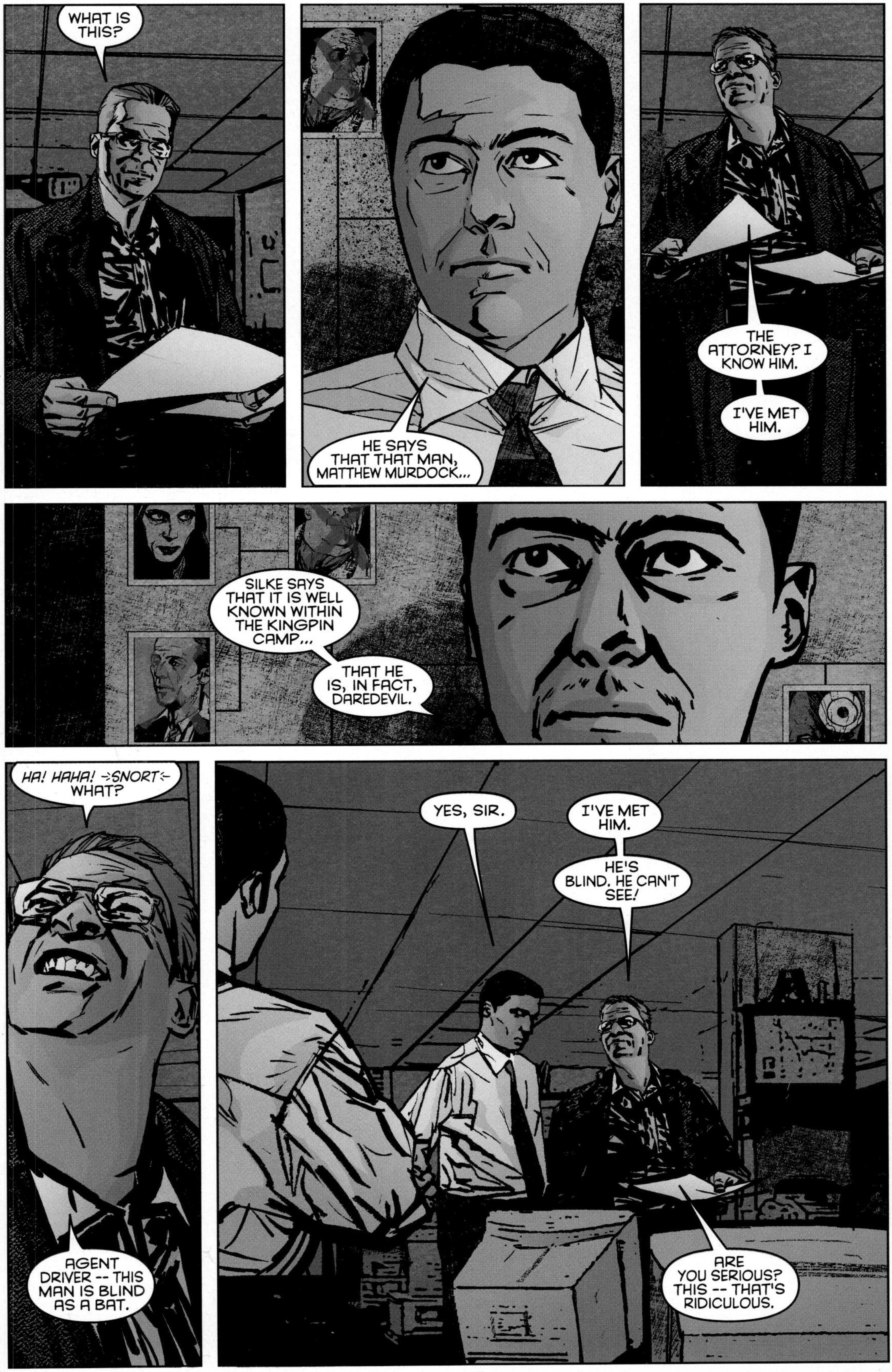
WHAT IS THIS?
HE SAYS THAT THAT MAN, MATTHEW MURDOCK...
THE ATTORNEY? I KNOW HIM.
I'VE MET HIM.
SILKE SAYS THAT IT IS WELL KNOWN WITHIN THE KINGPIN CAMP...
THAT HE IS, IN FACT, DAREDEVIL.
HA! HAHA! ->SNORT<- WHAT?
AGENT DRIVER -- THIS MAN IS BLIND AS A BAT.
YES, SIR.
I'VE MET HIM.
HE'S BLIND. HE CAN'T SEE!
ARE YOU SERIOUS? THIS -- THAT'S RIDICULOUS.

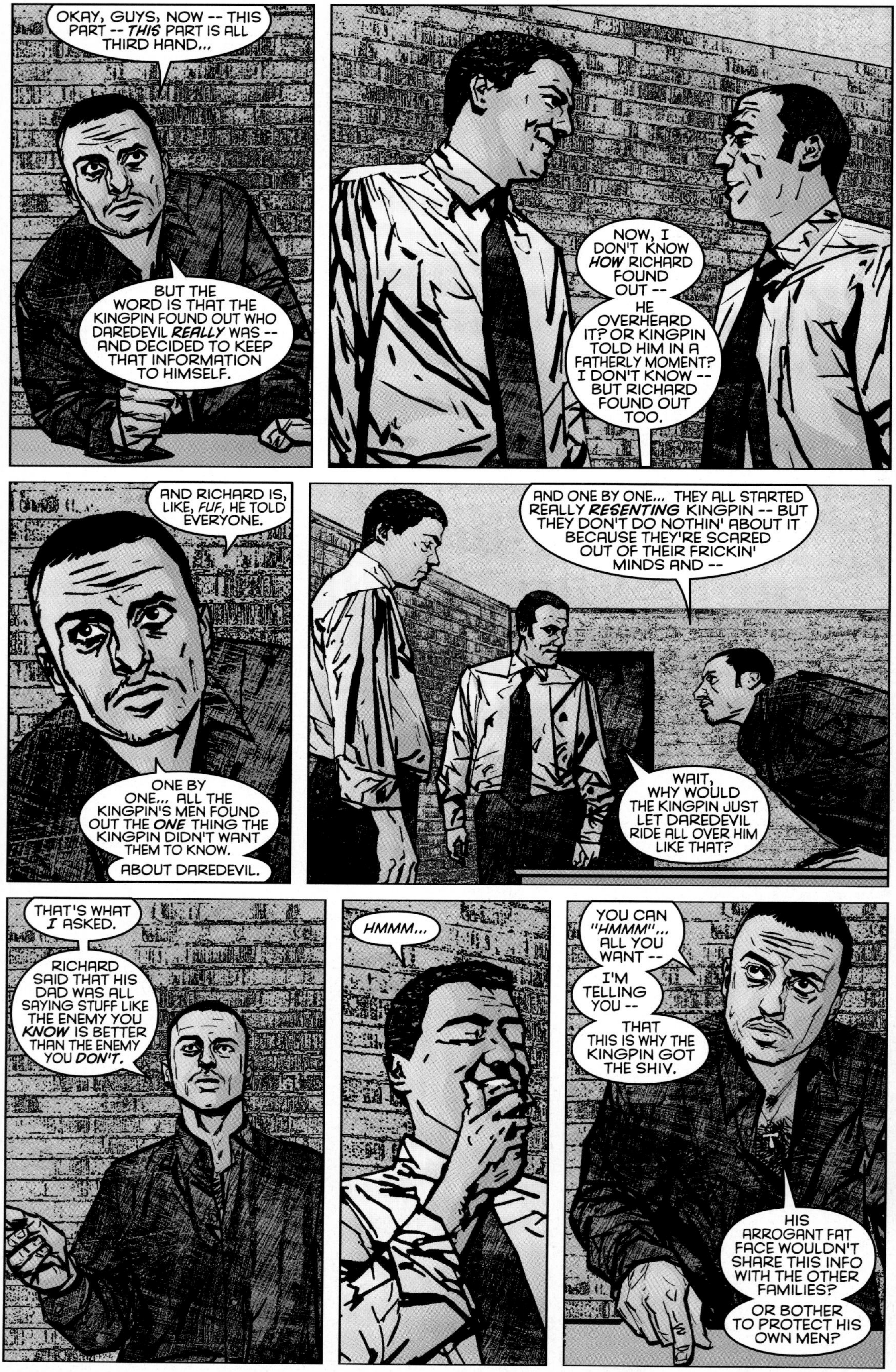
OKAY, GUYS, NOW -- THIS PART -- *THIS* PART IS ALL THIRD HAND...
BUT THE WORD IS THAT THE KINGPIN FOUND OUT WHO DAREDEVIL *REALLY* WAS -- AND DECIDED TO KEEP THAT INFORMATION TO HIMSELF.
NOW, I DON'T KNOW *HOW* RICHARD FOUND OUT --
HE OVERHEARD IT? OR KINGPIN TOLD HIM IN A FATHERLY MOMENT? I DON'T KNOW -- BUT RICHARD FOUND OUT TOO.
AND RICHARD IS, LIKE, *FUF*, HE TOLD EVERYONE.
ONE BY ONE... ALL THE KINGPIN'S MEN FOUND OUT THE *ONE* THING THE KINGPIN DIDN'T WANT THEM TO KNOW.
ABOUT DAREDEVIL.
AND ONE BY ONE... THEY ALL STARTED REALLY *RESENTING* KINGPIN -- BUT THEY DON'T DO NOTHIN' ABOUT IT BECAUSE THEY'RE SCARED OUT OF THEIR FRICKIN' MINDS AND --
WAIT, WHY WOULD THE KINGPIN JUST LET DAREDEVIL RIDE ALL OVER HIM LIKE THAT?
THAT'S WHAT *I* ASKED.
RICHARD SAID THAT HIS DAD WAS ALL SAYING STUFF LIKE THE ENEMY YOU *KNOW* IS BETTER THAN THE ENEMY YOU *DON'T*.
HMMM...
YOU CAN "*HMMM*"... ALL YOU WANT --
I'M TELLING YOU --
THAT THIS IS WHY THE KINGPIN GOT THE SHIV.
HIS ARROGANT FAT FACE WOULDN'T SHARE THIS INFO WITH THE OTHER FAMILIES?
OR BOTHER TO PROTECT HIS OWN MEN?

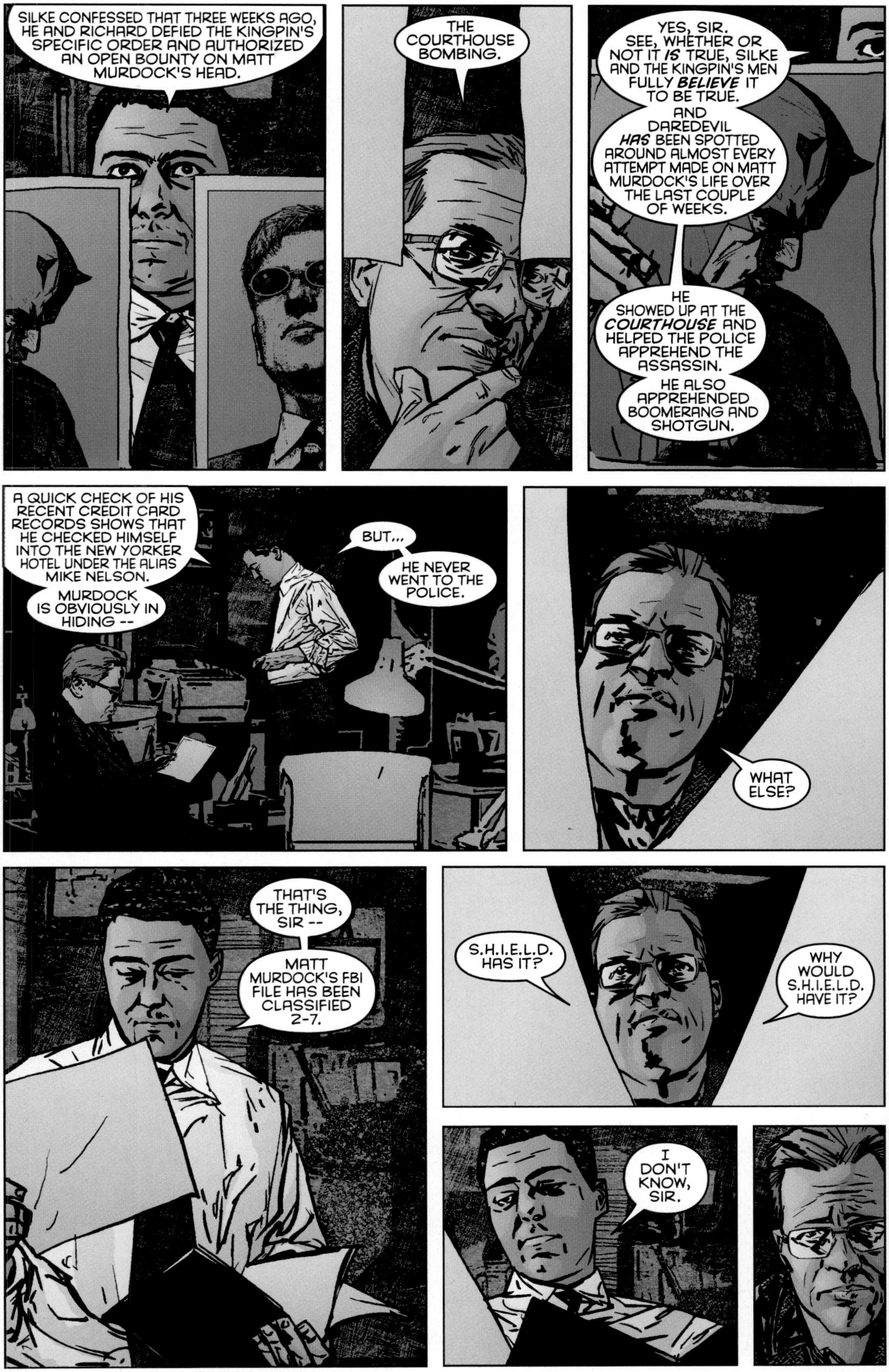
SILKE CONFESSED THAT THREE WEEKS AGO, HE AND RICHARD DEFIED THE KINGPIN'S SPECIFIC ORDER AND AUTHORIZED AN OPEN BOUNTY ON MATT MURDOCK'S HEAD.
THE COURTHOUSE BOMBING.
YES, SIR. SEE, WHETHER OR NOT IT IS TRUE, SILKE AND THE KINGPIN'S MEN FULLY BELIEVE IT TO BE TRUE.
AND DAREDEVIL HAS BEEN SPOTTED AROUND ALMOST EVERY ATTEMPT MADE ON MATT MURDOCK'S LIFE OVER THE LAST COUPLE OF WEEKS.
HE SHOWED UP AT THE COURTHOUSE AND HELPED THE POLICE APPREHEND THE ASSASSIN.
HE ALSO APPREHENDED BOOMERANG AND SHOTGUN.
A QUICK CHECK OF HIS RECENT CREDIT CARD RECORDS SHOWS THAT HE CHECKED HIMSELF INTO THE NEW YORKER HOTEL UNDER THE ALIAS MIKE NELSON.
MURDOCK IS OBVIOUSLY IN HIDING --
BUT...
HE NEVER WENT TO THE POLICE.
WHAT ELSE?
THAT'S THE THING, SIR --
MATT MURDOCK'S FBI FILE HAS BEEN CLASSIFIED 2-7.
S.H.I.E.L.D. HAS IT?
WHY WOULD S.H.I.E.L.D. HAVE IT?
I DON'T KNOW, SIR.

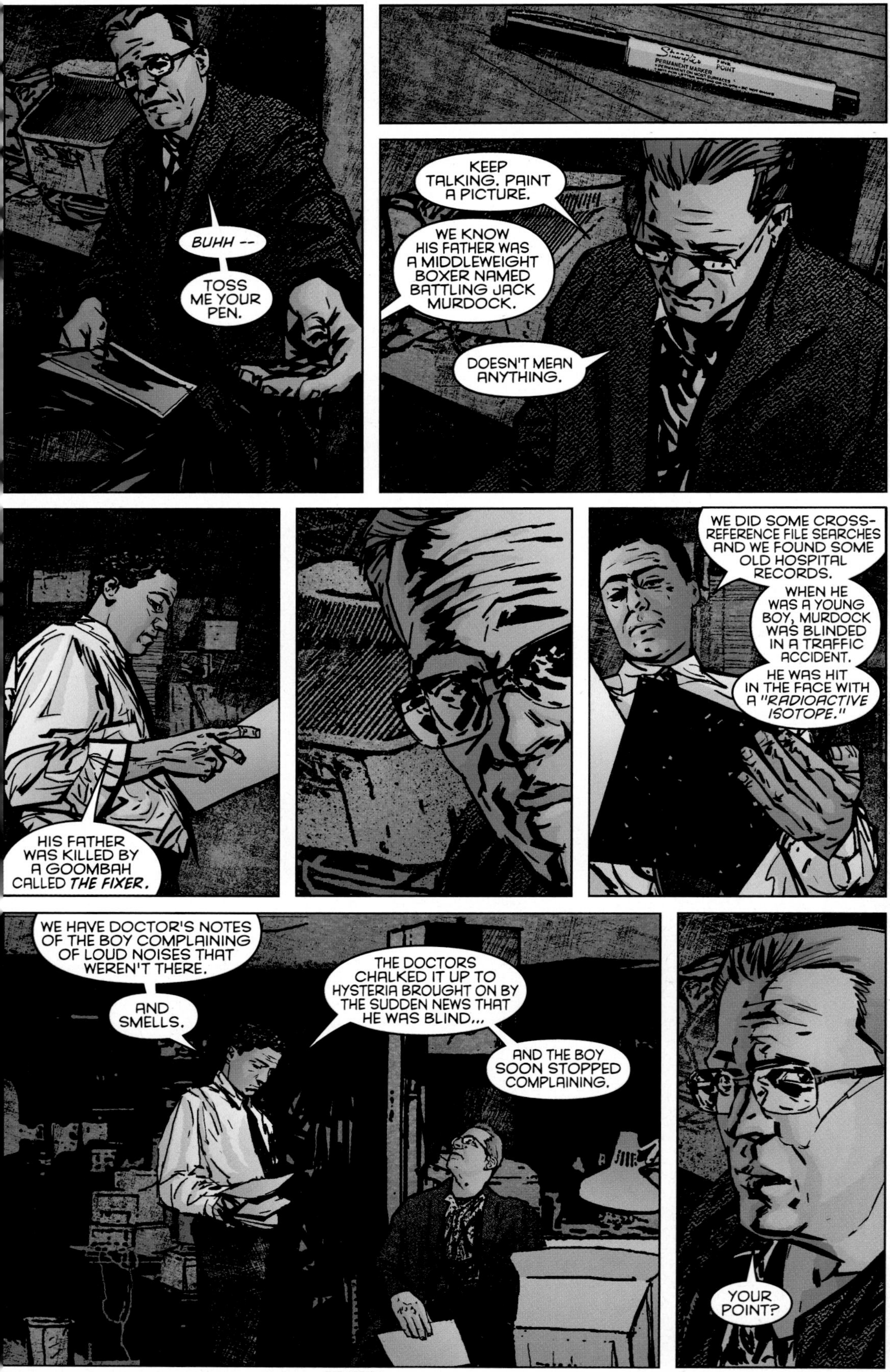

BUHH --
TOSS ME YOUR PEN.
SHARPIE FINE POINT PERMANENT MARKER
KEEP TALKING. PAINT A PICTURE.
WE KNOW HIS FATHER WAS A MIDDLEWEIGHT BOXER NAMED BATTLING JACK MURDOCK.
DOESN'T MEAN ANYTHING.
HIS FATHER WAS KILLED BY A GOOMBAH CALLED *THE FIXER*.
WE DID SOME CROSS-REFERENCE FILE SEARCHES AND WE FOUND SOME OLD HOSPITAL RECORDS.
WHEN HE WAS A YOUNG BOY, MURDOCK WAS BLINDED IN A TRAFFIC ACCIDENT.
HE WAS HIT IN THE FACE WITH A *"RADIOACTIVE ISOTOPE."*
WE HAVE DOCTOR'S NOTES OF THE BOY COMPLAINING OF LOUD NOISES THAT WEREN'T THERE.
AND SMELLS.
THE DOCTORS CHALKED IT UP TO HYSTERIA BROUGHT ON BY THE SUDDEN NEWS THAT HE WAS BLIND...
AND THE BOY SOON STOPPED COMPLAINING.
YOUR POINT?

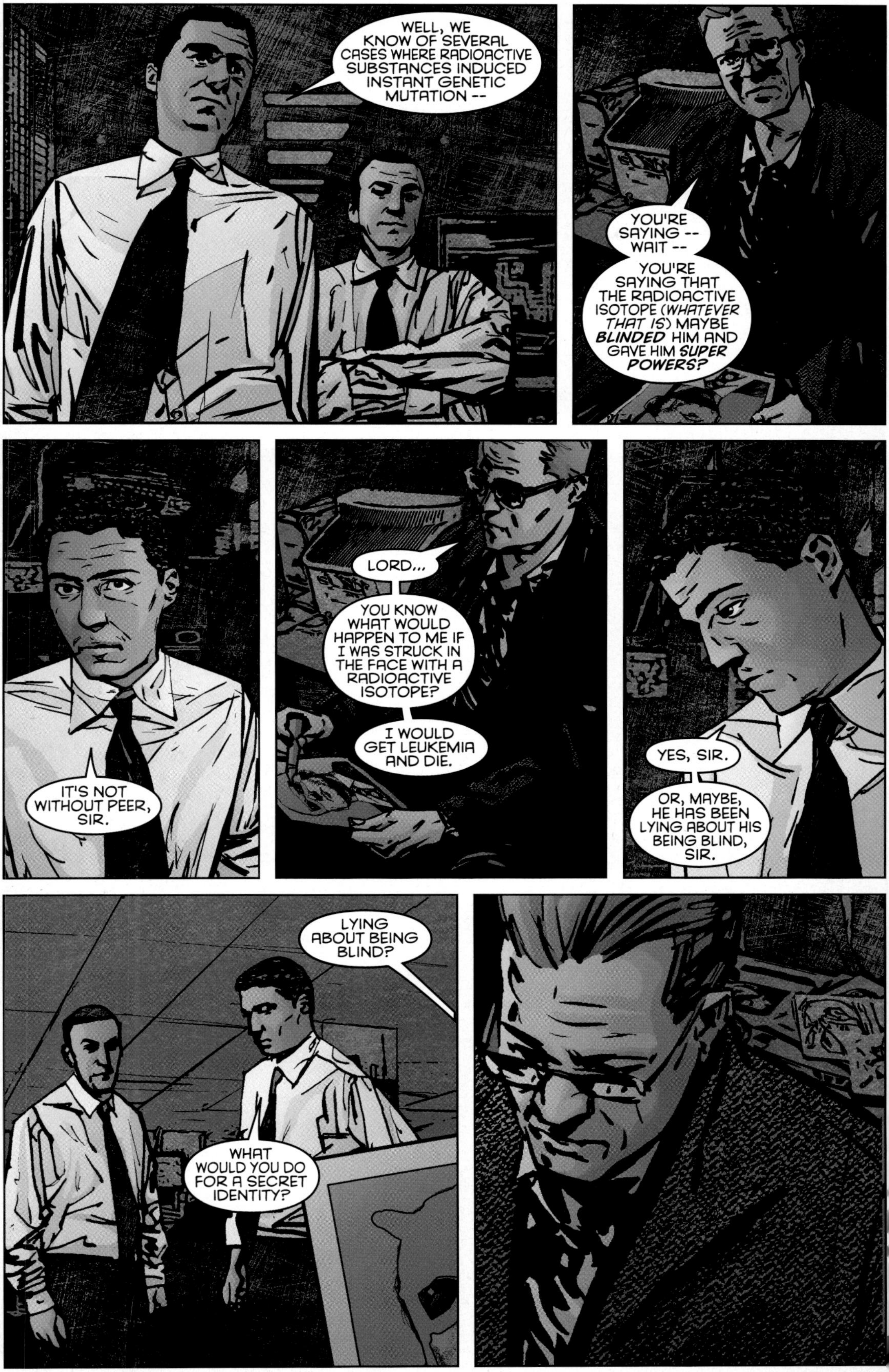
WELL, WE KNOW OF SEVERAL CASES WHERE RADIOACTIVE SUBSTANCES INDUCED INSTANT GENETIC MUTATION --
YOU'RE SAYING -- WAIT --
YOU'RE SAYING THAT THE RADIOACTIVE ISOTOPE (*WHATEVER THAT IS*) MAYBE ***BLINDED*** HIM AND GAVE HIM ***SUPER POWERS?***
IT'S NOT WITHOUT PEER, SIR.
LORD...
YOU KNOW WHAT WOULD HAPPEN TO ME IF I WAS STRUCK IN THE FACE WITH A RADIOACTIVE ISOTOPE?
I WOULD GET LEUKEMIA AND DIE.
YES, SIR.
OR, MAYBE, HE HAS BEEN LYING ABOUT HIS BEING BLIND, SIR.
LYING ABOUT BEING BLIND?
WHAT WOULD YOU DO FOR A SECRET IDENTITY?

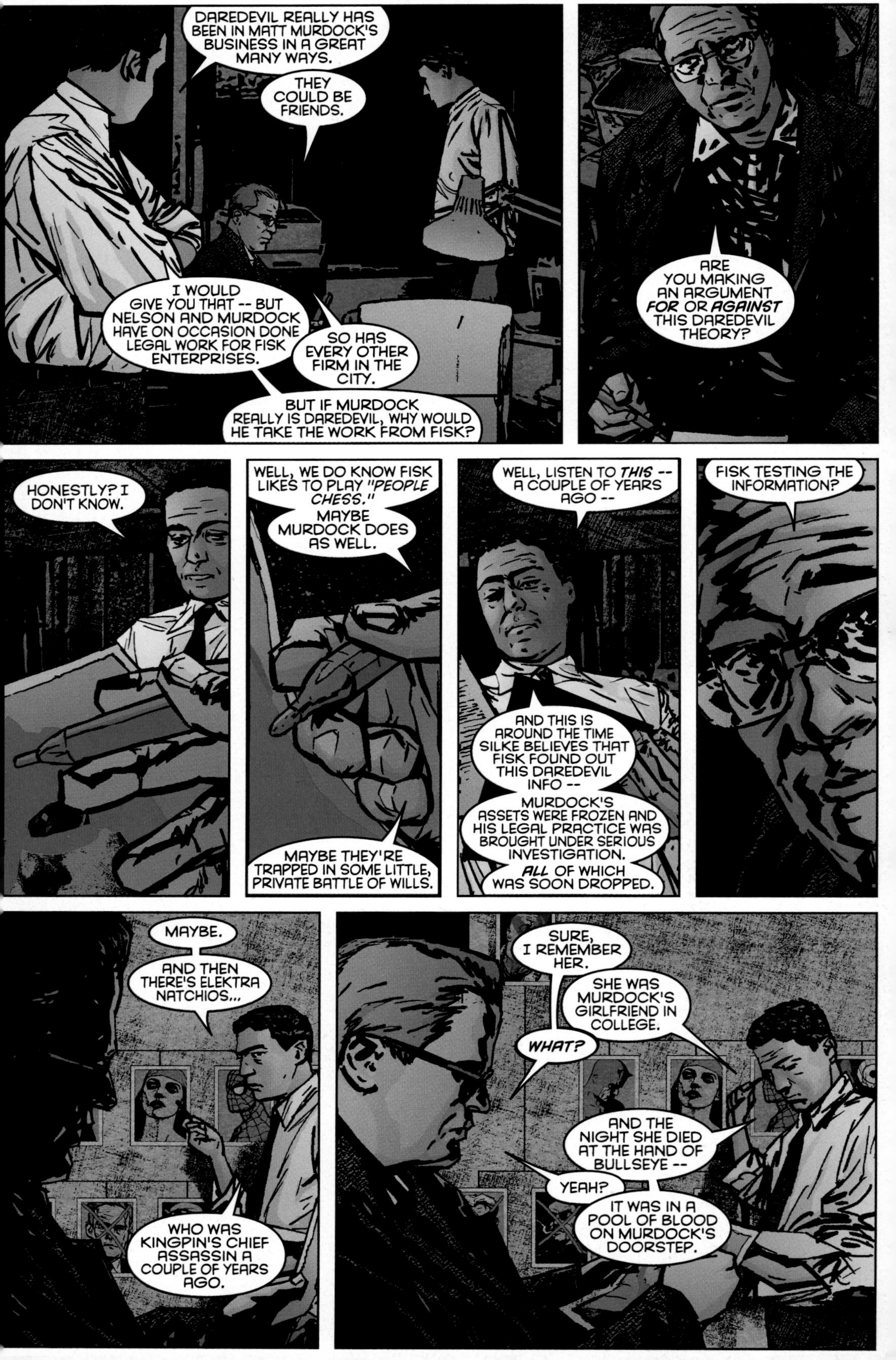
DAREDEVIL REALLY HAS BEEN IN MATT MURDOCK'S BUSINESS IN A GREAT MANY WAYS.
THEY COULD BE FRIENDS.
I WOULD GIVE YOU THAT -- BUT NELSON AND MURDOCK HAVE ON OCCASION DONE LEGAL WORK FOR FISK ENTERPRISES.
SO HAS EVERY OTHER FIRM IN THE CITY.
BUT IF MURDOCK REALLY IS DAREDEVIL, WHY WOULD HE TAKE THE WORK FROM FISK?
ARE YOU MAKING AN ARGUMENT FOR OR AGAINST THIS DAREDEVIL THEORY?
HONESTLY? I DON'T KNOW.
WELL, WE DO KNOW FISK LIKES TO PLAY "PEOPLE CHESS."
MAYBE MURDOCK DOES AS WELL.
MAYBE THEY'RE TRAPPED IN SOME LITTLE, PRIVATE BATTLE OF WILLS.
WELL, LISTEN TO THIS -- A COUPLE OF YEARS AGO --
AND THIS IS AROUND THE TIME SILKE BELIEVES THAT FISK FOUND OUT THIS DAREDEVIL INFO --
MURDOCK'S ASSETS WERE FROZEN AND HIS LEGAL PRACTICE WAS BROUGHT UNDER SERIOUS INVESTIGATION.
ALL OF WHICH WAS SOON DROPPED.
FISK TESTING THE INFORMATION?
MAYBE.
AND THEN THERE'S ELEKTRA NATCHIOS...
WHO WAS KINGPIN'S CHIEF ASSASSIN A COUPLE OF YEARS AGO.
SURE, I REMEMBER HER.
SHE WAS MURDOCK'S GIRLFRIEND IN COLLEGE.
WHAT?
AND THE NIGHT SHE DIED AT THE HAND OF BULLSEYE --
YEAH?
IT WAS IN A POOL OF BLOOD ON MURDOCK'S DOORSTEP.

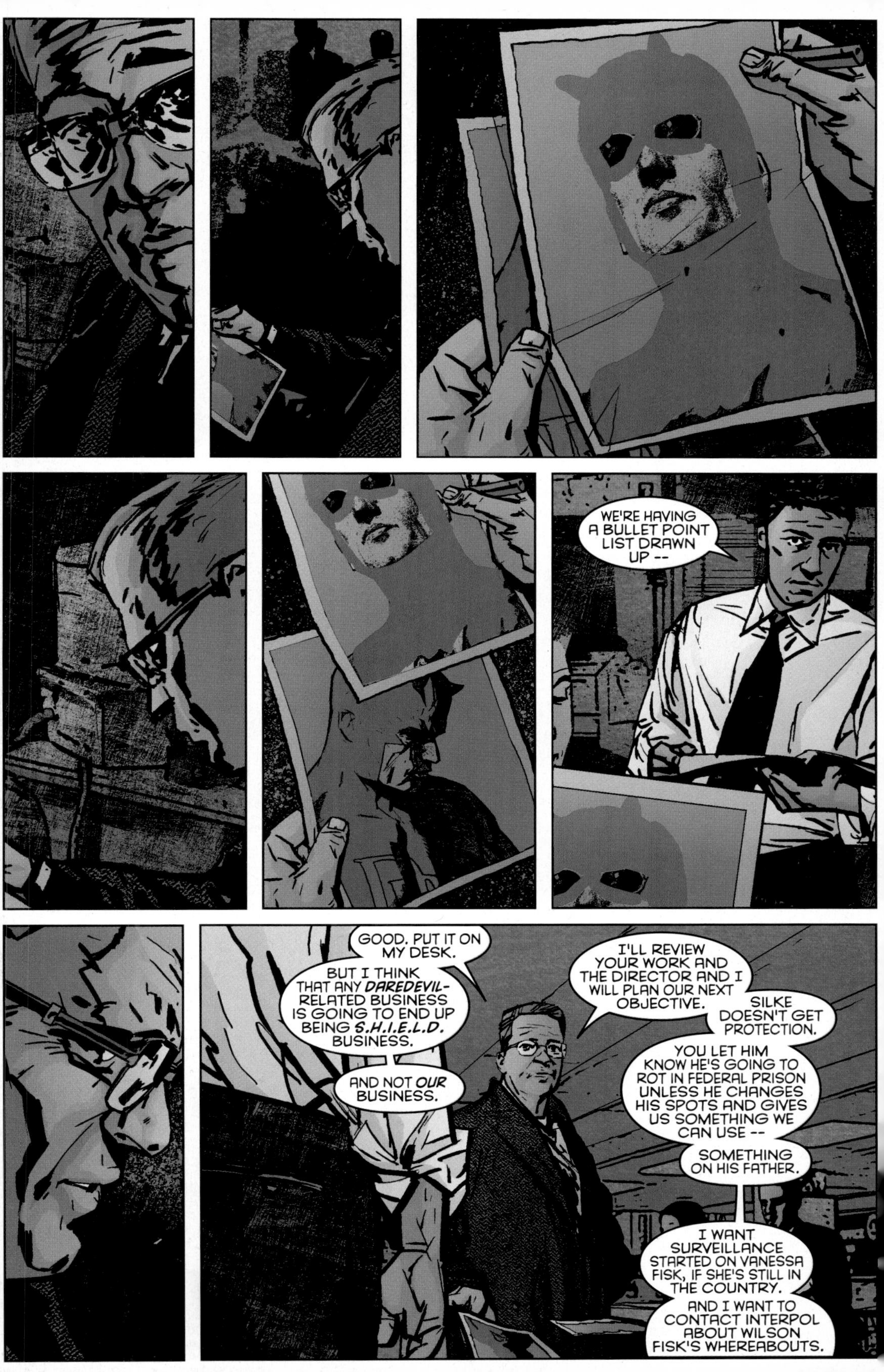
WE'RE HAVING A BULLET POINT LIST DRAWN UP --
GOOD. PUT IT ON MY DESK.
BUT I THINK THAT ANY *DAREDEVIL*-RELATED BUSINESS IS GOING TO END UP BEING *S.H.I.E.L.D.* BUSINESS.
AND NOT *OUR* BUSINESS.
I'LL REVIEW YOUR WORK AND THE DIRECTOR AND I WILL PLAN OUR NEXT OBJECTIVE.
SILKE DOESN'T GET PROTECTION.
YOU LET HIM KNOW HE'S GOING TO ROT IN FEDERAL PRISON UNLESS HE CHANGES HIS SPOTS AND GIVES US SOMETHING WE CAN USE --
SOMETHING ON HIS FATHER.
I WANT SURVEILLANCE STARTED ON VANESSA FISK, IF SHE'S STILL IN THE COUNTRY.
AND I WANT TO CONTACT INTERPOL ABOUT WILSON FISK'S WHEREABOUTS.

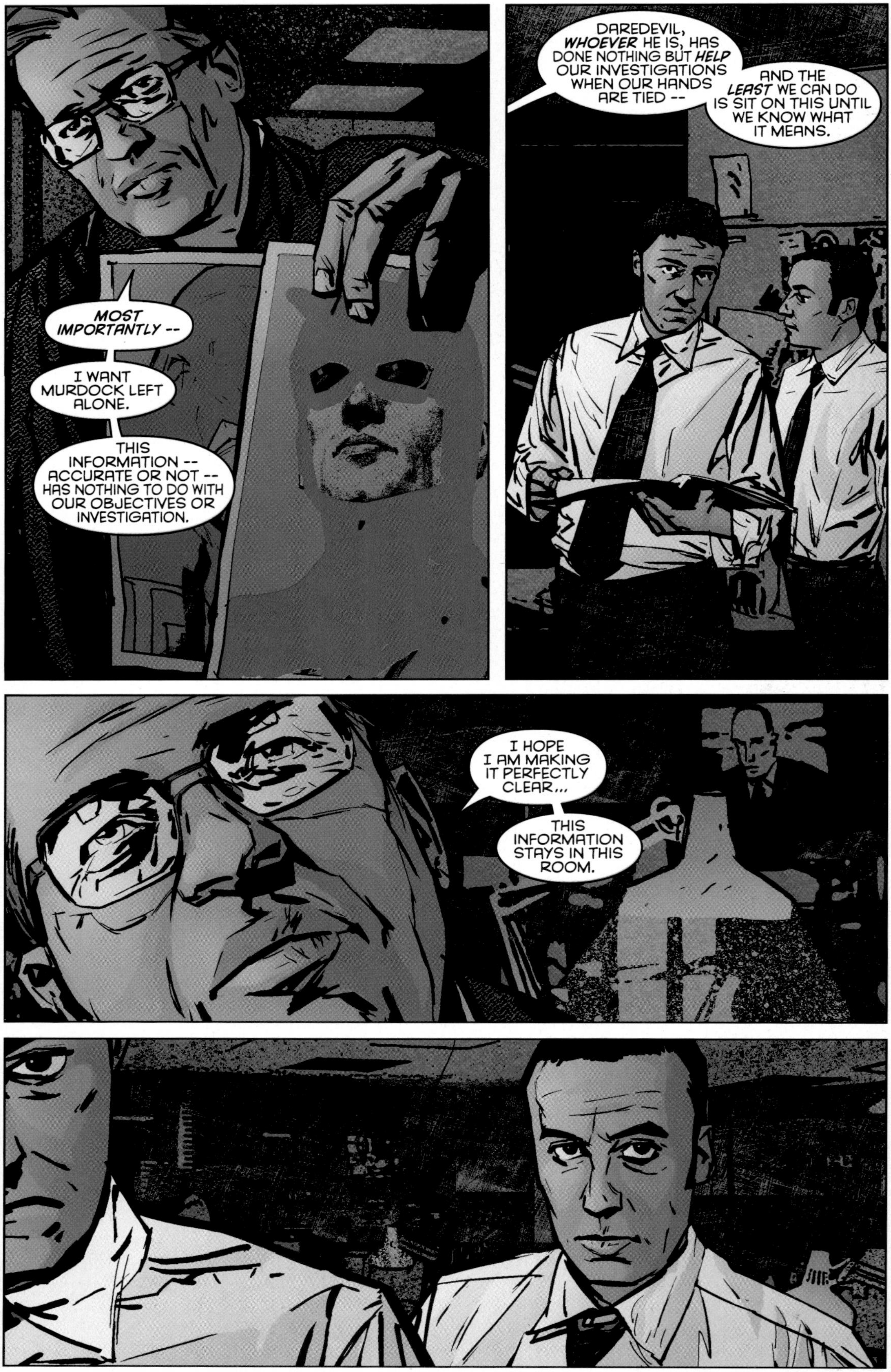

MOST IMPORTANTLY --
I WANT MURDOCK LEFT ALONE.
THIS INFORMATION -- ACCURATE OR NOT -- HAS NOTHING TO DO WITH OUR OBJECTIVES OR INVESTIGATION.
DAREDEVIL, *WHOEVER* HE IS, HAS DONE NOTHING BUT *HELP* OUR INVESTIGATIONS WHEN OUR HANDS ARE TIED --
AND THE *LEAST* WE CAN DO IS SIT ON THIS UNTIL WE KNOW WHAT IT MEANS.
I HOPE I AM MAKING IT PERFECTLY CLEAR...
THIS INFORMATION STAYS IN THIS ROOM.

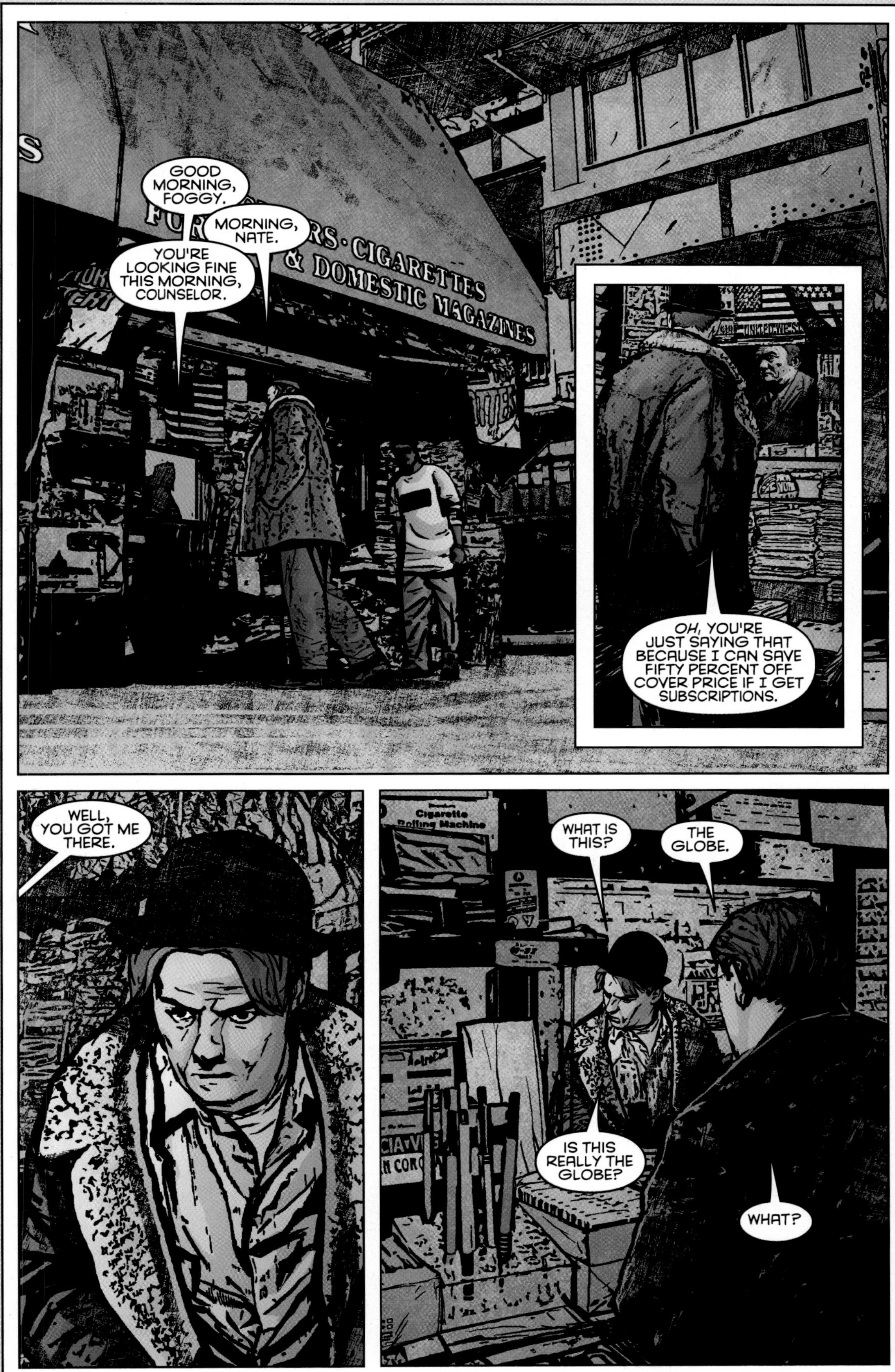
GOOD MORNING, FOGGY.
MORNING, NATE.
YOU'RE LOOKING FINE THIS MORNING, COUNSELOR.
FURS · CIGARETTES & DOMESTIC MAGAZINES
OH, YOU'RE JUST SAYING THAT BECAUSE I CAN SAVE FIFTY PERCENT OFF COVER PRICE IF I GET SUBSCRIPTIONS.
WELL, YOU GOT ME THERE.
Cigarette Rolling Machine
WHAT IS THIS?
THE GLOBE.
IS THIS REALLY THE GLOBE?
WHAT?

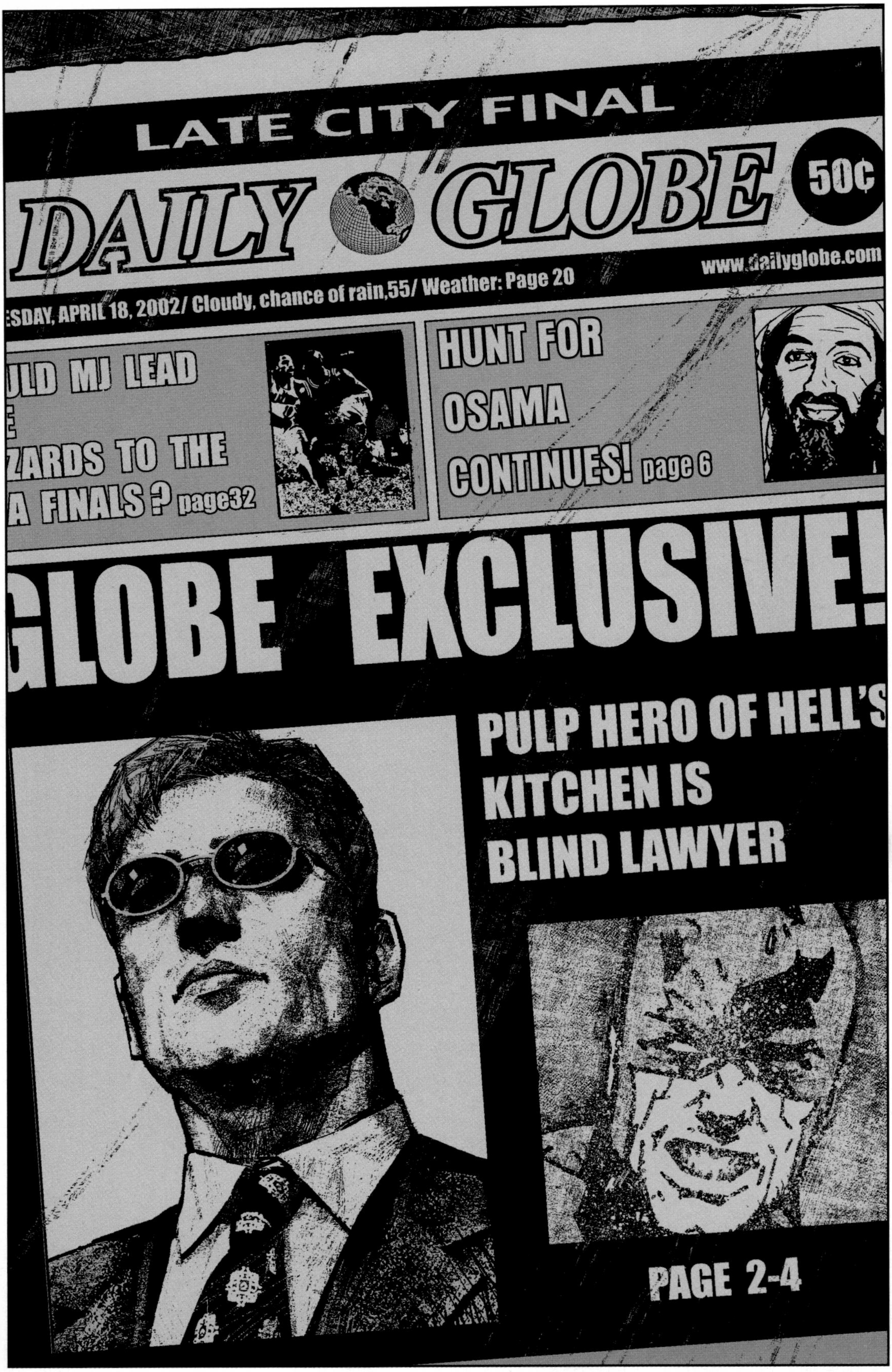
LATE CITY FINAL
DAILY GLOBE
50¢
www.dailyglobe.com
ESDAY, APRIL 18, 2002/ Cloudy, chance of rain,55/ Weather: Page 20
ULD MJ LEAD
E
ZARDS TO THE
A FINALS ? page32
HUNT FOR
OSAMA
CONTINUES! page 6
GLOBE EXCLUSIVE!
PULP HERO OF HELL'S
KITCHEN IS
BLIND LAWYER
PAGE 2-4

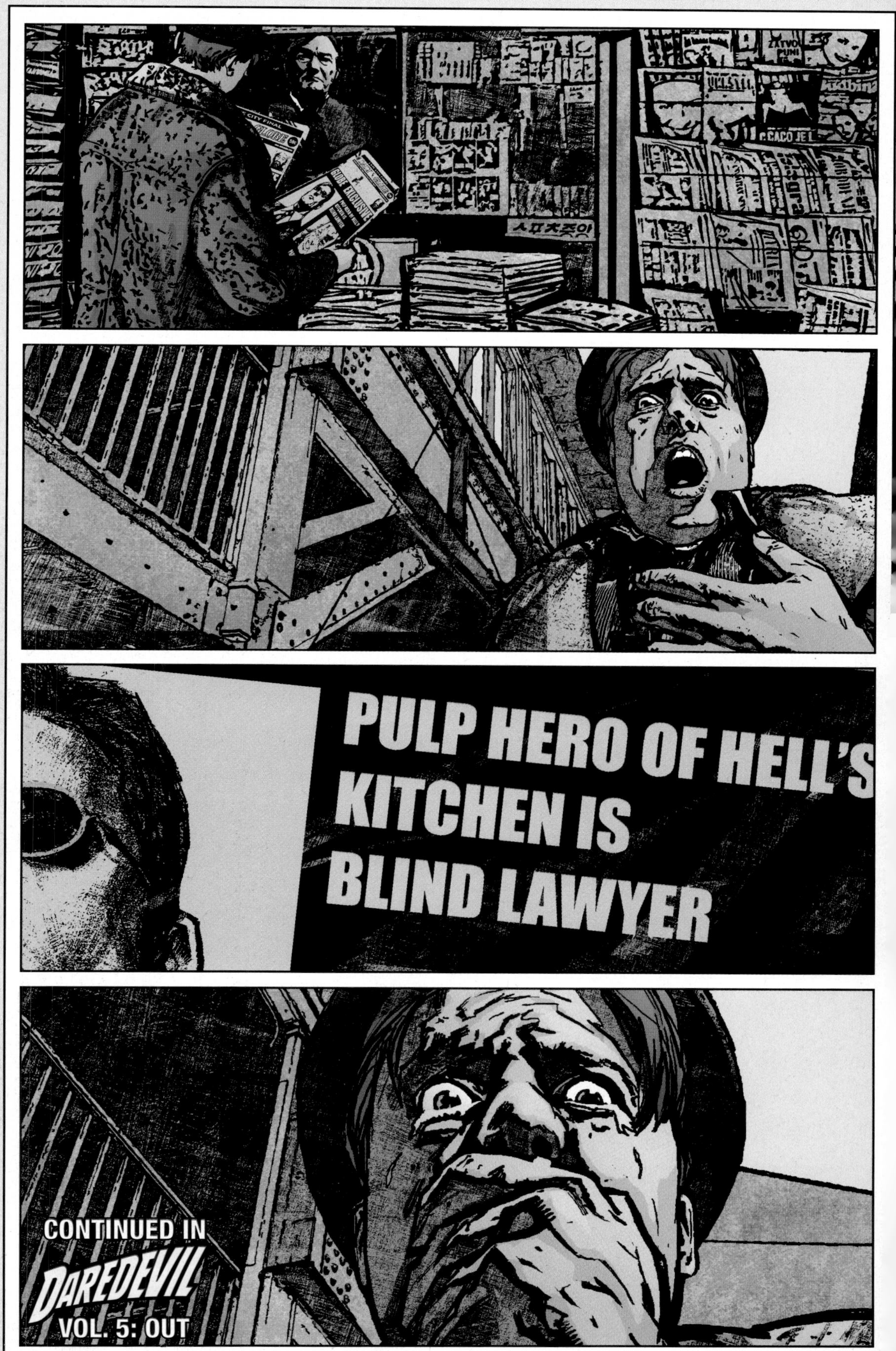
PULP HERO OF HELL'S KITCHEN IS BLIND LAWYER
CONTINUED IN
DAREDEVIL
VOL. 5: OUT

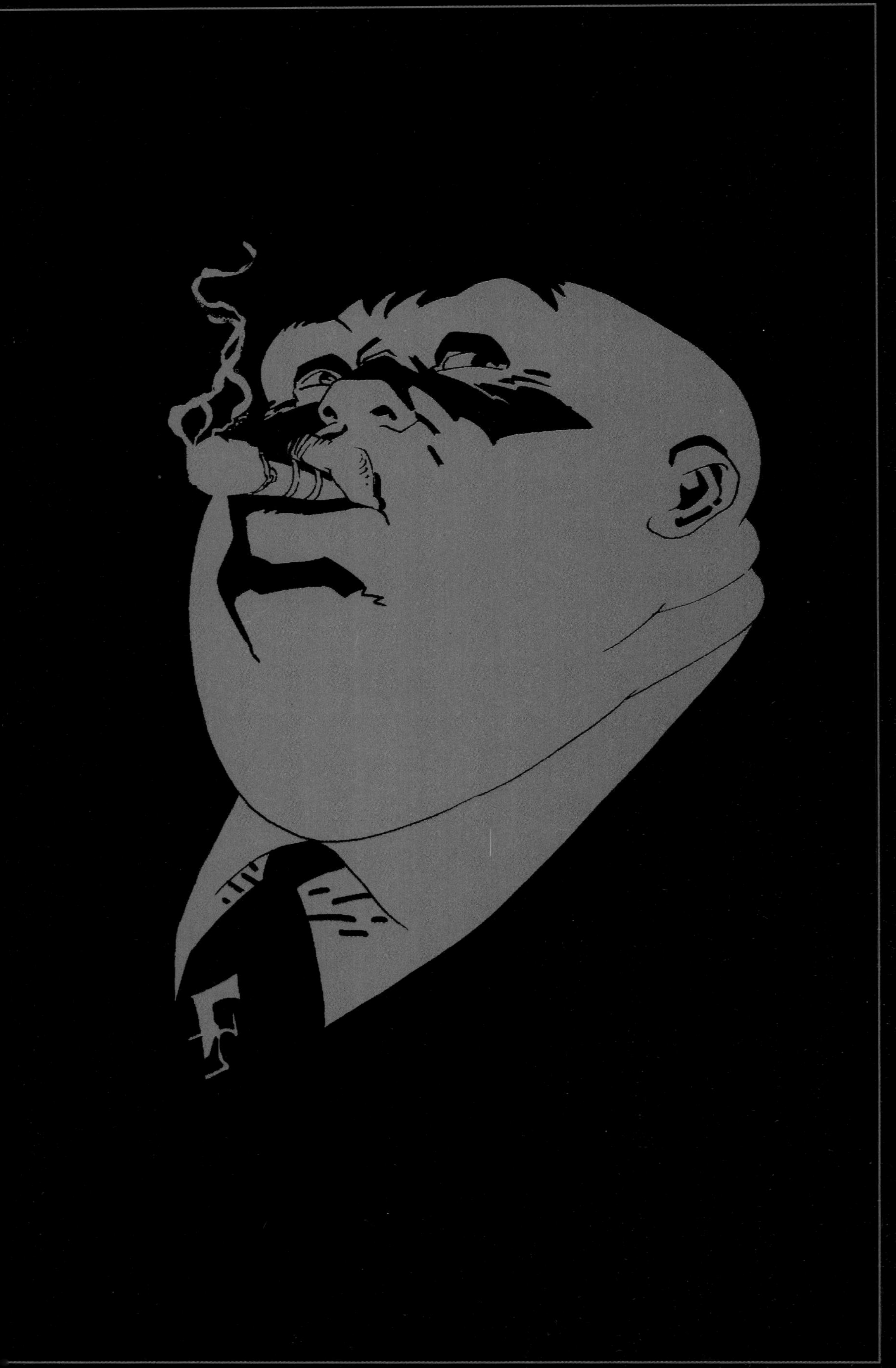

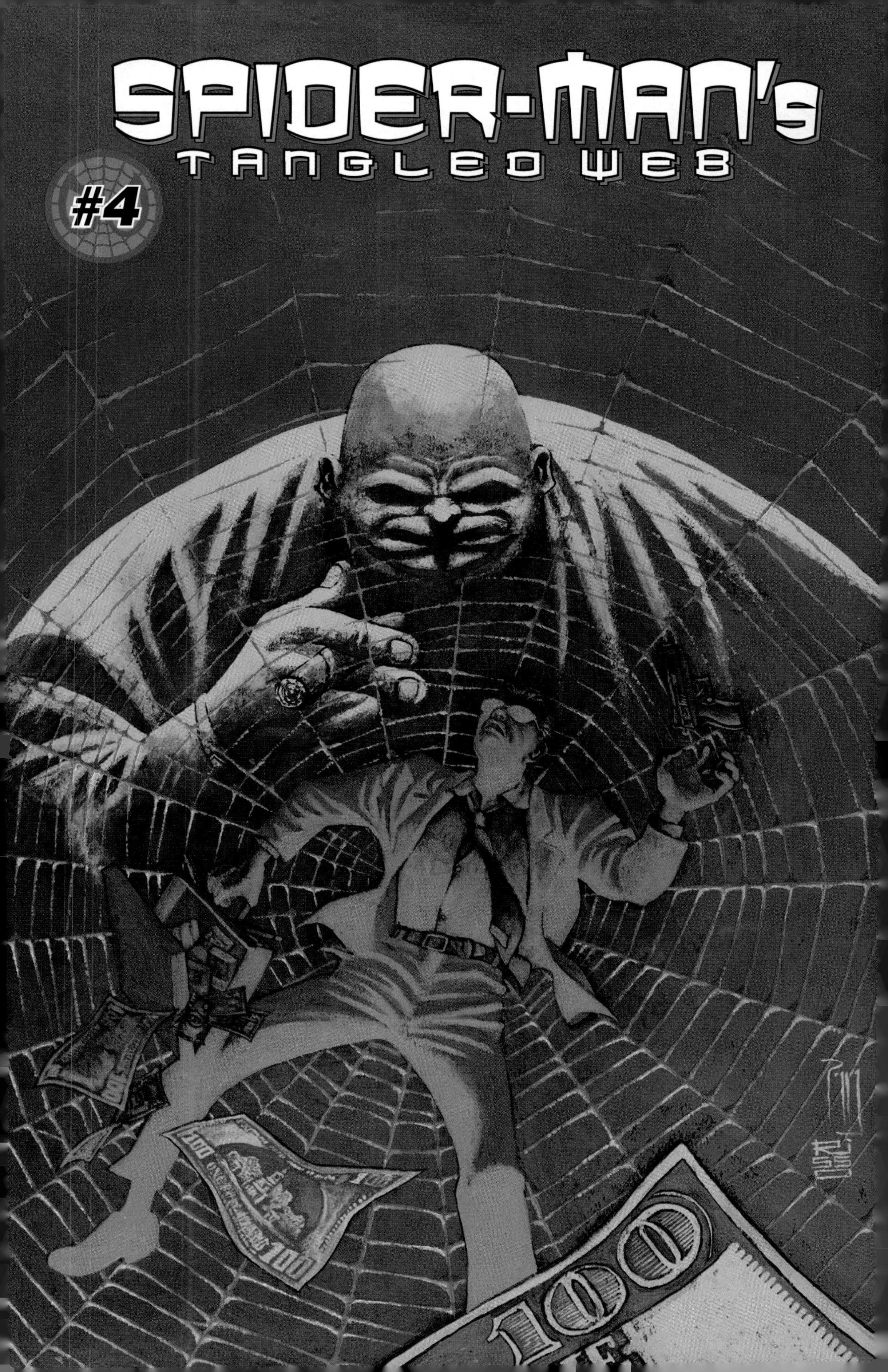
SPIDER-MAN's
TANGLED WEB
#4

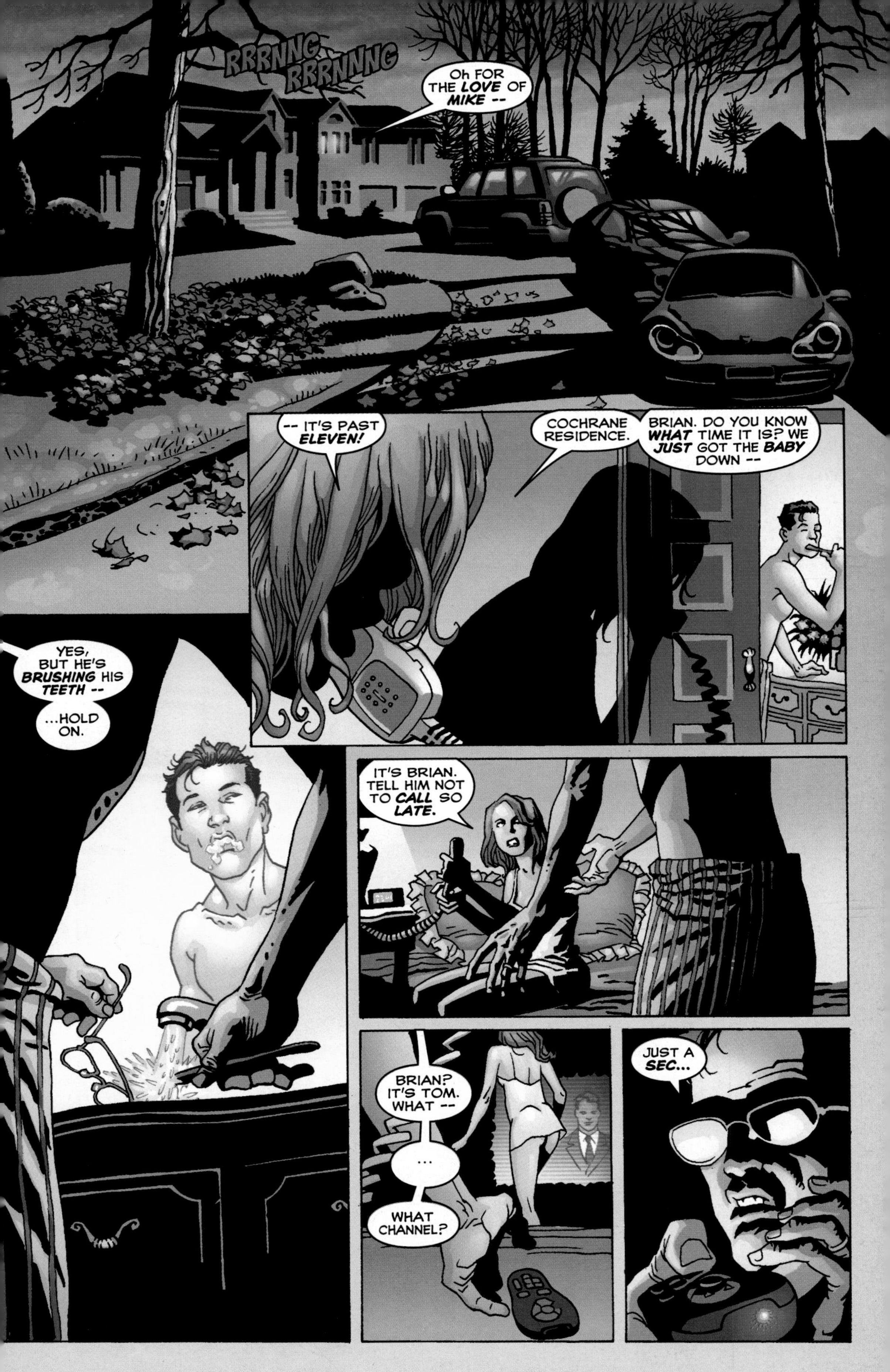
RRRNNG RRRNNNG
Oh FOR THE LOVE OF MIKE --
-- IT'S PAST ELEVEN!
COCHRANE RESIDENCE.
BRIAN. DO YOU KNOW WHAT TIME IT IS? WE JUST GOT THE BABY DOWN --
YES, BUT HE'S BRUSHING HIS TEETH --
...HOLD ON.
IT'S BRIAN. TELL HIM NOT TO CALL SO LATE.
BRIAN? IT'S TOM. WHAT --
...
WHAT CHANNEL?
JUST A SEC...

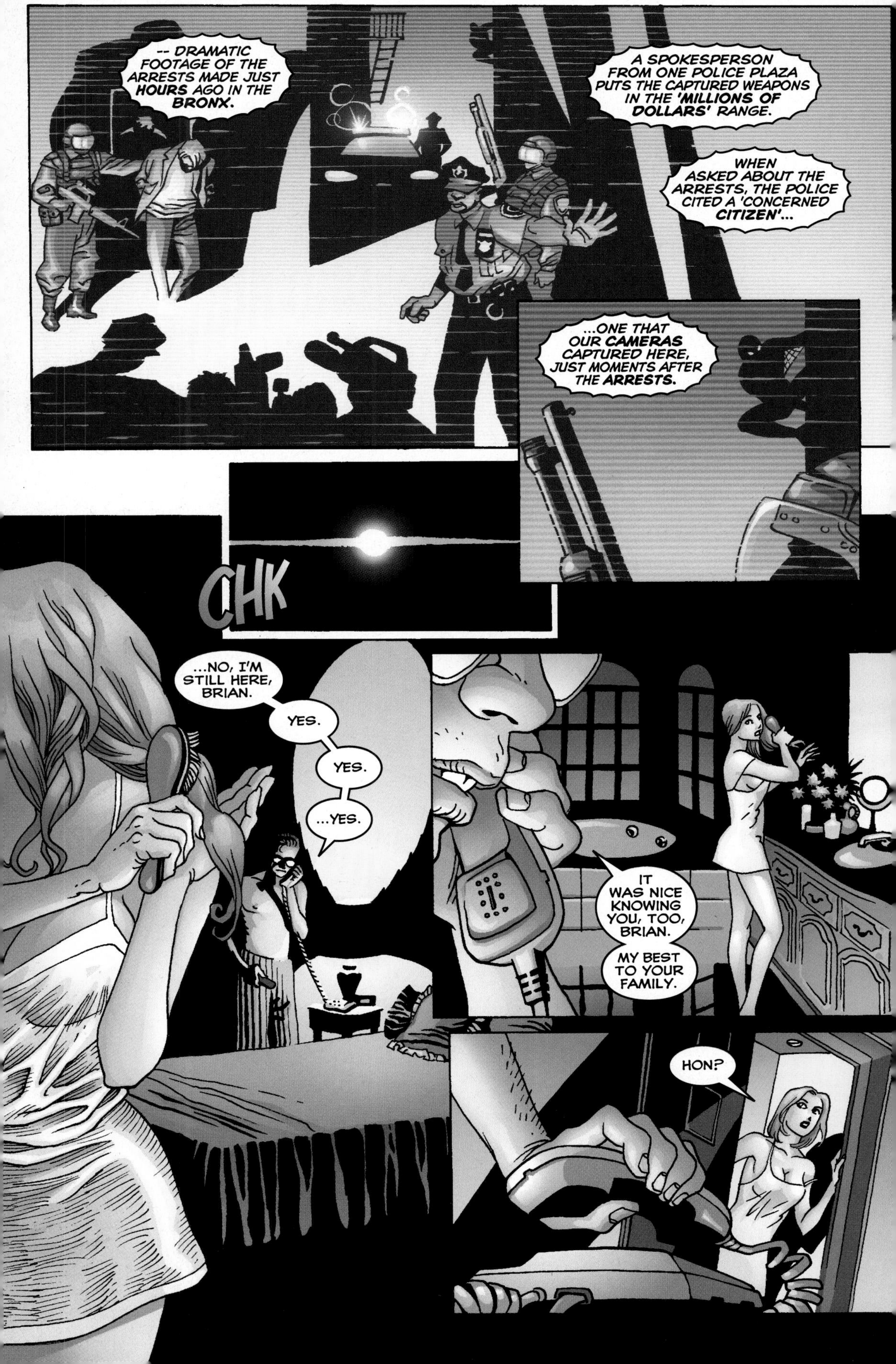
-- DRAMATIC FOOTAGE OF THE ARRESTS MADE JUST HOURS AGO IN THE BRONX.
A SPOKESPERSON FROM ONE POLICE PLAZA PUTS THE CAPTURED WEAPONS IN THE 'MILLIONS OF DOLLARS' RANGE.
WHEN ASKED ABOUT THE ARRESTS, THE POLICE CITED A 'CONCERNED CITIZEN'...
...ONE THAT OUR CAMERAS CAPTURED HERE, JUST MOMENTS AFTER THE ARRESTS.
CHK
...NO, I'M STILL HERE, BRIAN.
YES.
YES.
...YES.
IT WAS NICE KNOWING YOU, TOO, BRIAN.
MY BEST TO YOUR FAMILY.
HON?

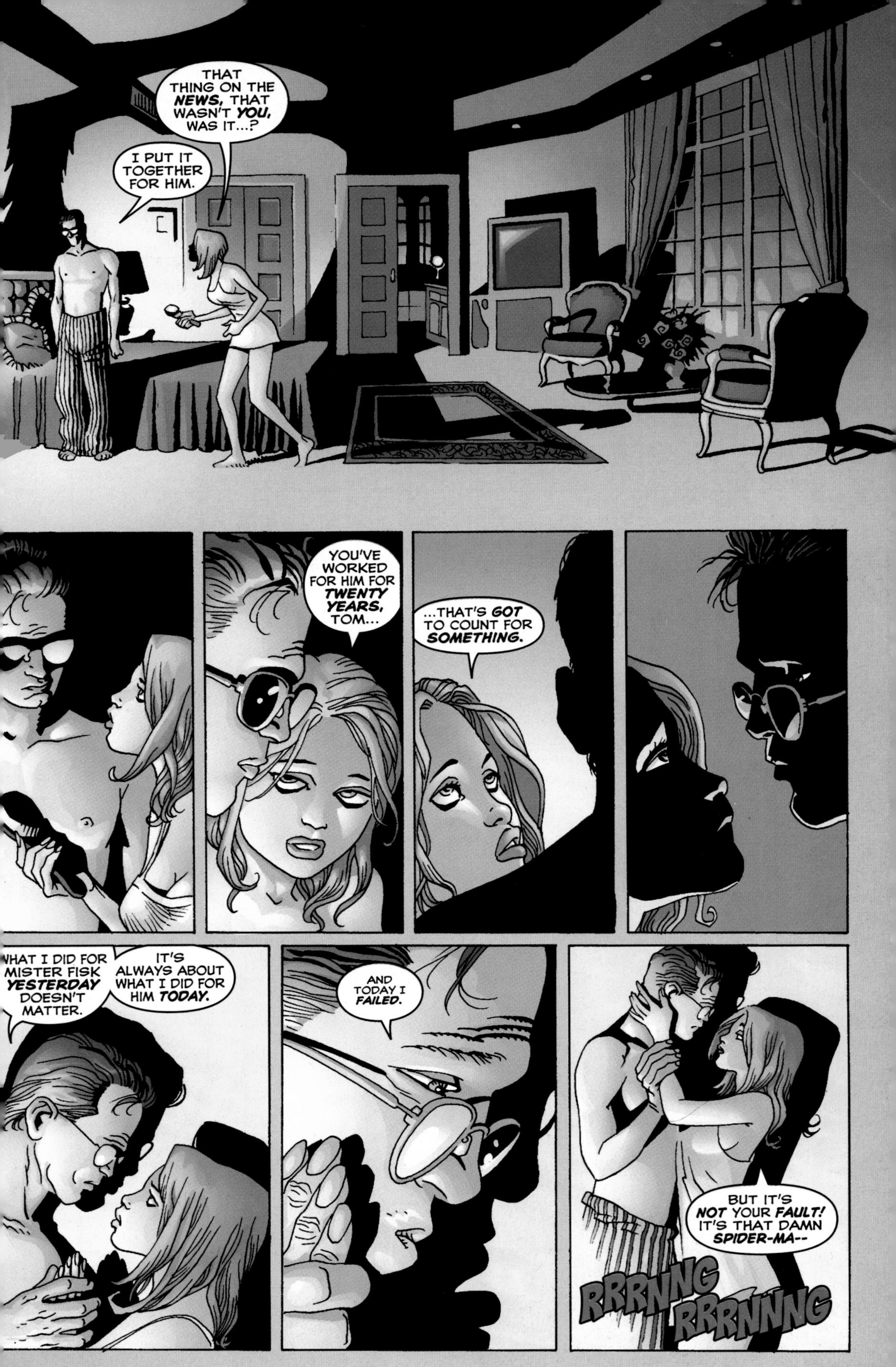
THAT THING ON THE NEWS, THAT WASN'T YOU, WAS IT...?
I PUT IT TOGETHER FOR HIM.
YOU'VE WORKED FOR HIM FOR TWENTY YEARS, TOM...
...THAT'S GOT TO COUNT FOR SOMETHING.
WHAT I DID FOR MISTER FISK YESTERDAY DOESN'T MATTER.
IT'S ALWAYS ABOUT WHAT I DID FOR HIM TODAY.
AND TODAY I FAILED.
BUT IT'S NOT YOUR FAULT! IT'S THAT DAMN SPIDER-MA--
RRRNNG
RRRNNNG

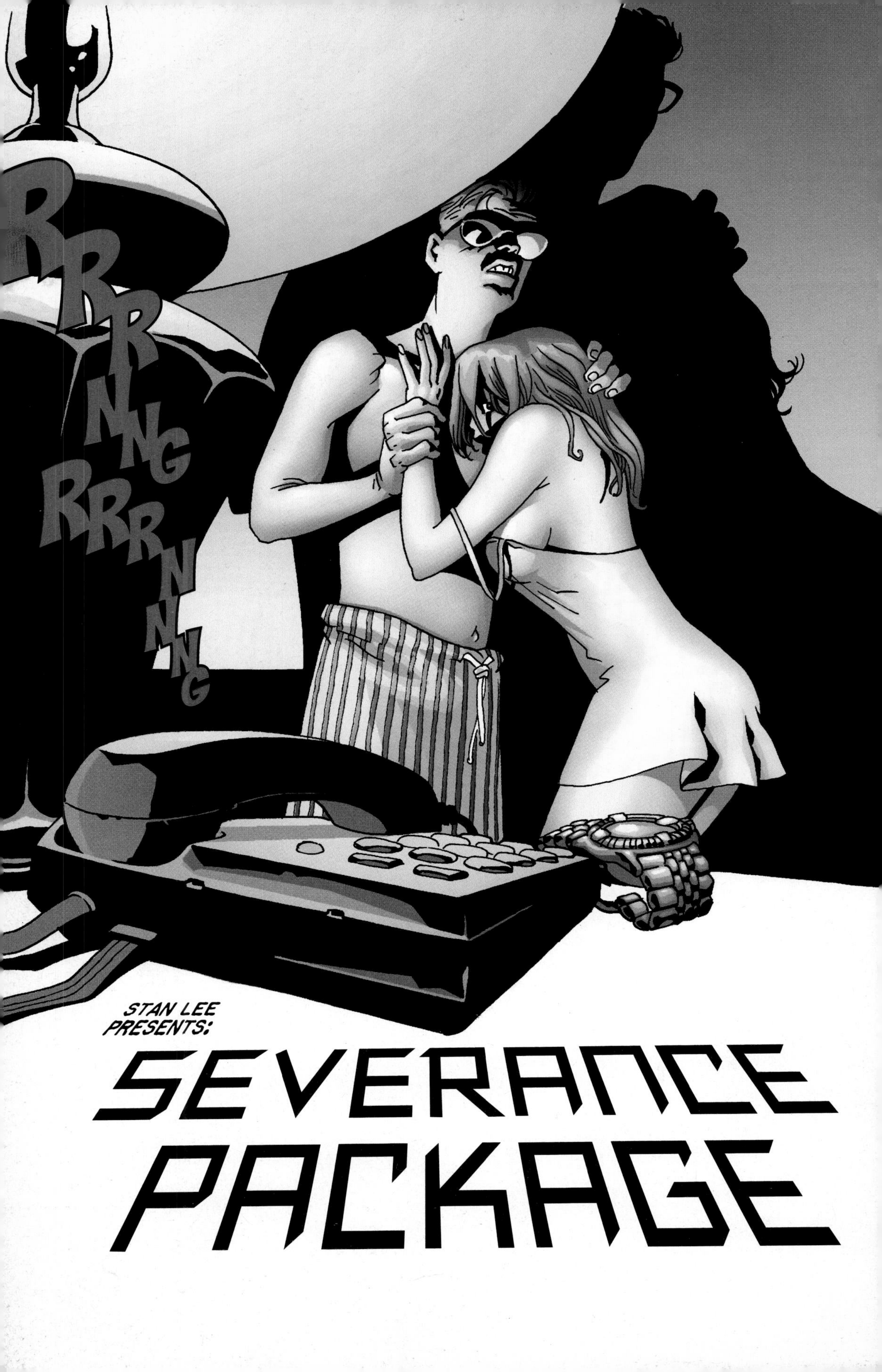
RRRNNG
RRRNNNG
STAN LEE PRESENTS:
SEVERANCE PACKAGE

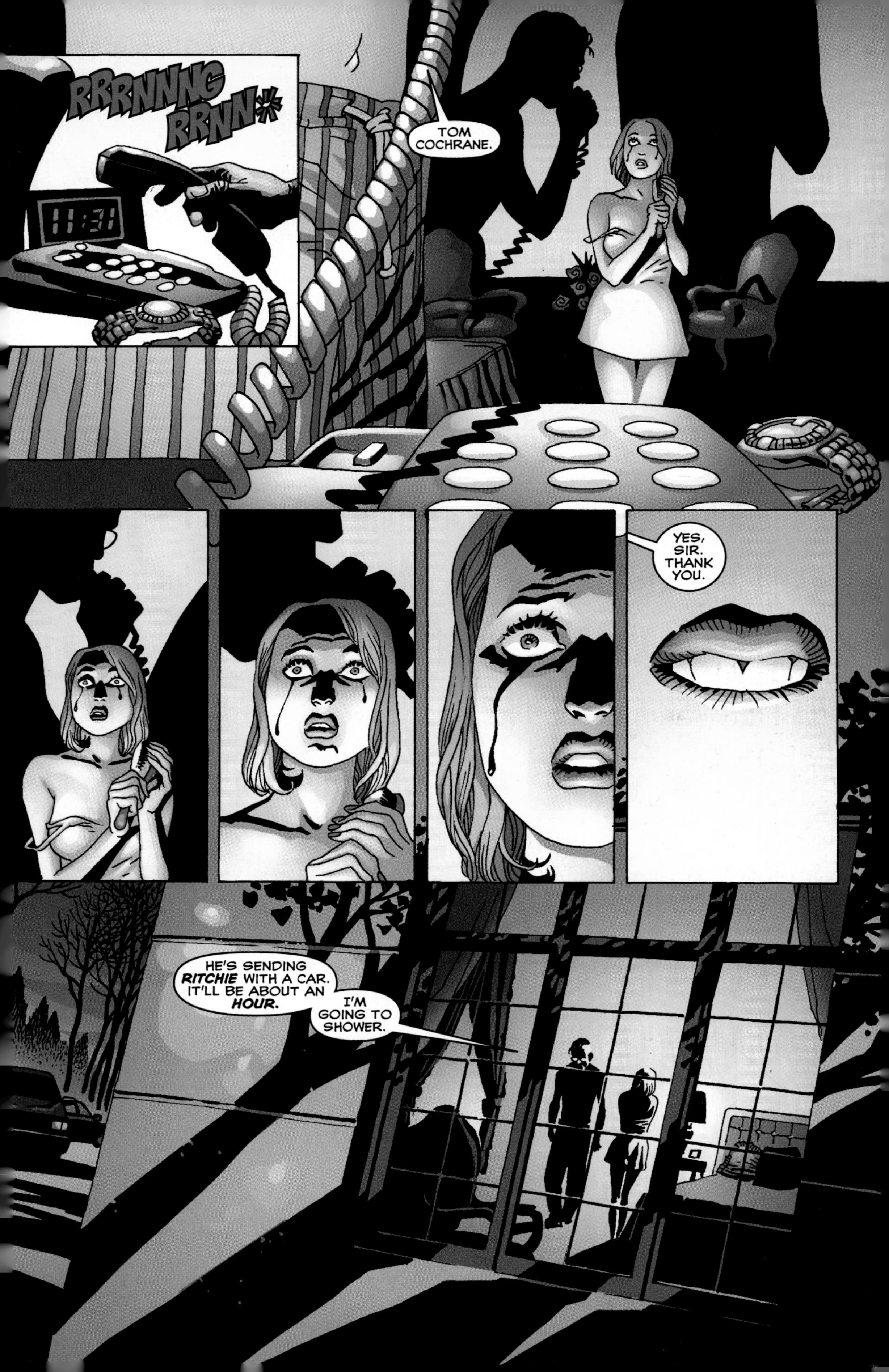
RRRNNNG RRNN*
TOM COCHRANE.
YES, SIR. THANK YOU.
HE'S SENDING RITCHIE WITH A CAR. IT'LL BE ABOUT AN HOUR.
I'M GOING TO SHOWER.

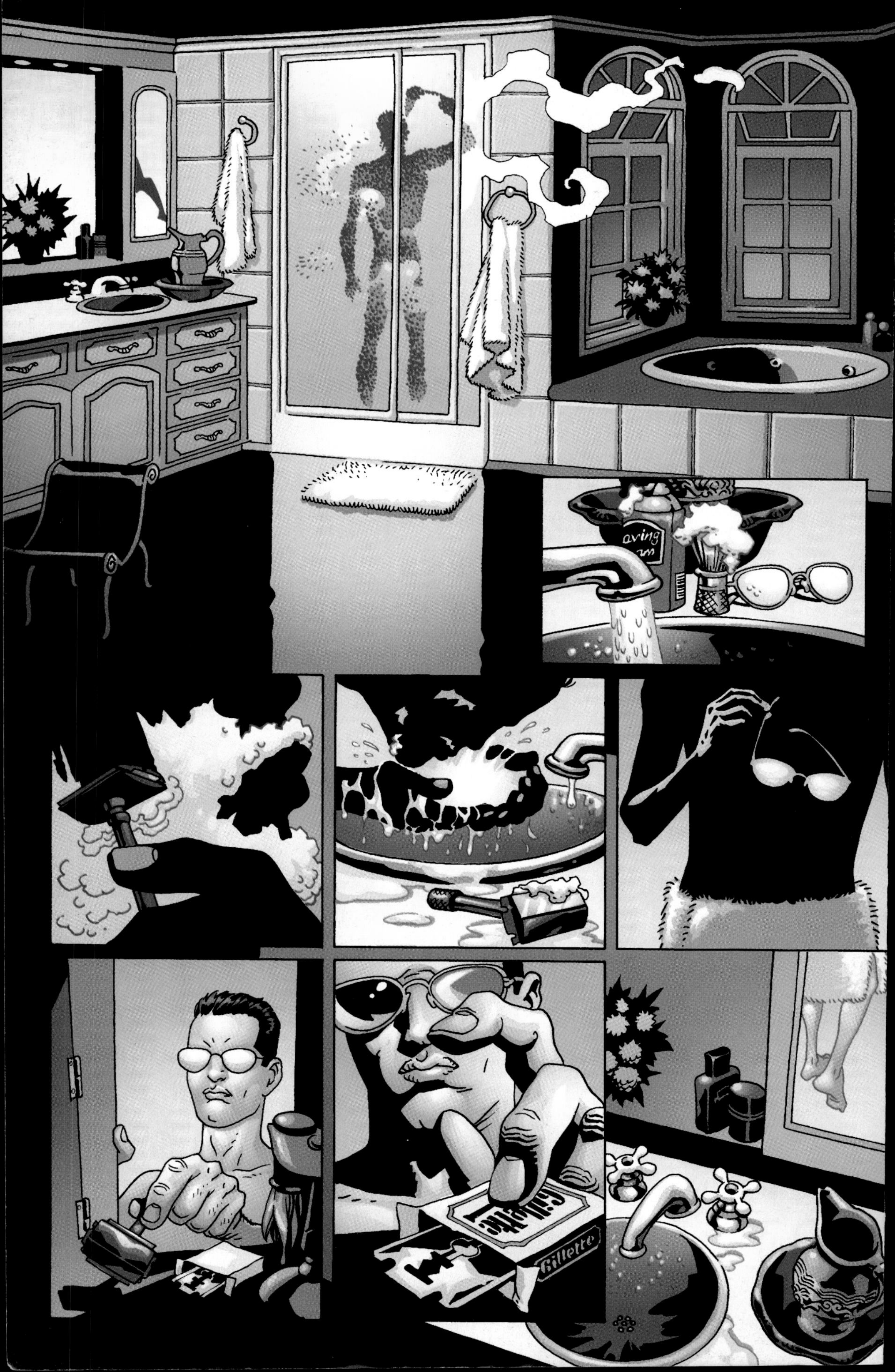
Gillette

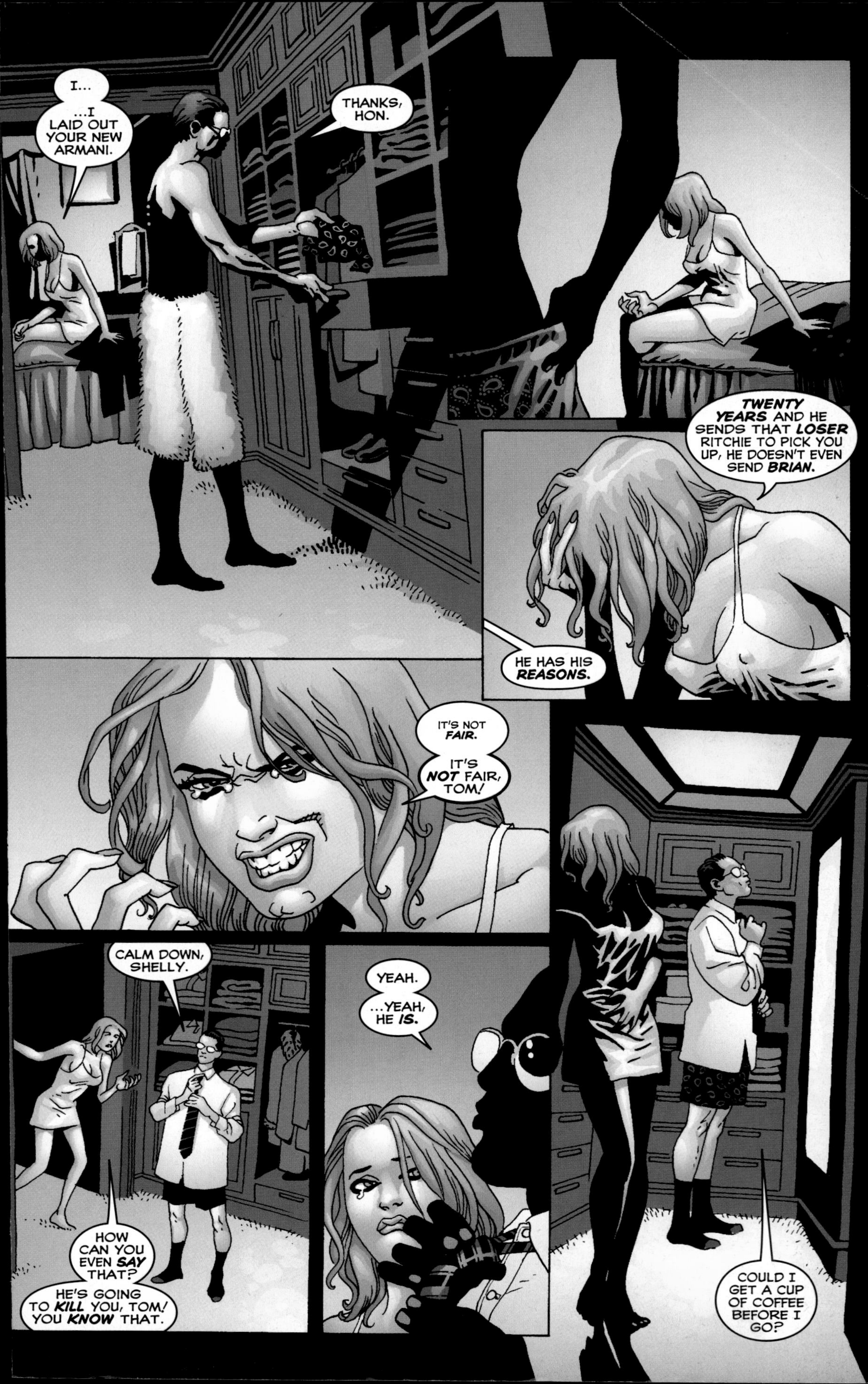
I...
...I LAID OUT YOUR NEW ARMANI.
THANKS, HON.
TWENTY YEARS AND HE SENDS THAT LOSER RITCHIE TO PICK YOU UP, HE DOESN'T EVEN SEND BRIAN.
HE HAS HIS REASONS.
IT'S NOT FAIR.
IT'S NOT FAIR, TOM!
CALM DOWN, SHELLY.
HOW CAN YOU EVEN SAY THAT?
HE'S GOING TO KILL YOU, TOM! YOU KNOW THAT.
YEAH.
...YEAH, HE IS.
COULD I GET A CUP OF COFFEE BEFORE I GO?

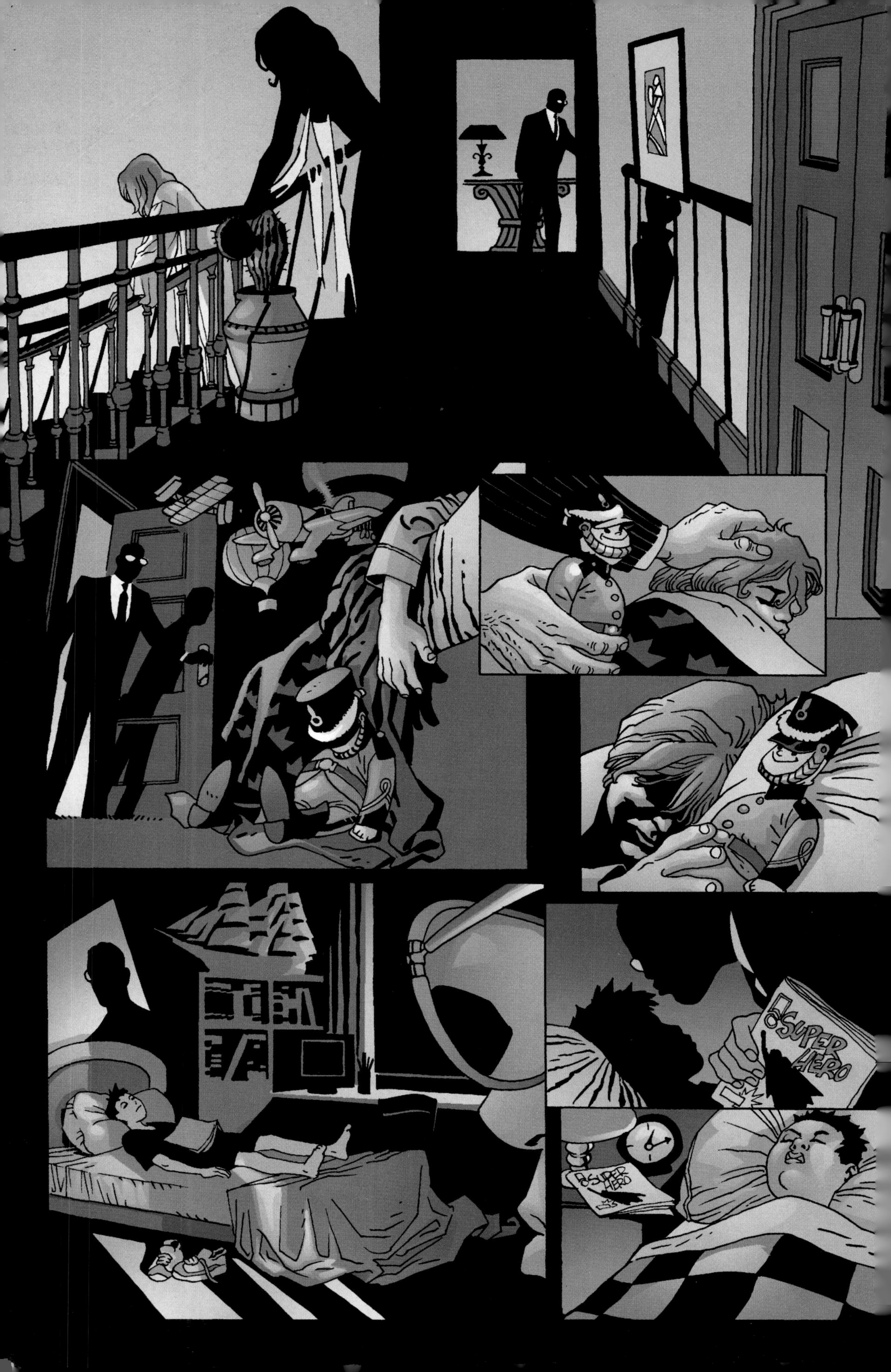
SUPER HERO
SUPER HERO

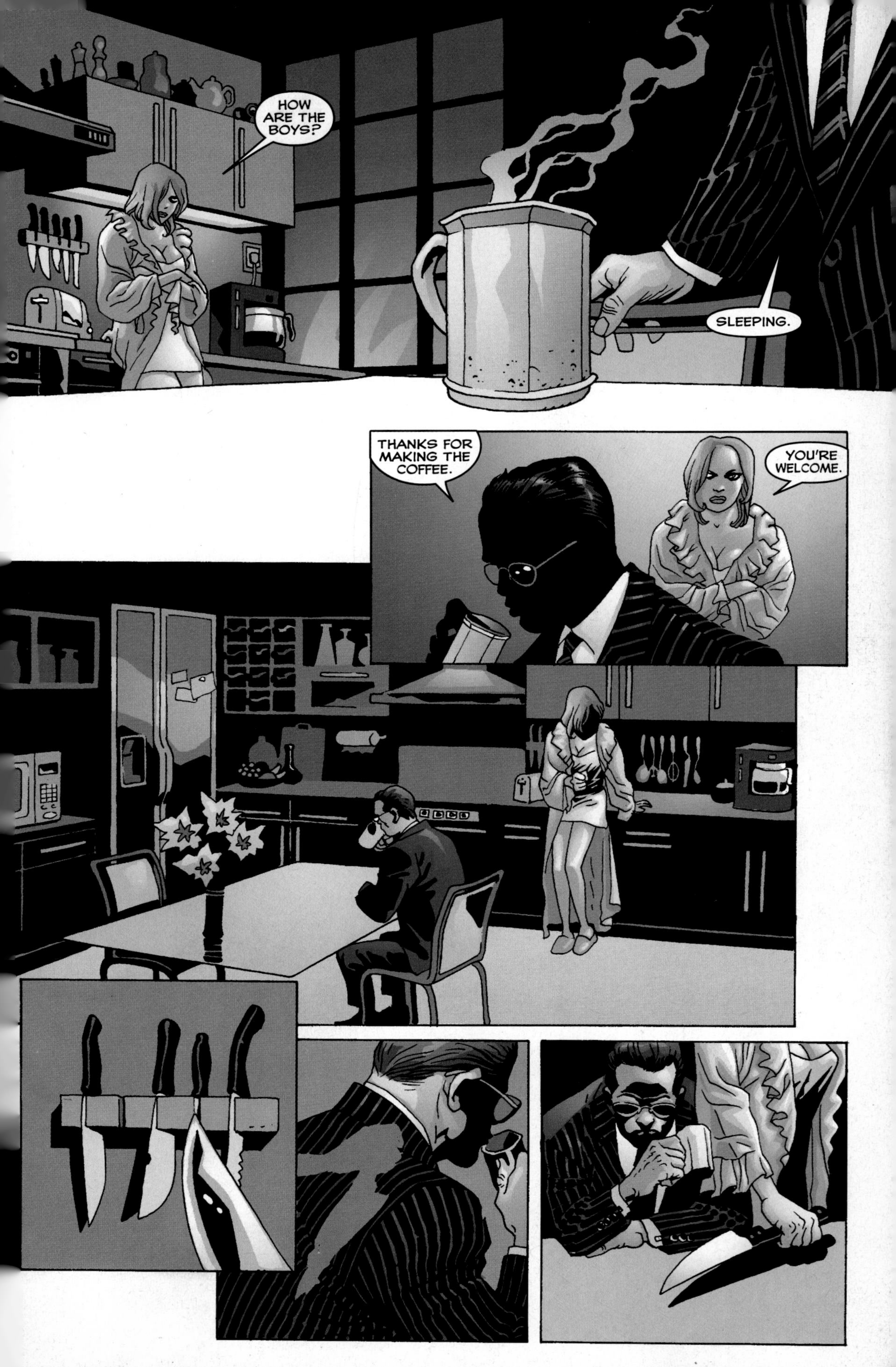
HOW ARE THE BOYS?
SLEEPING.
THANKS FOR MAKING THE COFFEE.
YOU'RE WELCOME.

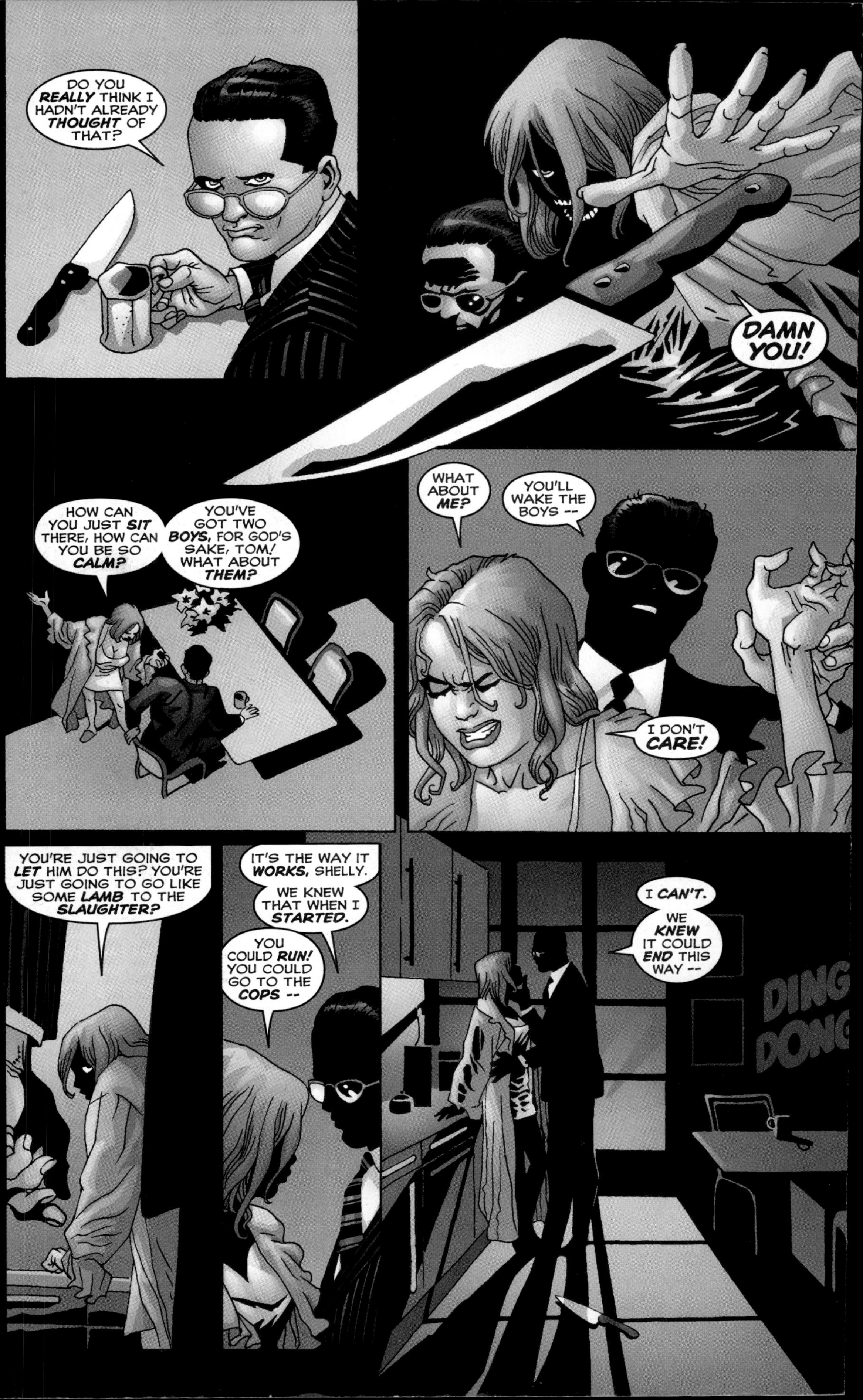

DO YOU REALLY THINK I HADN'T ALREADY THOUGHT OF THAT?
DAMN YOU!
HOW CAN YOU JUST SIT THERE, HOW CAN YOU BE SO CALM?
YOU'VE GOT TWO BOYS, FOR GOD'S SAKE, TOM! WHAT ABOUT THEM?
WHAT ABOUT ME?
YOU'LL WAKE THE BOYS --
I DON'T CARE!
YOU'RE JUST GOING TO LET HIM DO THIS? YOU'RE JUST GOING TO GO LIKE SOME LAMB TO THE SLAUGHTER?
IT'S THE WAY IT WORKS, SHELLY.
WE KNEW THAT WHEN I STARTED.
YOU COULD RUN! YOU COULD GO TO THE COPS --
I CAN'T.
WE KNEW IT COULD END THIS WAY --
DING DONG

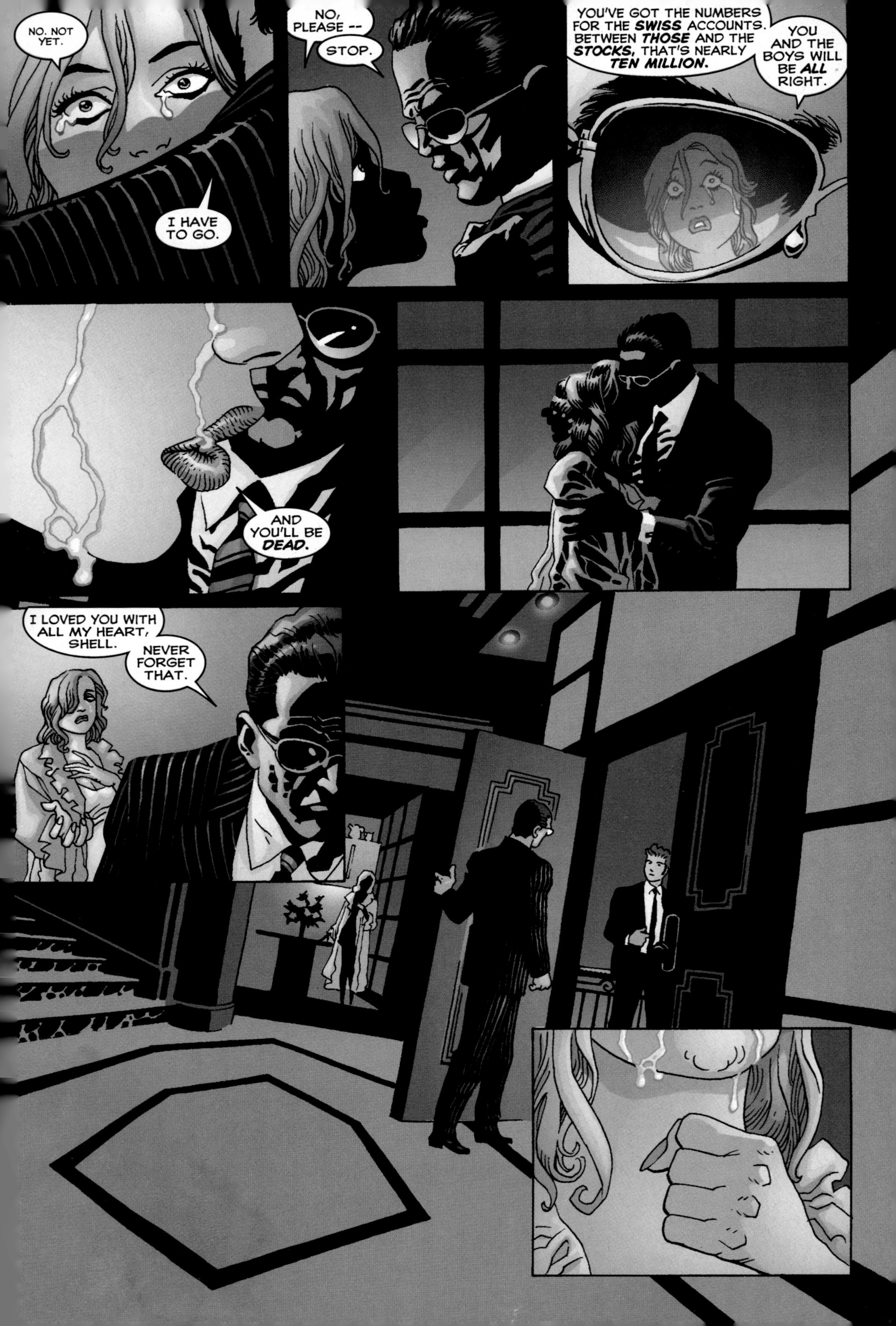

NO. NOT YET.
I HAVE TO GO.
NO, PLEASE --
STOP.
YOU'VE GOT THE NUMBERS FOR THE **SWISS** ACCOUNTS. BETWEEN **THOSE** AND THE **STOCKS,** THAT'S NEARLY **TEN MILLION.**
YOU AND THE BOYS WILL BE **ALL** RIGHT.
AND YOU'LL BE **DEAD.**
I LOVED YOU WITH ALL MY HEART, SHELL.
NEVER FORGET THAT.

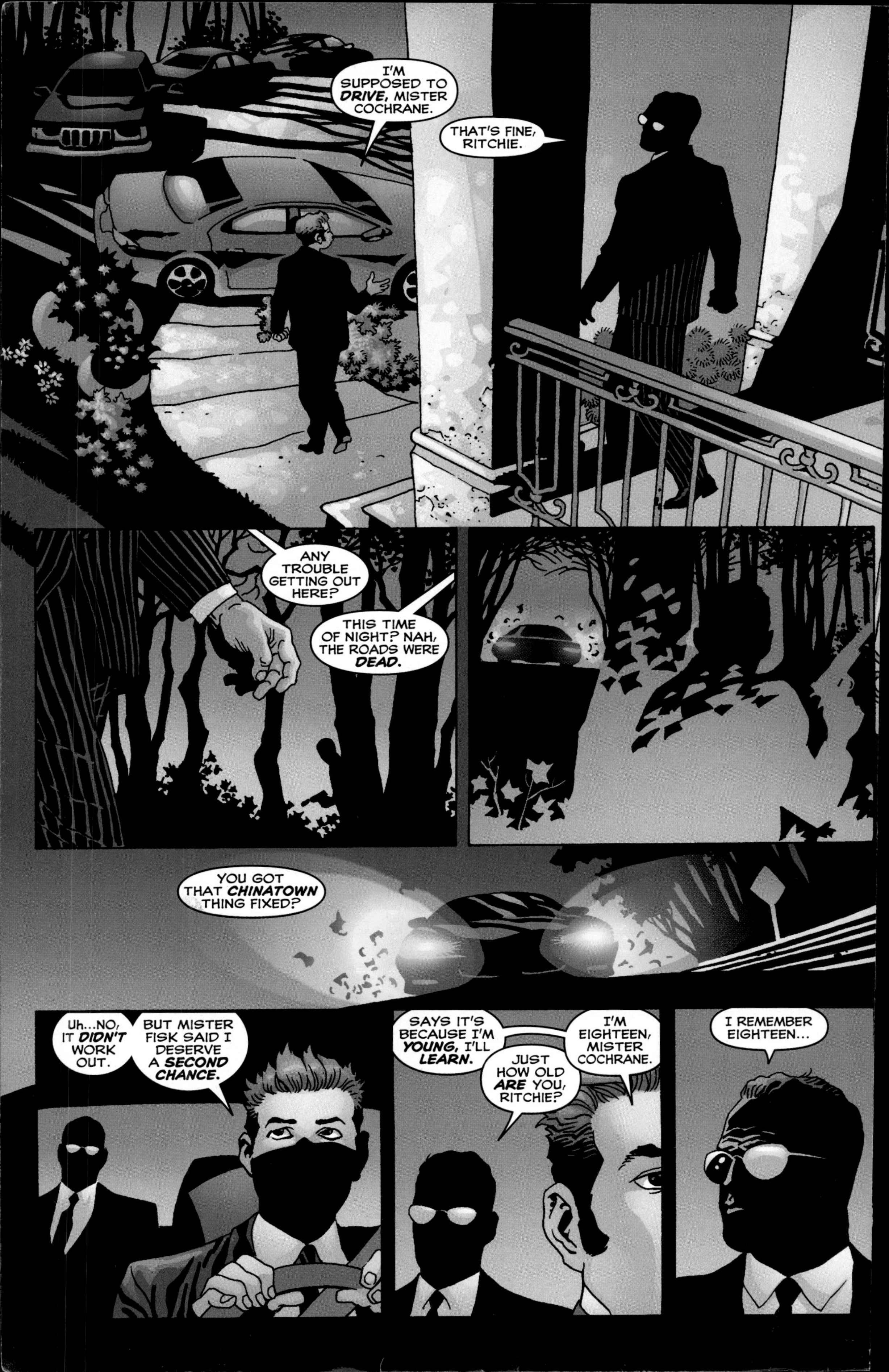
I'M SUPPOSED TO DRIVE, MISTER COCHRANE.
THAT'S FINE, RITCHIE.
ANY TROUBLE GETTING OUT HERE?
THIS TIME OF NIGHT? NAH, THE ROADS WERE DEAD.
YOU GOT THAT CHINATOWN THING FIXED?
Uh...NO, IT DIDN'T WORK OUT.
BUT MISTER FISK SAID I DESERVE A SECOND CHANCE.
SAYS IT'S BECAUSE I'M YOUNG, I'LL LEARN.
JUST HOW OLD ARE YOU, RITCHIE?
I'M EIGHTEEN, MISTER COCHRANE.
I REMEMBER EIGHTEEN...

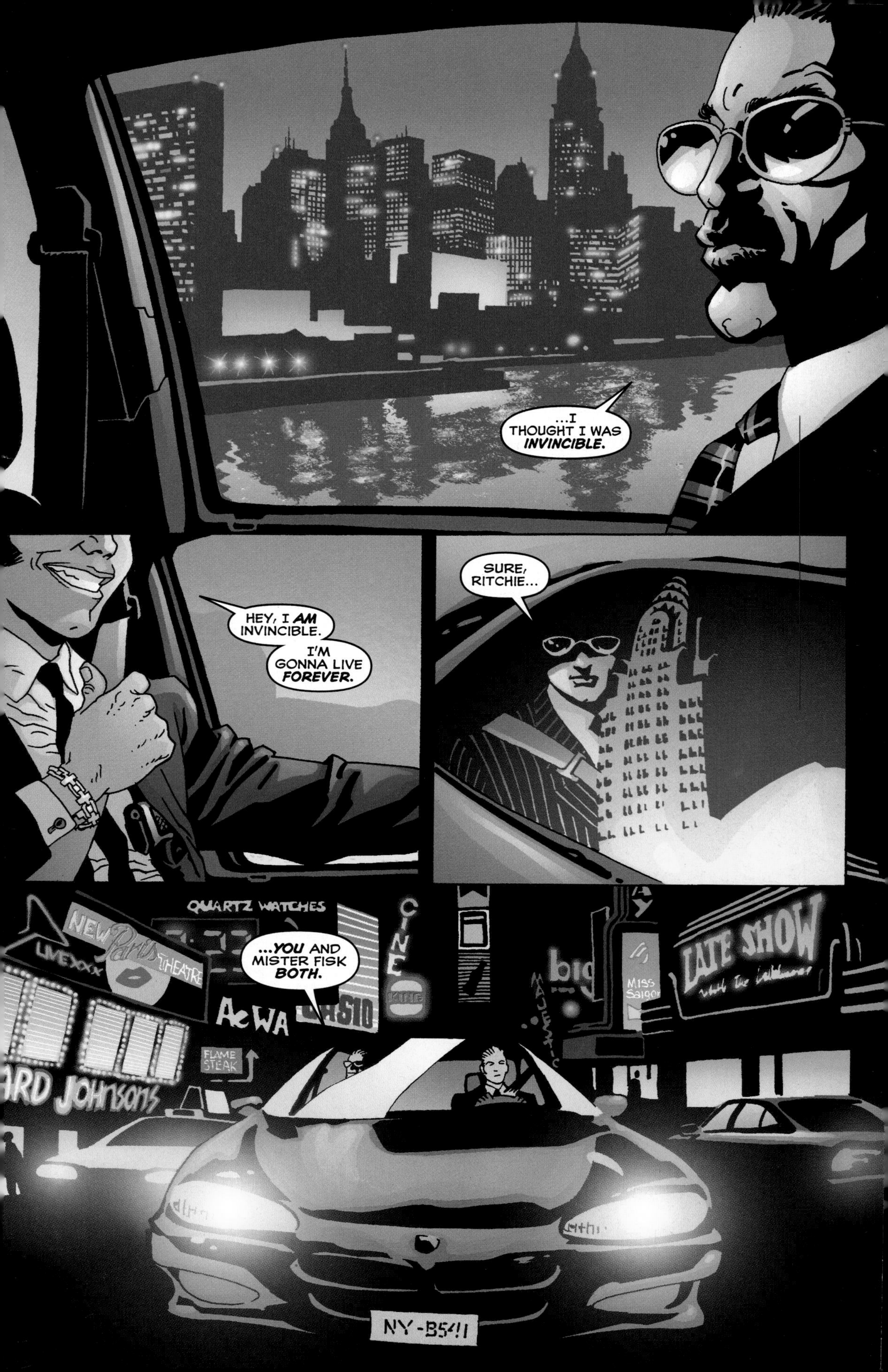
...I THOUGHT I WAS *INVINCIBLE.*
HEY, I *AM* INVINCIBLE.
I'M GONNA LIVE *FOREVER.*
SURE, RITCHIE...
...*YOU* AND MISTER FISK *BOTH.*
QUARTZ WATCHES
NEW Paris THEATRE
LIVE XXX
CINE
LATE SHOW
MISS SAIGON
FLAME STEAK
ARD JOHNSONS
NY-B541

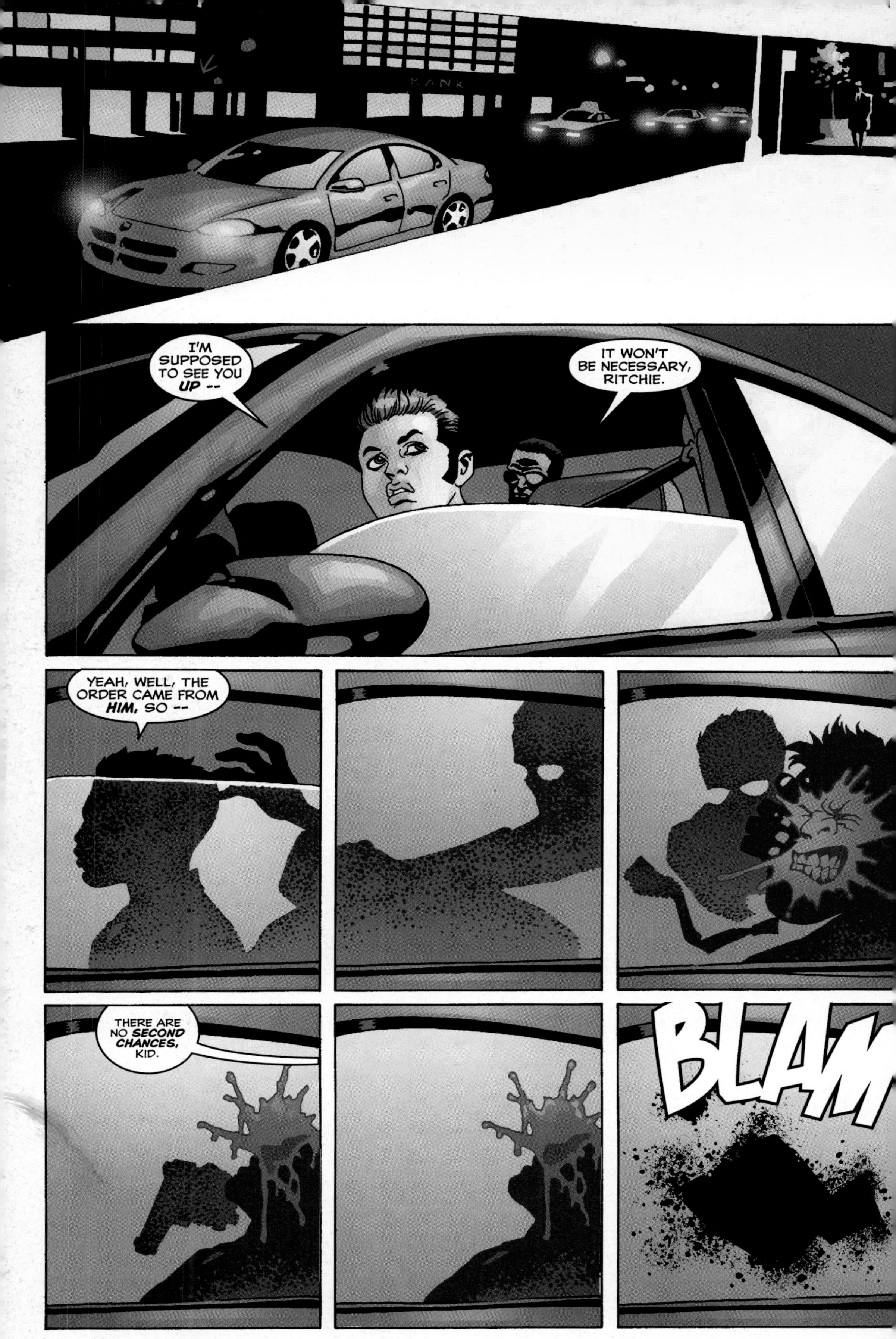
BANK
I'M SUPPOSED TO SEE YOU UP --
IT WON'T BE NECESSARY, RITCHIE.
YEAH, WELL, THE ORDER CAME FROM HIM, SO --
THERE ARE NO SECOND CHANCES, KID.
BLAM

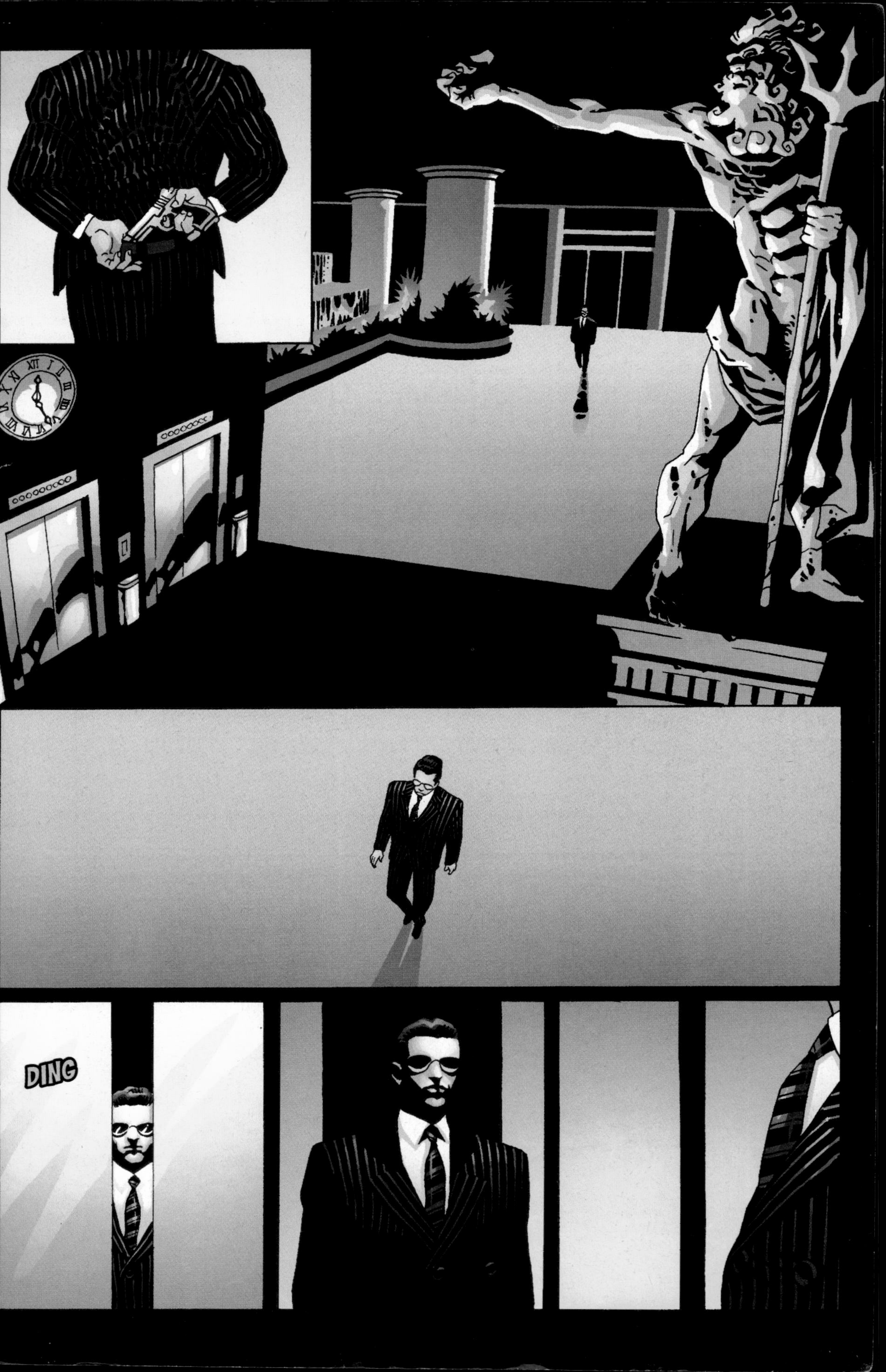
DING

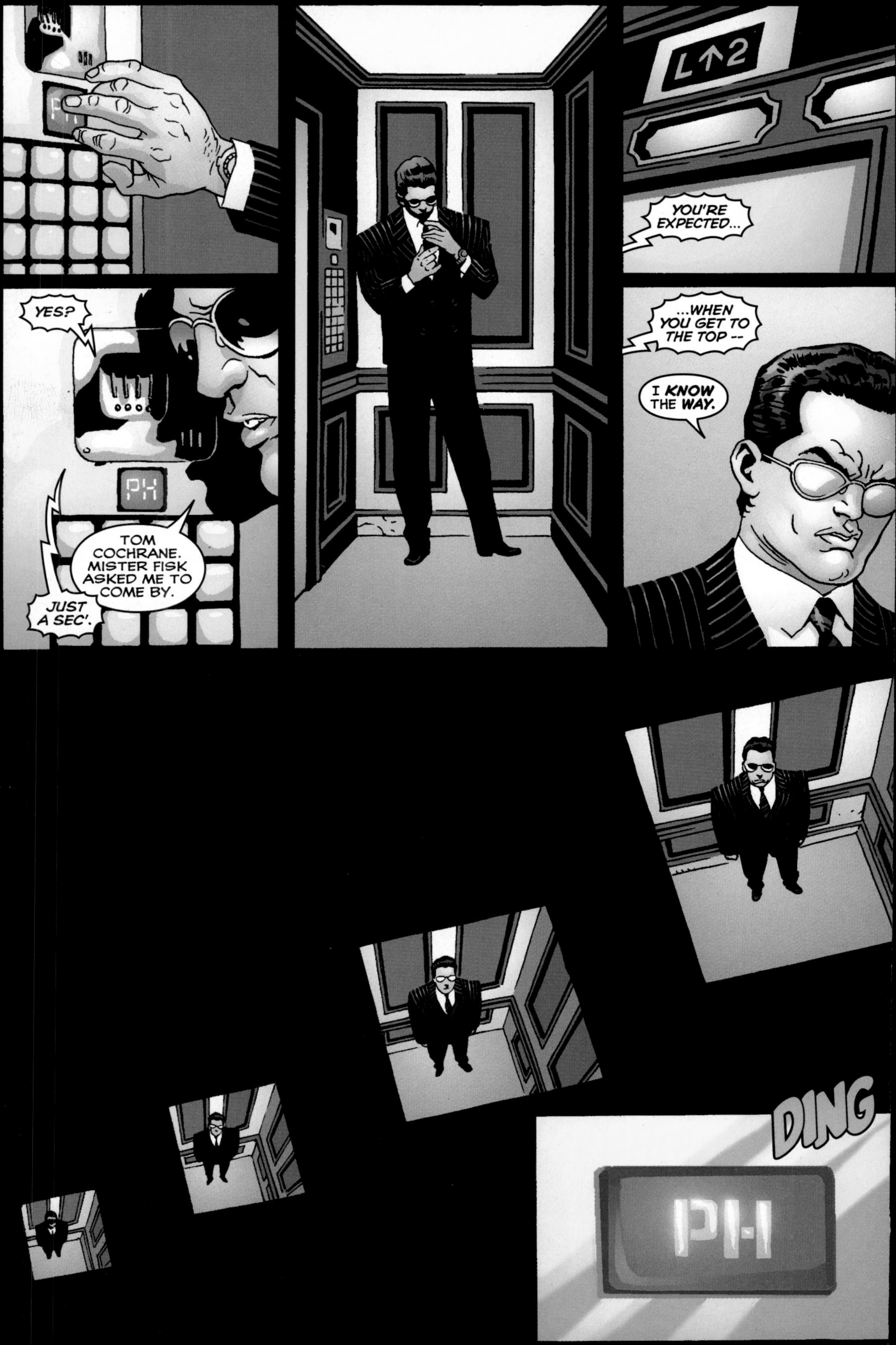
YOU'RE EXPECTED...
YES?
TOM COCHRANE. MISTER FISK ASKED ME TO COME BY.
JUST A SEC'.
...WHEN YOU GET TO THE TOP --
I KNOW THE WAY.
DING

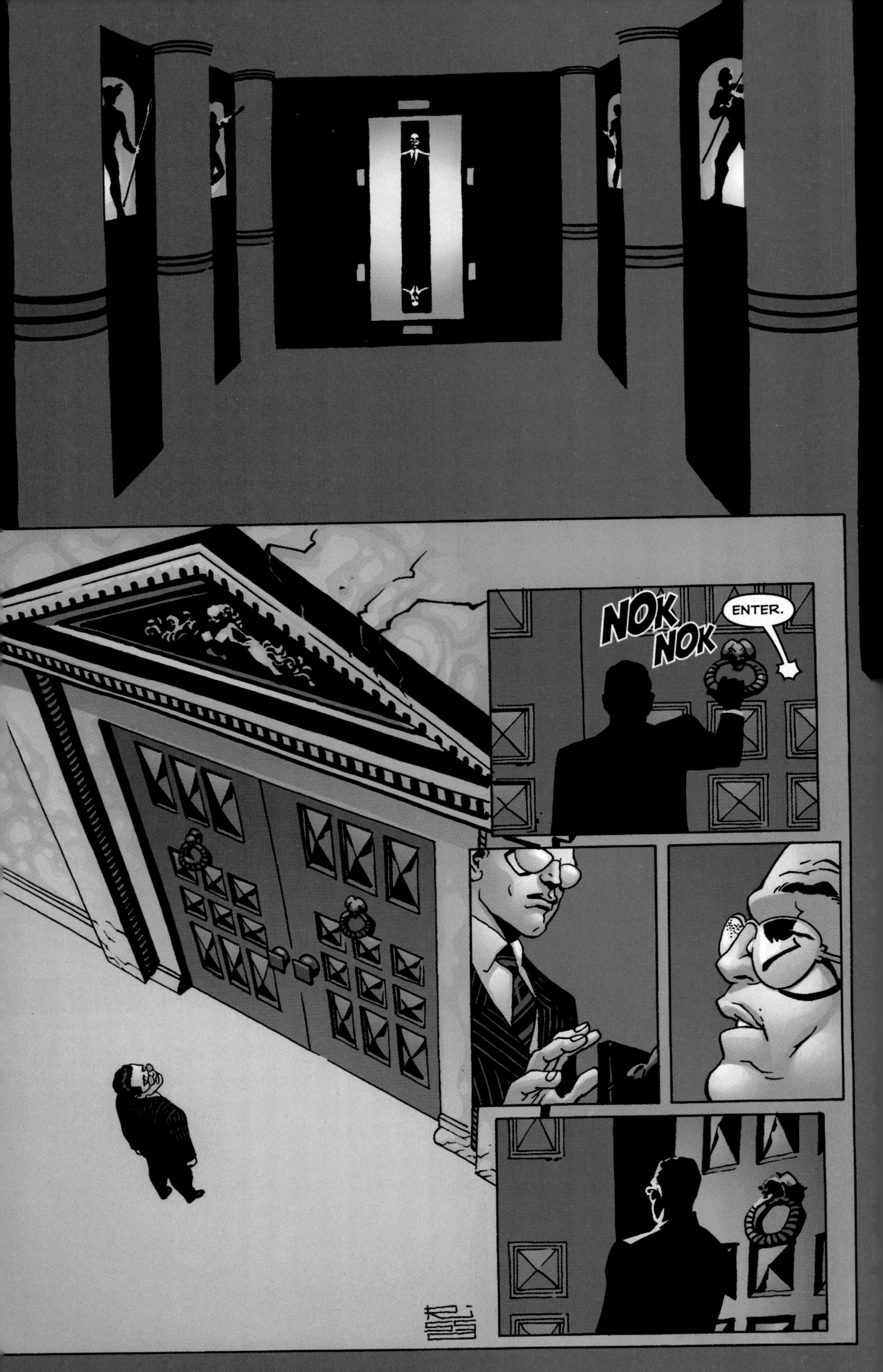
NOK NOK
ENTER.

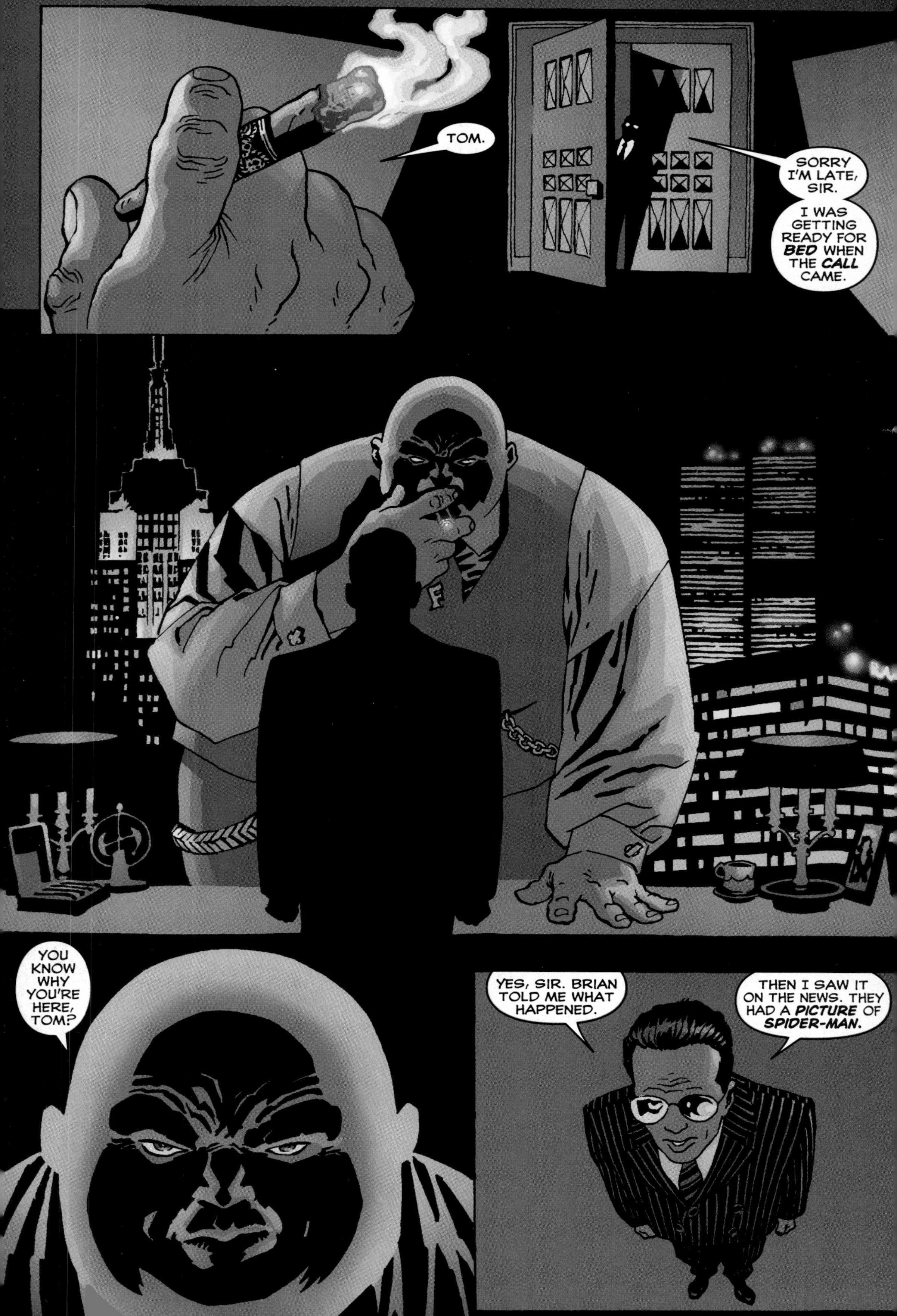
TOM.
SORRY I'M LATE, SIR.
I WAS GETTING READY FOR BED WHEN THE CALL CAME.
YOU KNOW WHY YOU'RE HERE, TOM?
YES, SIR. BRIAN TOLD ME WHAT HAPPENED.
THEN I SAW IT ON THE NEWS. THEY HAD A PICTURE OF SPIDER-MAN.

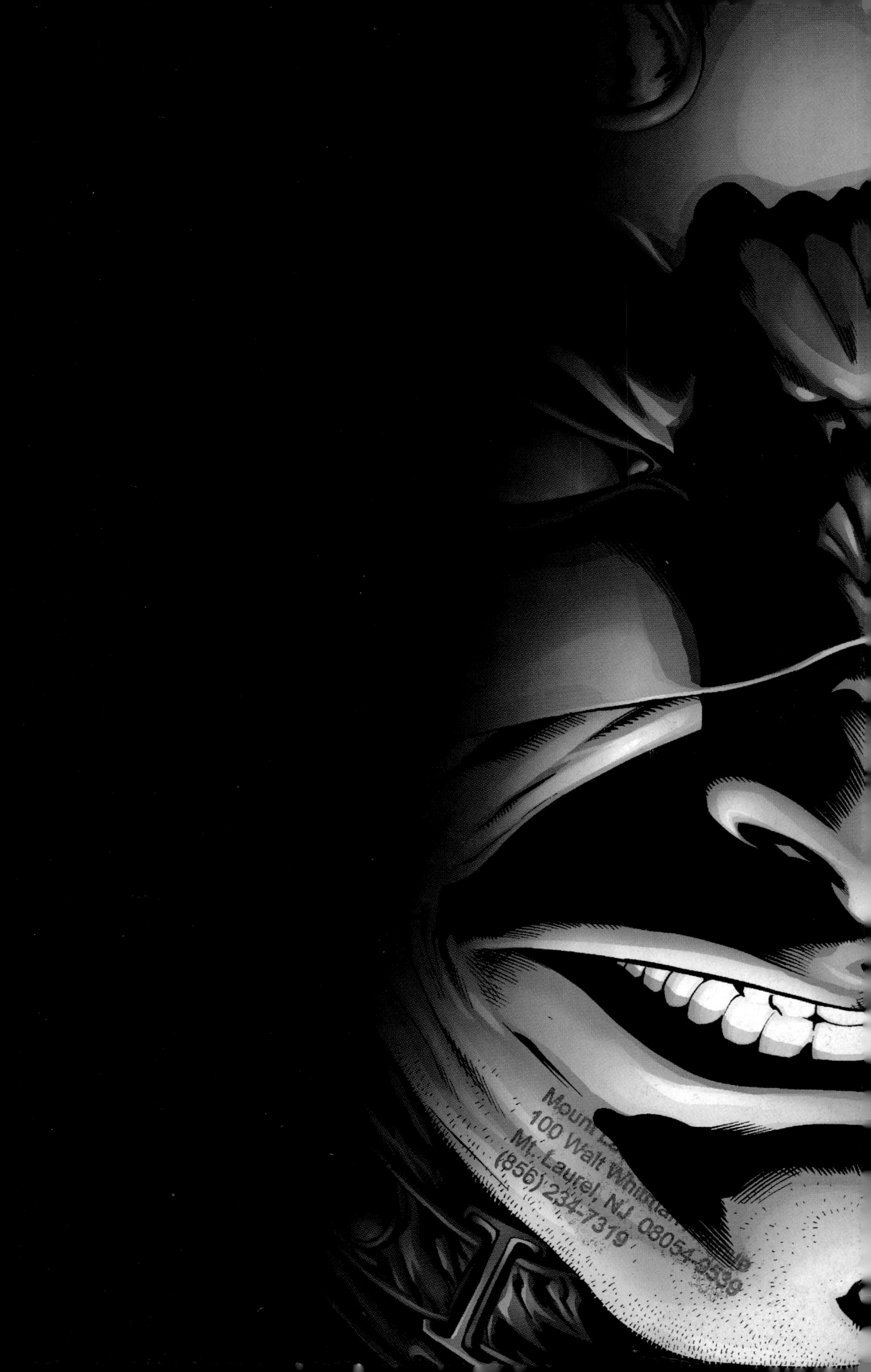

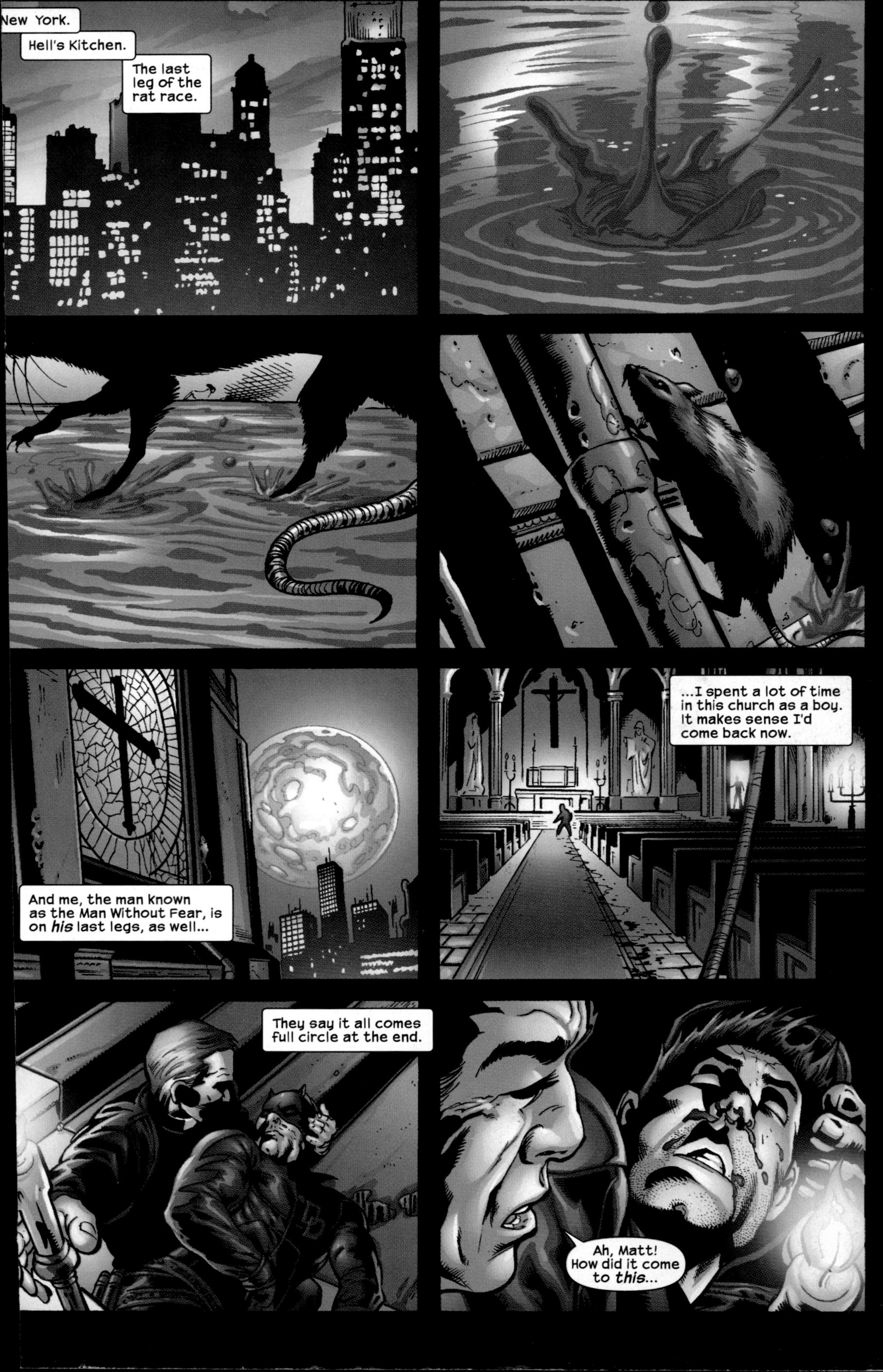
New York.
Hell's Kitchen.
The last leg of the rat race.
And me, the man known as the Man Without Fear, is on *his* last legs, as well...
...I spent a lot of time in this church as a boy. It makes sense I'd come back now.
They say it all comes full circle at the end.
Ah, Matt! How did it come to *this*...

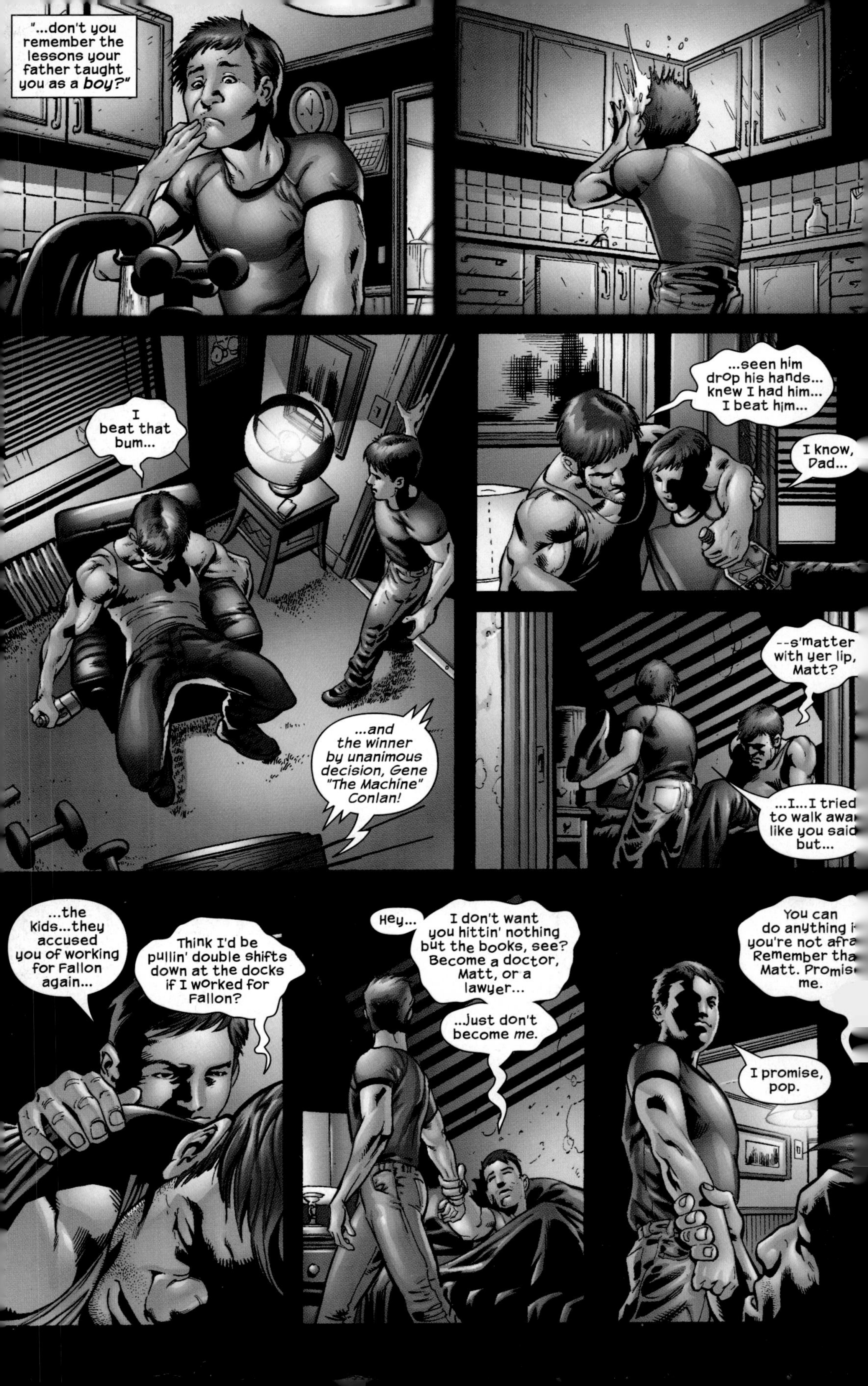
"...don't you remember the lessons your father taught you as a *boy?*"
I beat that bum...
...and the winner by unanimous decision, Gene "The Machine" Conlan!
...seen him drop his hands... knew I had him... I beat him...
I know, Dad...
--s'matter with yer lip, Matt?
...I...I tried to walk awa like you said but...
...the kids...they accused you of working for Fallon again...
Think I'd be pullin' double shifts down at the docks if I worked for Fallon?
Hey...
I don't want you hittin' nothing but the books, see? Become a doctor, Matt, or a lawyer...
...just don't become *me.*
You can do anything i you're not afra Remember tha Matt. Promis me.
I promise, pop.

The next day...

...I was looking for my dad.

Jack Murdock?

He ain't worked here in months, kid. Now beat it, huh?

...p-please... you gotta t-tell Fallon I need more time!

Ain't just Fallon...

...It's *Kingpin* says yer all outta time!

--Dad?

NO!

Matt!

Wait!

KREEEEEHHHH!

KARR RAINGGG!

SSSSSSSSS...

MATT!

Matt, are you all right!

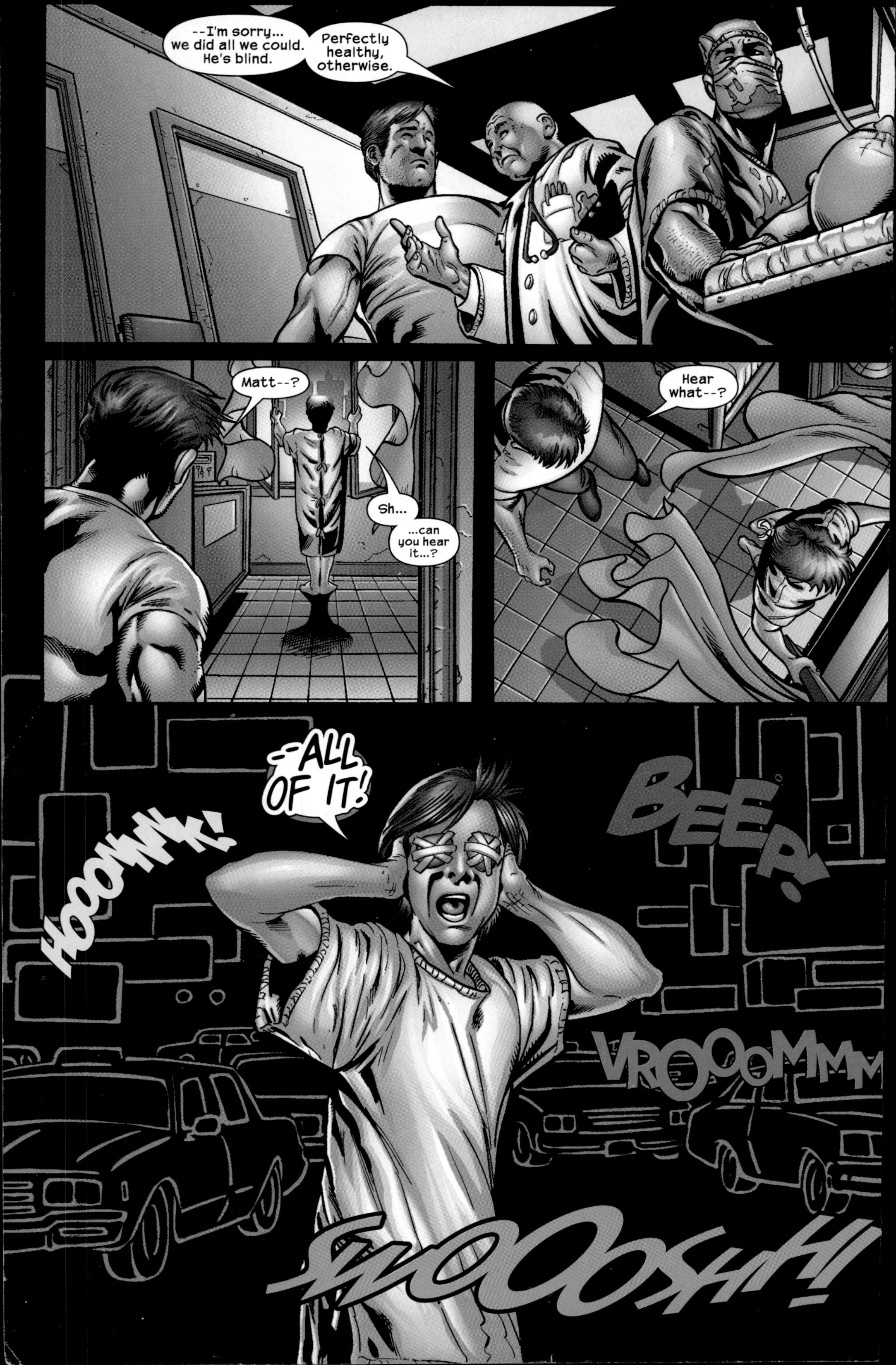
--I'm sorry... we did all we could. He's blind.
Perfectly healthy, otherwise.
Matt--?
Sh...
...can you hear it...?
Hear what--?
--ALL OF IT!
HOOONK!
BEEP!
VROOOMMM
SWOOSH!

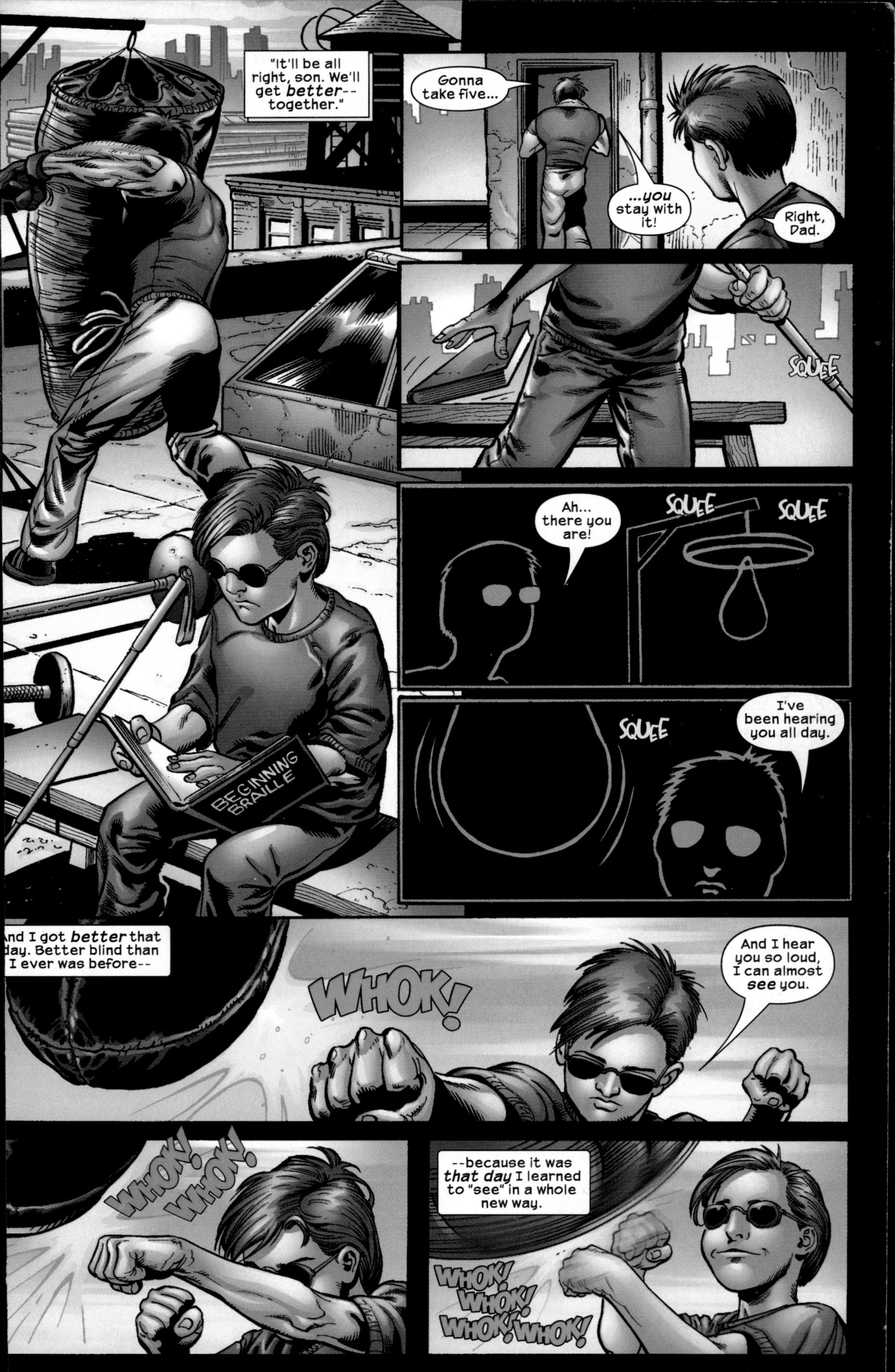
"It'll be all right, son. We'll get *better*-- together."
Gonna take five...
...*you* stay with it!
Right, Dad.
SQUEE
Ah... there you are!
SQUEE
SQUEE
BEGINNING BRAILLE
SQUEE
I've been hearing you all day.
And I got *better* that day. Better blind than I ever was before--
WHOK!
And I hear you so loud, I can almost *see* you.
WHOK! WHOK!
--because it was *that day* I learned to "see" in a whole new way.
WHOK! WHOK! WHOK! WHOK!

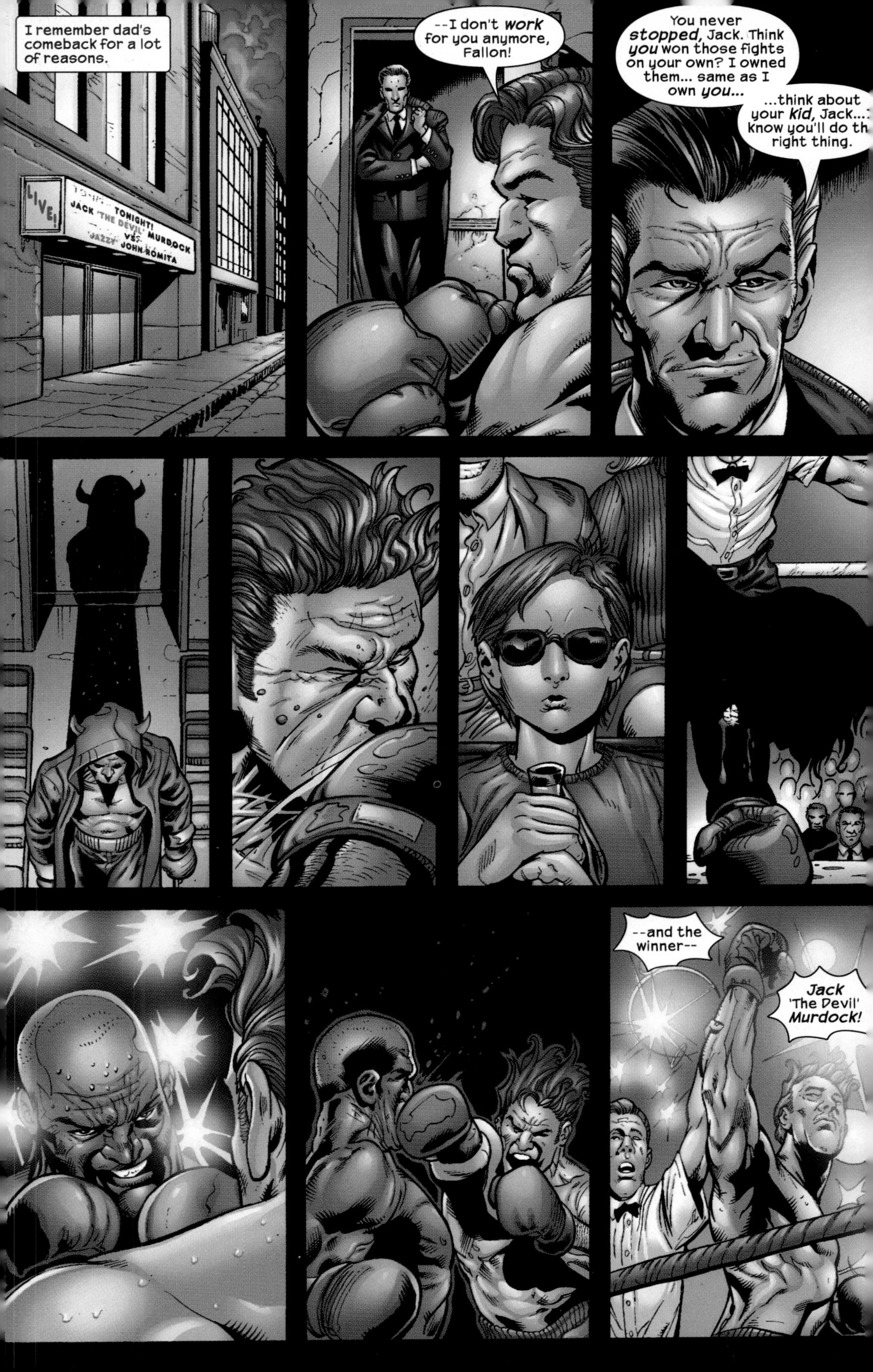

I remember dad's comeback for a lot of reasons.
LIVE!
TONIGHT! JACK 'THE DEVIL' MURDOCK VS. 'JAZZY' JOHN ROMITA
--I don't *work* for you anymore, Fallon!
You never *stopped*, Jack. Think *you* won those fights on your own? I owned them... same as I own *you*...
...think about your *kid*, Jack... I know you'll do the right thing.
--and the winner--
Jack 'The Devil' *Murdock!*

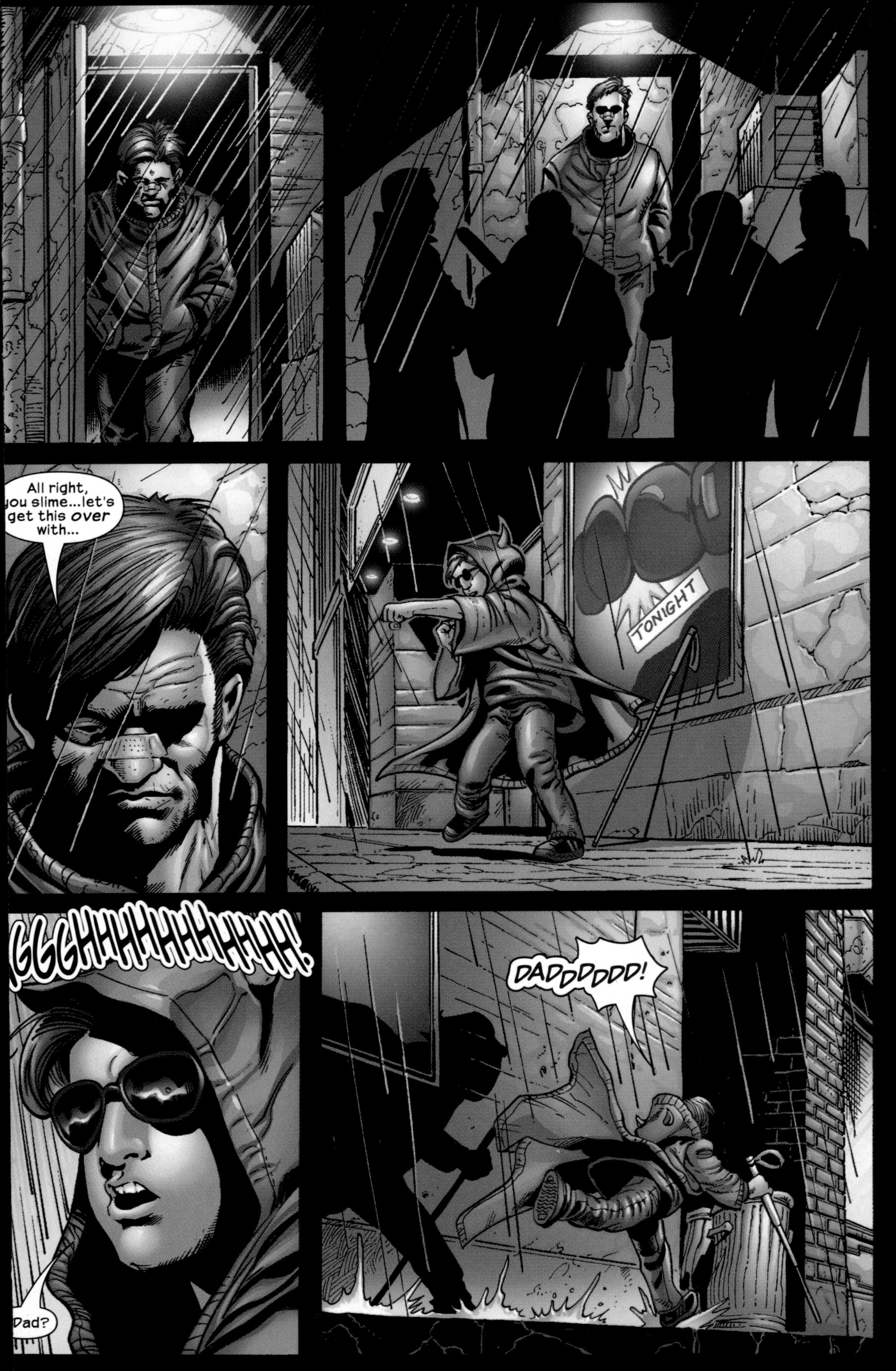
All right, you slime...let's get this *over* with...
TONIGHT
GGGHHHHHHHHHHH!
Dad?
DADDDDDD!

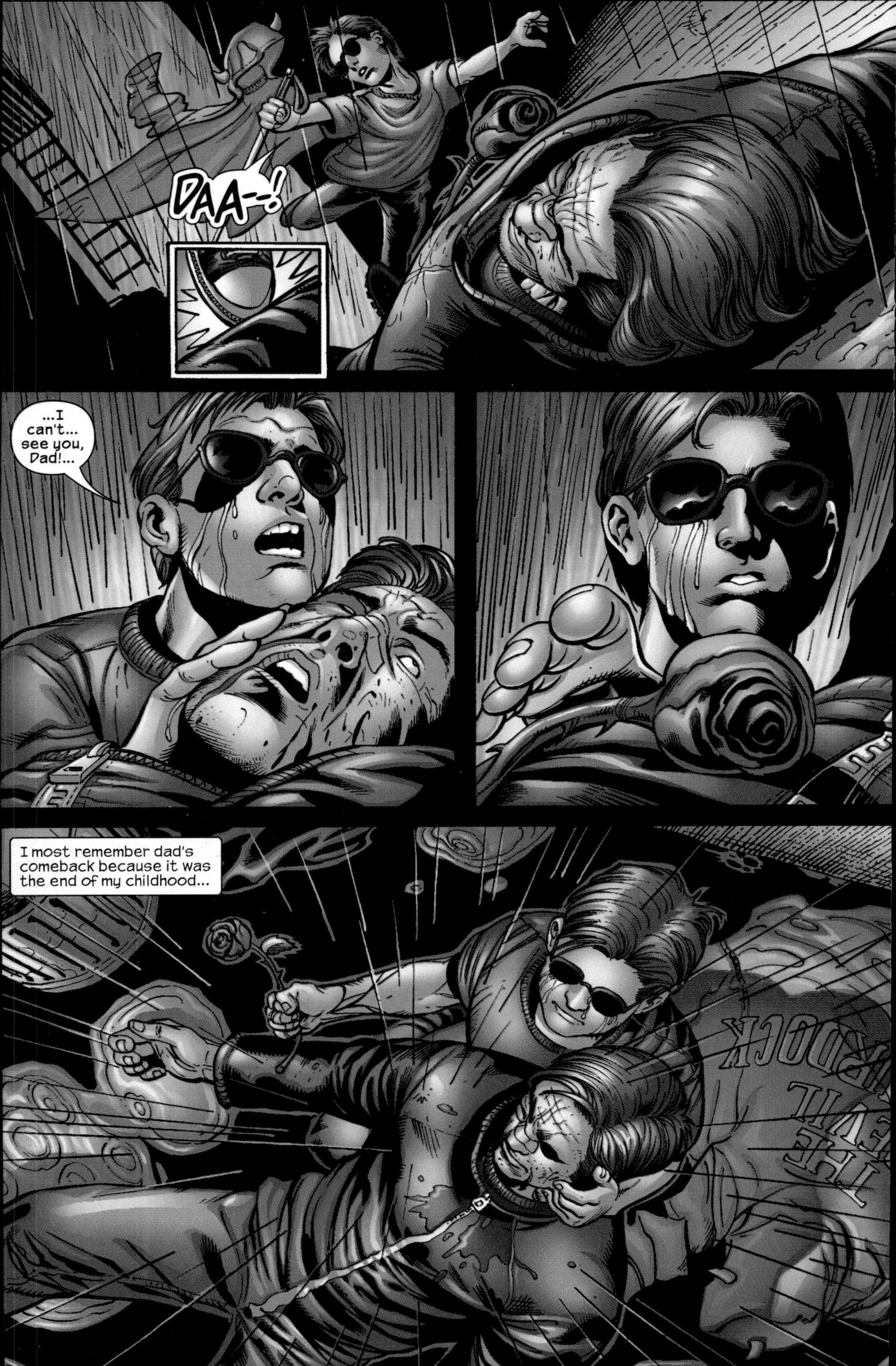
DAA--!
...I can't... see you, Dad!...
I most remember dad's comeback because it was the end of my childhood...

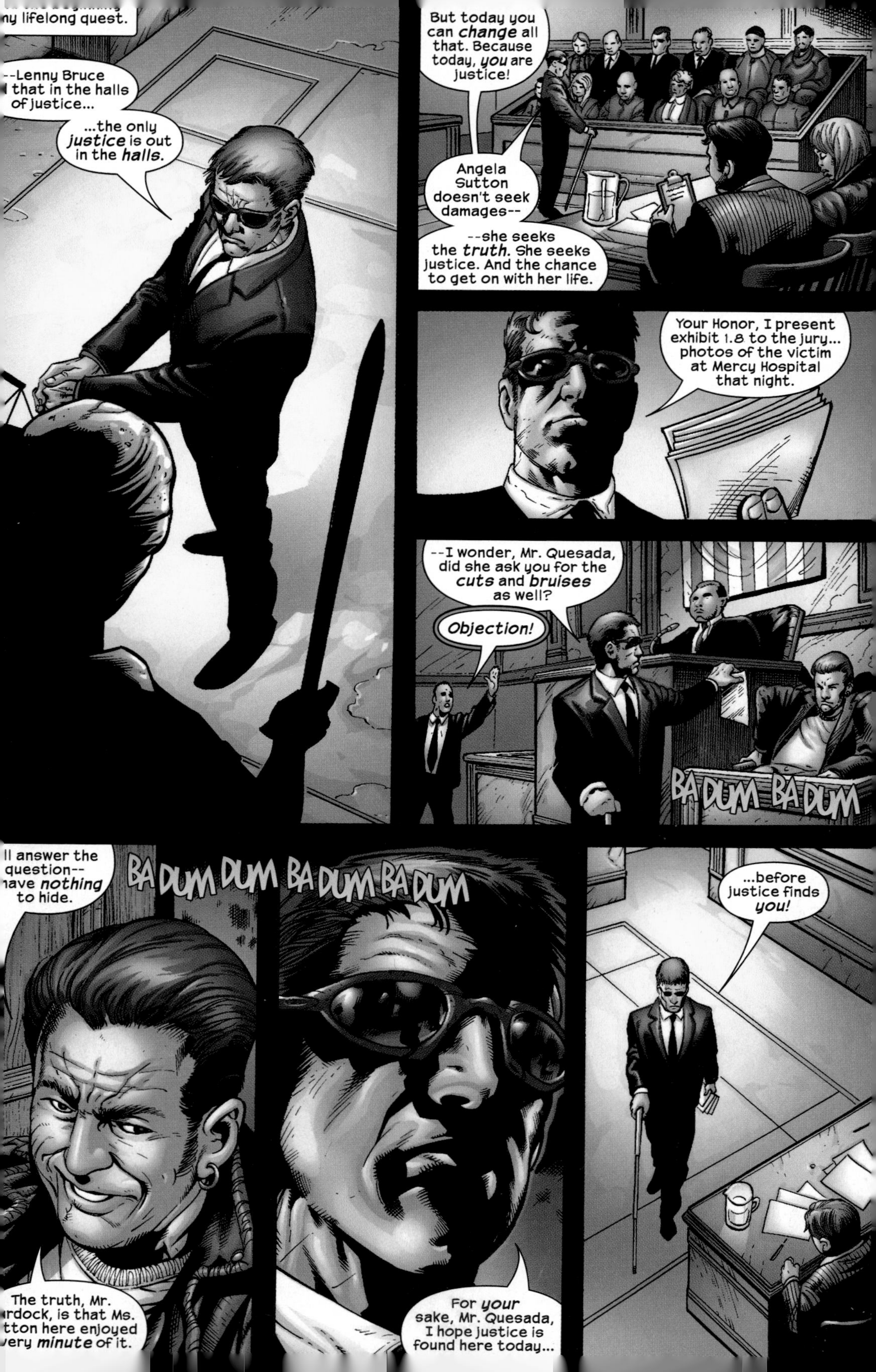

ny lifelong quest.
--Lenny Bruce
that in the halls of justice...
...the only *justice* is out in the *halls.*
But today you can *change* all that. Because today, *you* are justice!
Angela Sutton doesn't seek damages--
--she seeks the *truth.* She seeks justice. And the chance to get on with her life.
Your Honor, I present exhibit 1.8 to the jury... photos of the victim at Mercy Hospital that night.
--I wonder, Mr. Quesada, did she ask you for the *cuts* and *bruises* as well?
Objection!
BA DUM BA DUM
ll answer the question--
ave *nothing* to hide.
BA DUM DUM BA DUM BA DUM
The truth, Mr.
rdock, is that Ms.
tton here enjoyed
very *minute* of it.
For *your* sake, Mr. Quesada, I hope justice is found here today...
...before justice finds *you!*

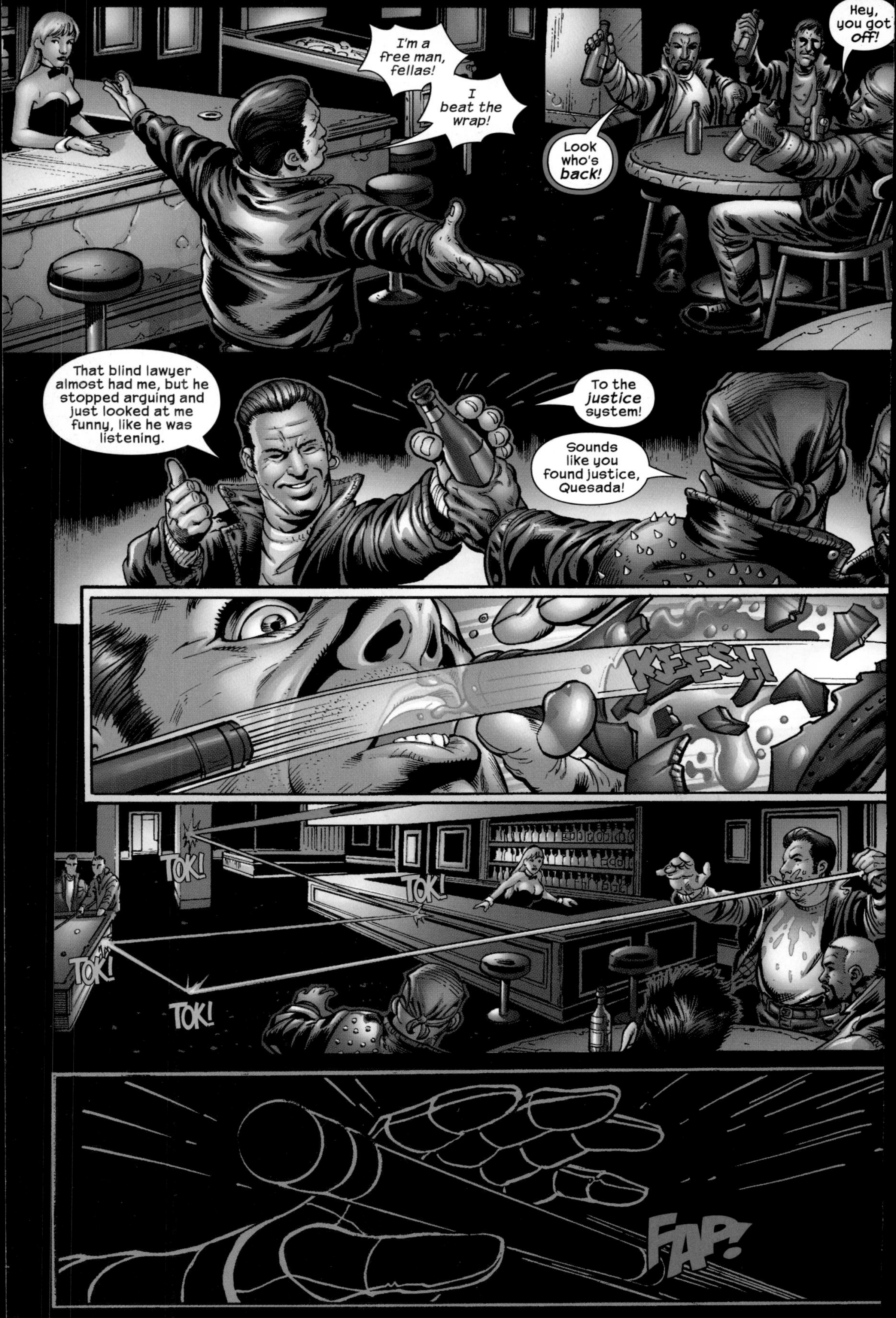
I'm a free man, fellas!
I beat the wrap!
Look who's back!
Hey, you got off!
That blind lawyer almost had me, but he stopped arguing and just looked at me funny, like he was listening.
To the justice system!
Sounds like you found justice, Quesada!
KEESH
TOK!
TOK!
TOK!
TOK!
FAP!

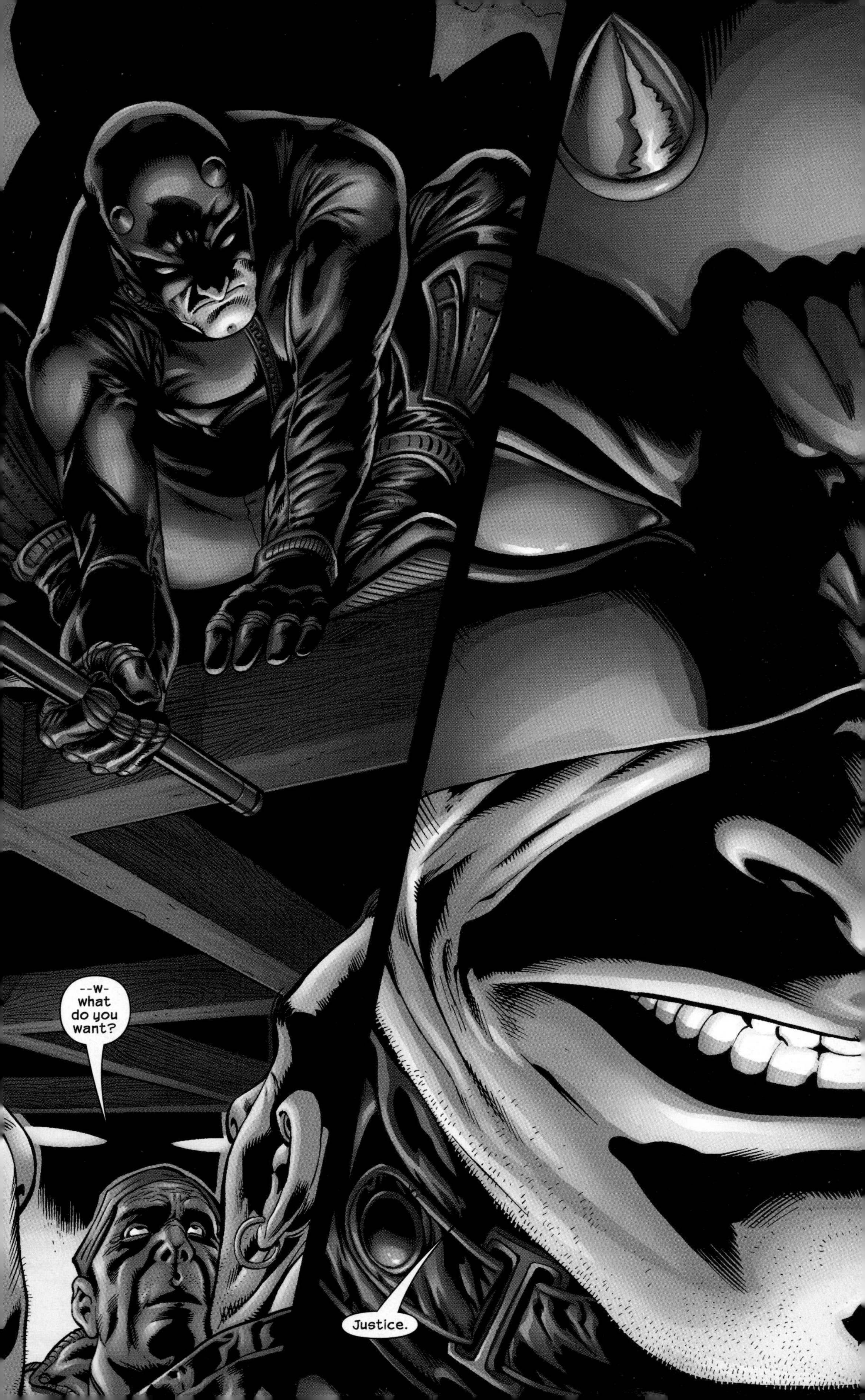
--W- what do you want?
Justice.

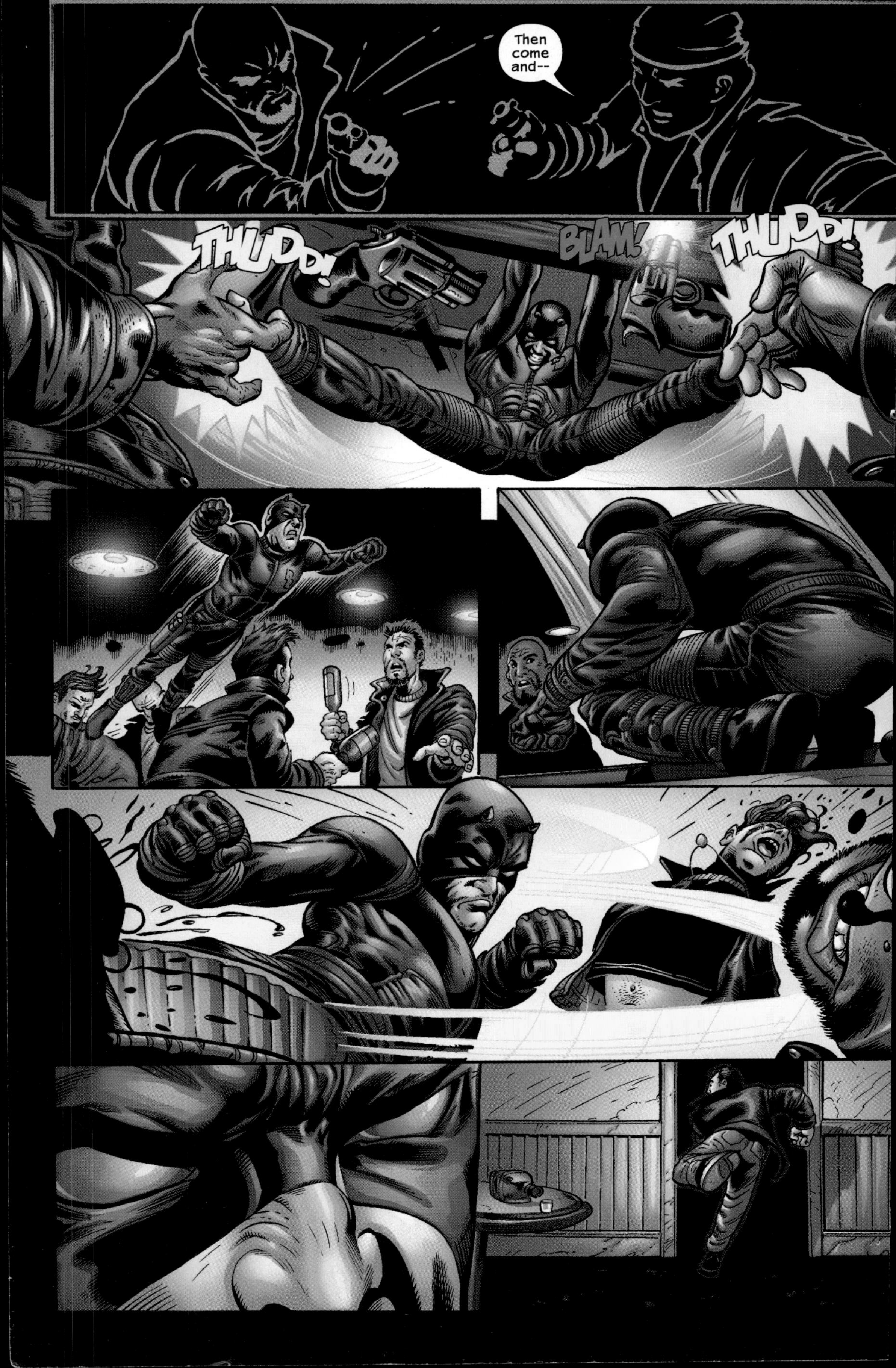
Then come and--
THUDD!
BLAM!
THUDD!

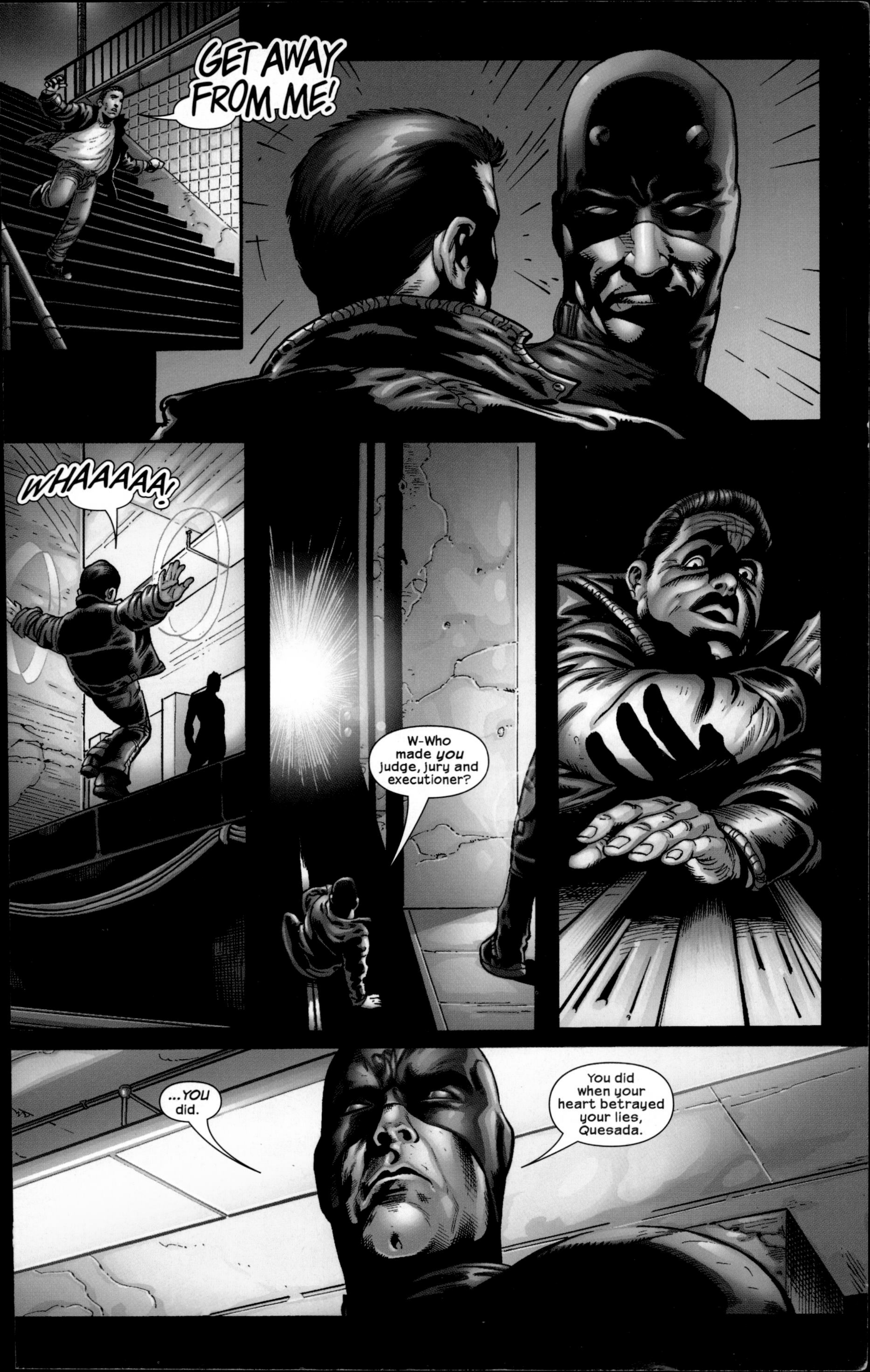
GET AWAY FROM ME!
WHAAAAAA!
W-Who made *you* judge, jury and executioner?
...YOU did.
You did when your heart betrayed your lies, Quesada.

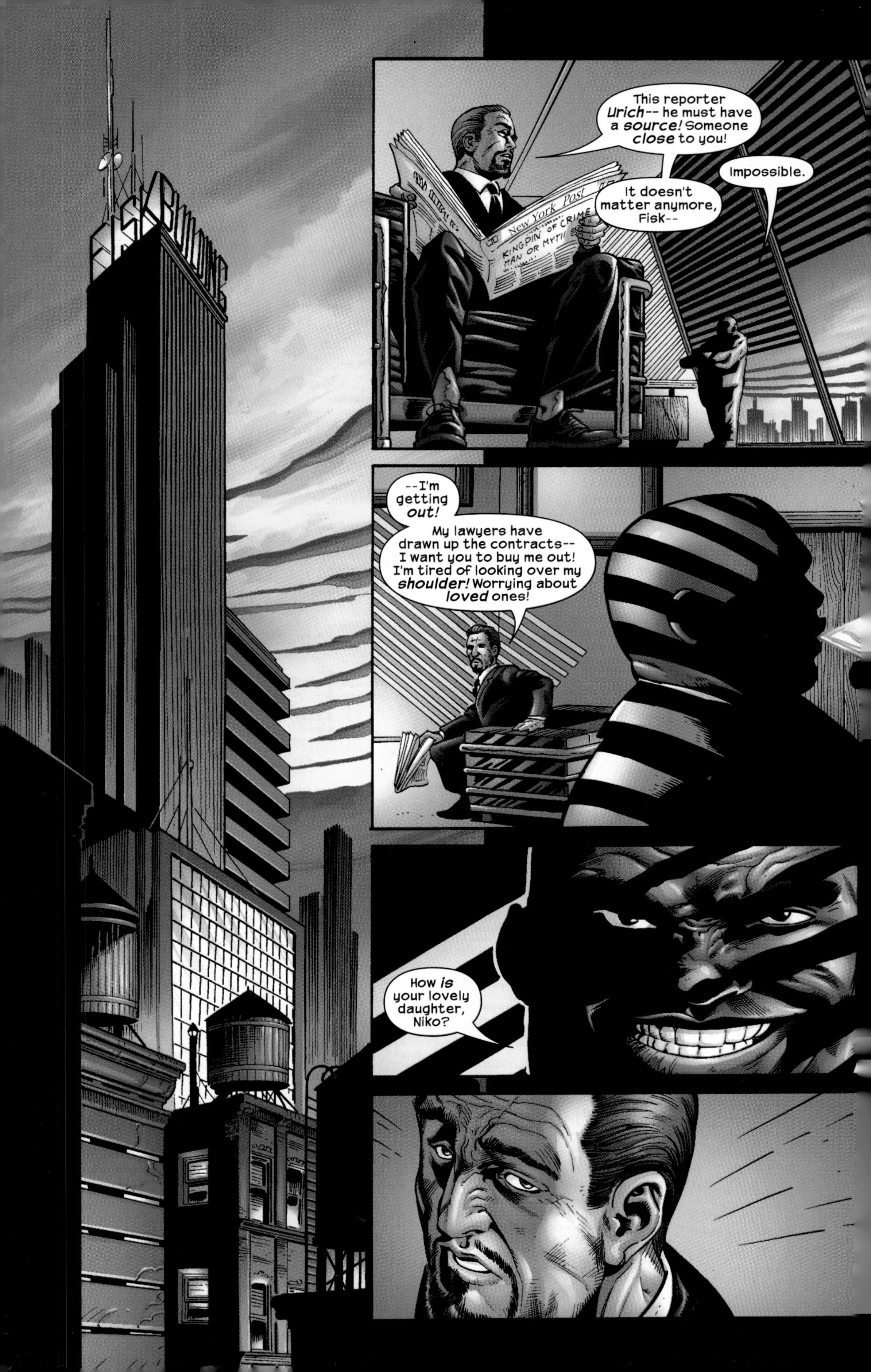
FISK BUILDING
This reporter Urich-- he must have a source! Someone close to you!
Impossible.
It doesn't matter anymore, Fisk--
New York Post
KINGPIN OF CRIME MAN OR MYTH
--I'm getting out!
My lawyers have drawn up the contracts-- I want you to buy me out! I'm tired of looking over my shoulder! Worrying about loved ones!
How is your lovely daughter, Niko?

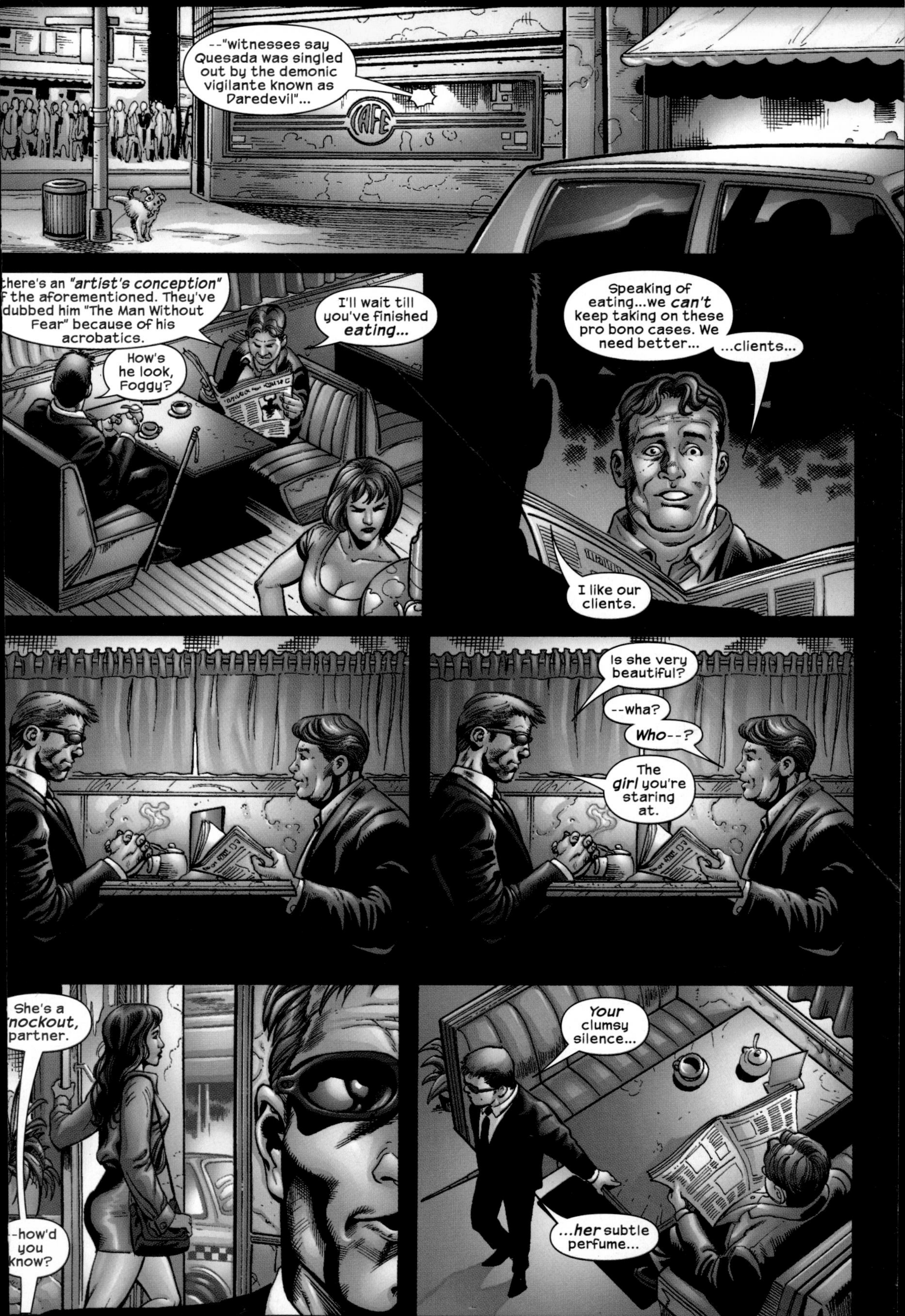
--"witnesses say Quesada was singled out by the demonic vigilante known as Daredevil"...
CAFE
there's an *"artist's conception"* f the aforementioned. They've dubbed him "The Man Without Fear" because of his acrobatics.
I'll wait till you've finished *eating...*
How's he look, Foggy?
Speaking of eating...we *can't* keep taking on these pro bono cases. We need better...
...clients...
I like our clients.
Is she very beautiful?
--wha?
Who--?
The *girl* you're staring at.
She's a *nockout,* partner.
-how'd you know?
Your clumsy silence...
...*her* subtle perfume...

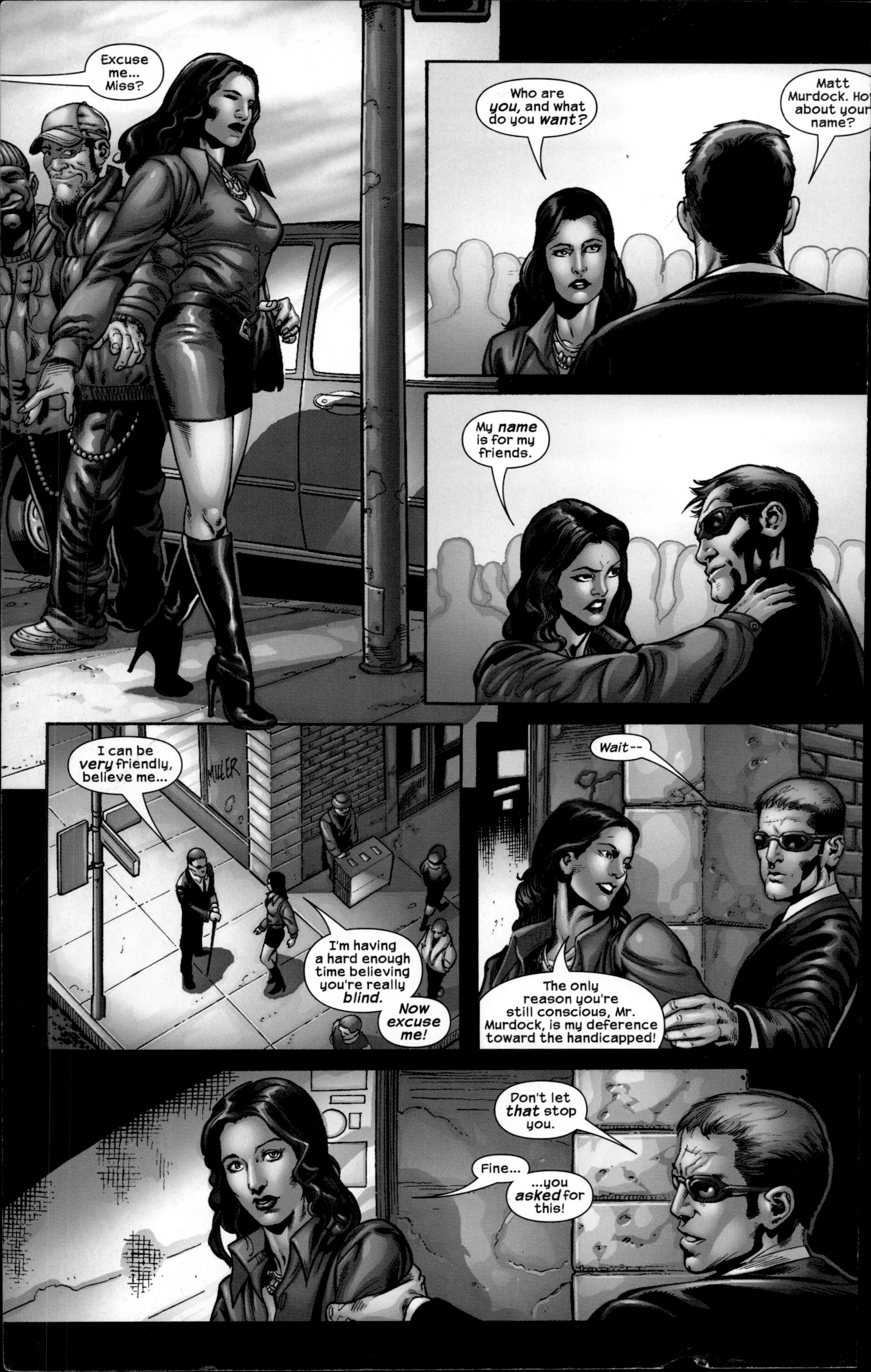
Excuse me... Miss?
Who are *you*, and what do you *want*?
Matt Murdock. How about your name?
My *name* is for my friends.
I can be *very* friendly, believe me...
I'm having a hard enough time believing you're really *blind*.
Now excuse me!
Wait--
The only reason you're still conscious, Mr. Murdock, is my deference toward the handicapped!
Don't let *that* stop you.
Fine...
...you *asked* for this!

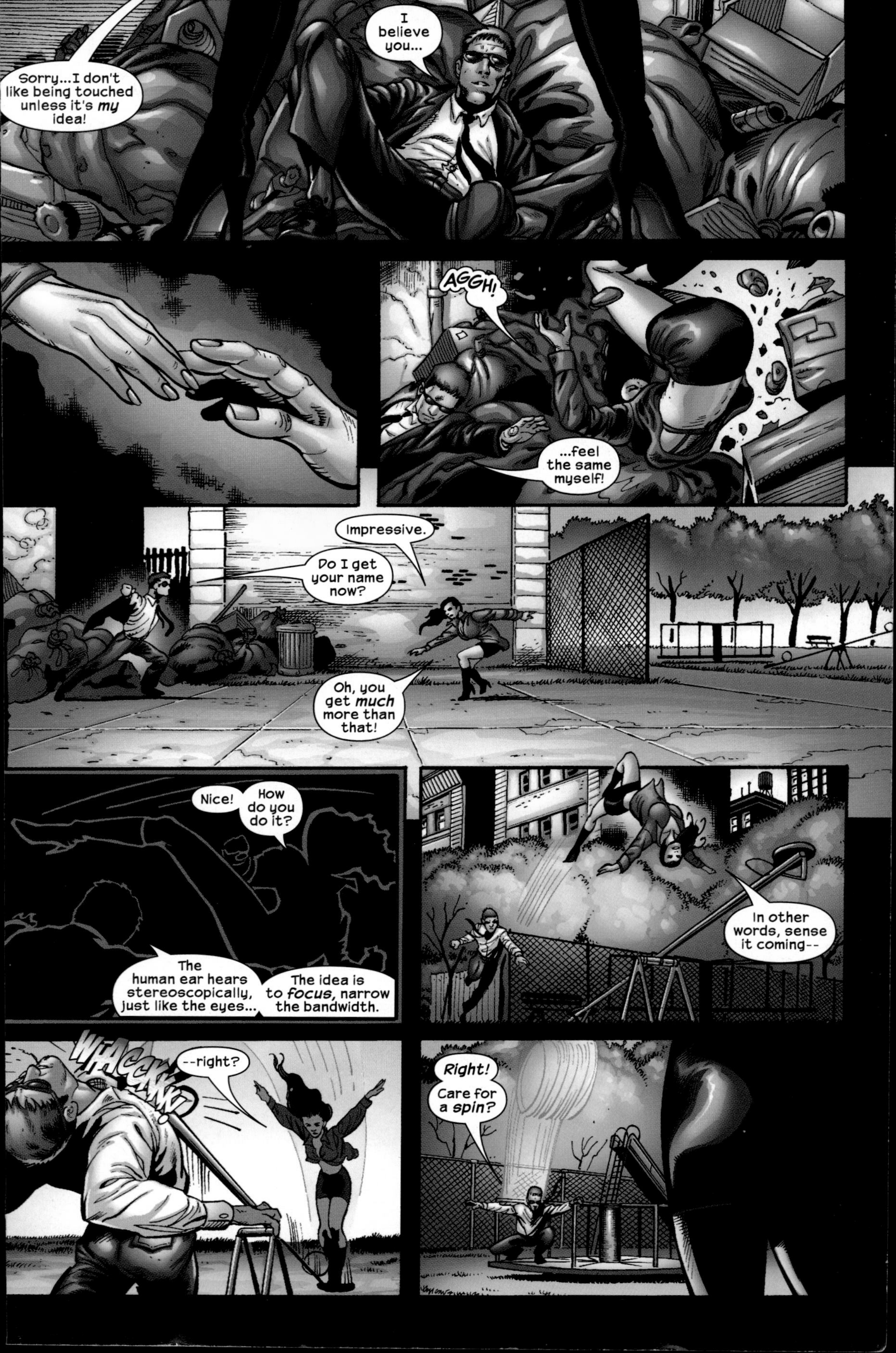
Sorry...I don't like being touched unless it's *my* idea!
I believe you...
AGGH!
...feel the same myself!
Impressive.
Do I get your name now?
Oh, you get *much* more than that!
Nice!
How do you do it?
The human ear hears stereoscopically, just like the eyes...
The idea is to *focus*, narrow the bandwidth.
In other words, sense it coming--
WHACKK!
--right?
Right!
Care for a *spin*?

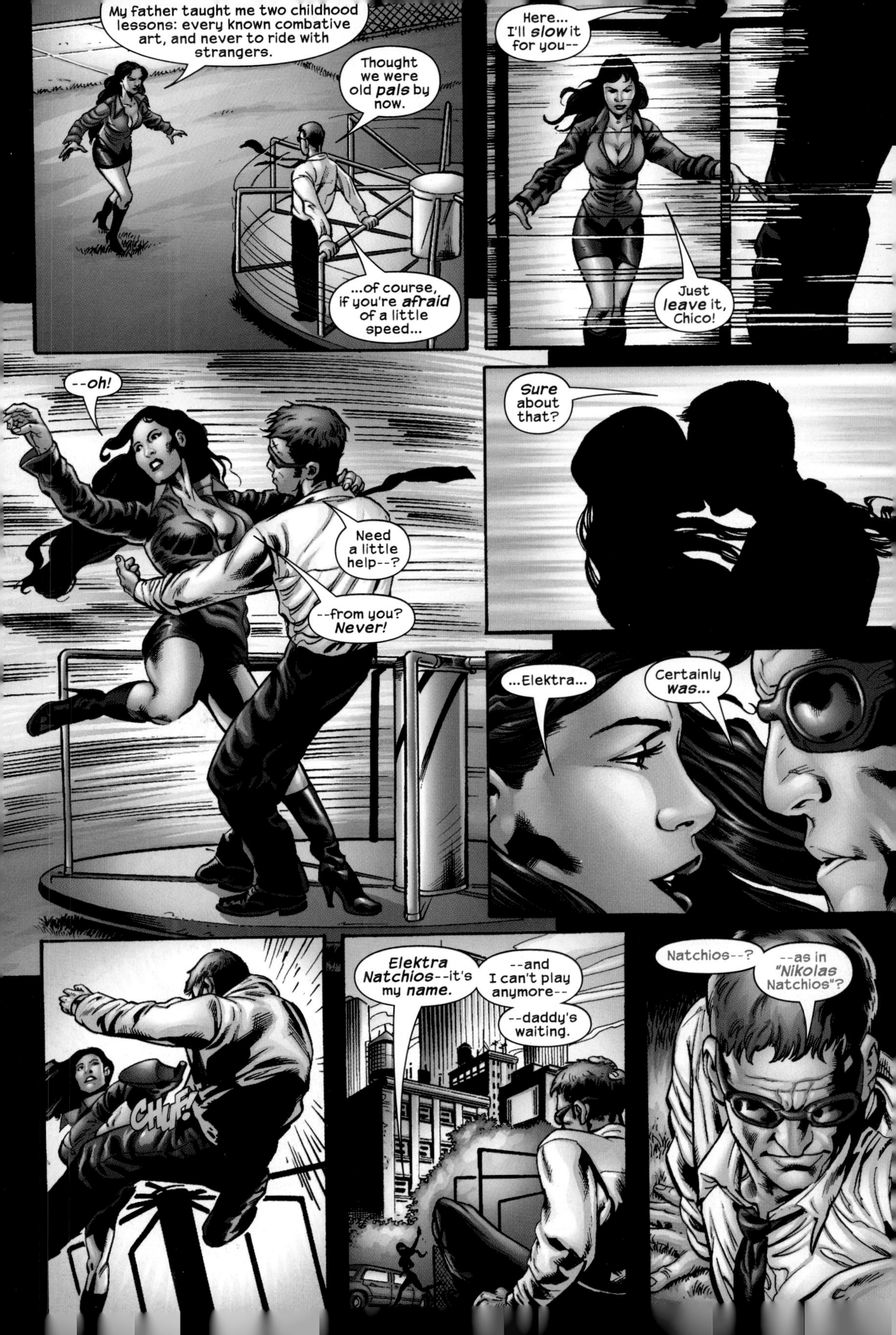
My father taught me two childhood lessons: every known combative art, and never to ride with strangers.
Thought we were old *pals* by now.
...of course, if you're *afraid* of a little speed...
Here... I'll *slow* it for you--
Just *leave* it, Chico!
--*oh!*
Need a little help--?
--from you? *Never!*
Sure about that?
...Elektra...
Certainly *was...*
CHUF!
Elektra Natchios--it's my *name.*
--and I can't play anymore--
--daddy's waiting.
Natchios--?
--as in *"Nikolas* Natchios"?

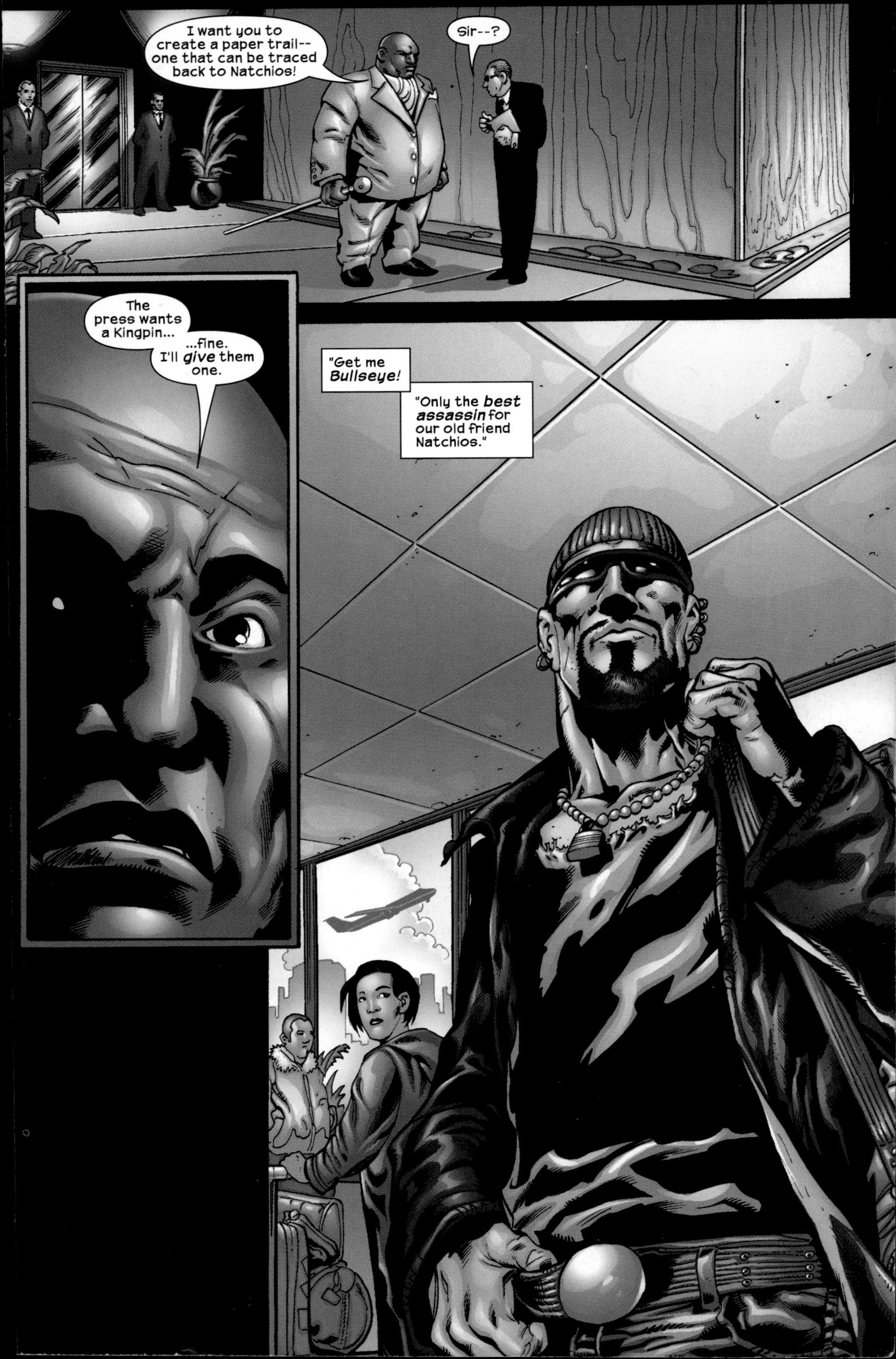

I want you to create a paper trail--one that can be traced back to Natchios!
Sir--?
The press wants a Kingpin...
...fine. I'll *give* them one.
"Get me *Bullseye!*
"Only the *best assassin* for our old friend Natchios."

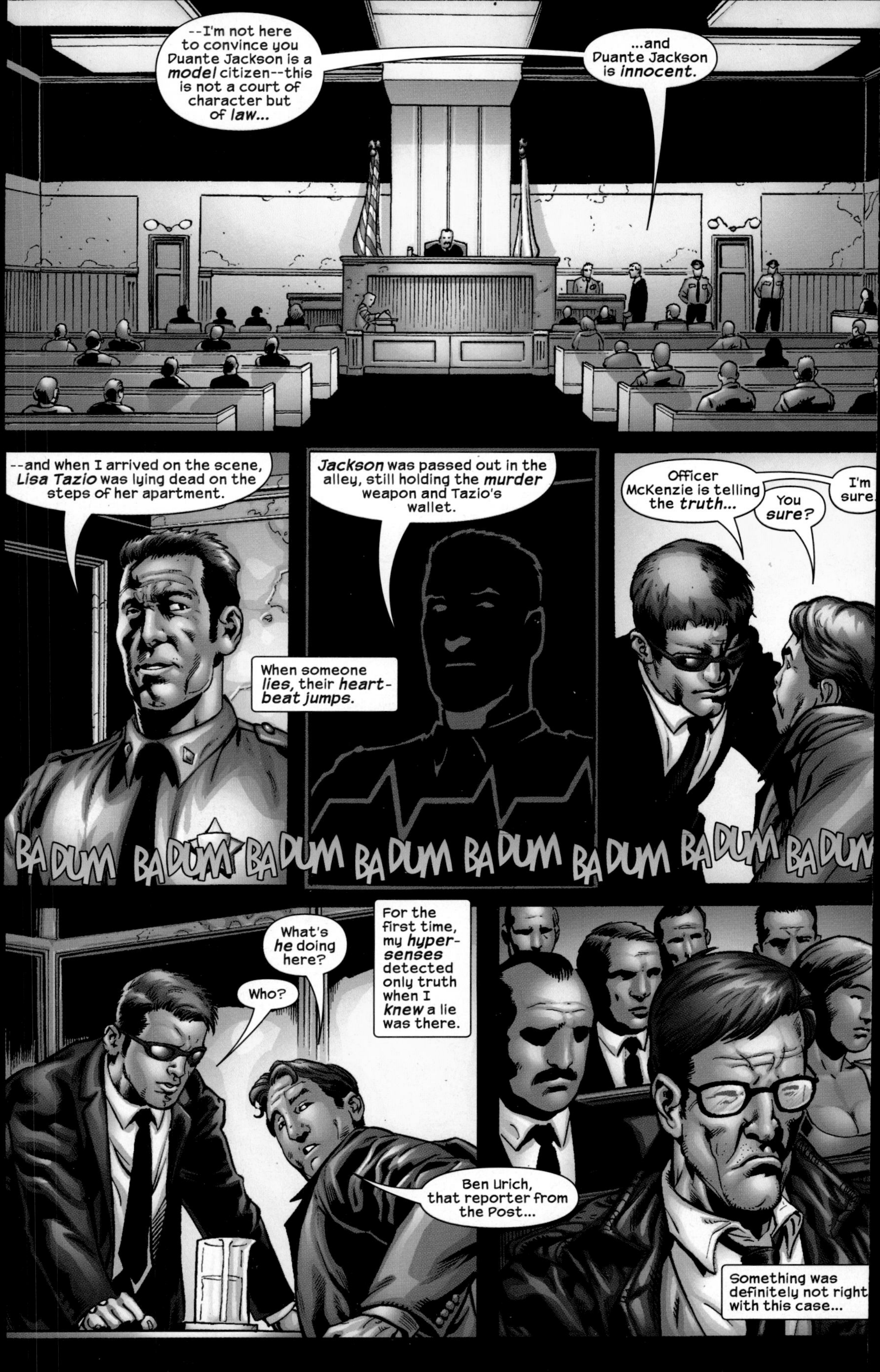
--I'm not here to convince you Duante Jackson is a *model* citizen--this is not a court of character but of *law*...
...and Duante Jackson is *innocent*.
--and when I arrived on the scene, *Lisa Tazio* was lying dead on the steps of her apartment.
Jackson was passed out in the alley, still holding the *murder* weapon and Tazio's wallet.
When someone *lies*, their *heart-beat jumps*.
Officer McKenzie is telling the *truth*...
You *sure?*
I'm sure.
BA DUM BA DUM BA DUM BA DUM BA DUM BA DUM BA DUM BA DUM
What's *he* doing here?
Who?
For the first time, my *hyper-senses* detected only truth when I *knew* a lie was there.
Ben Urich, that reporter from the Post...
Something was definitely not right with this case...

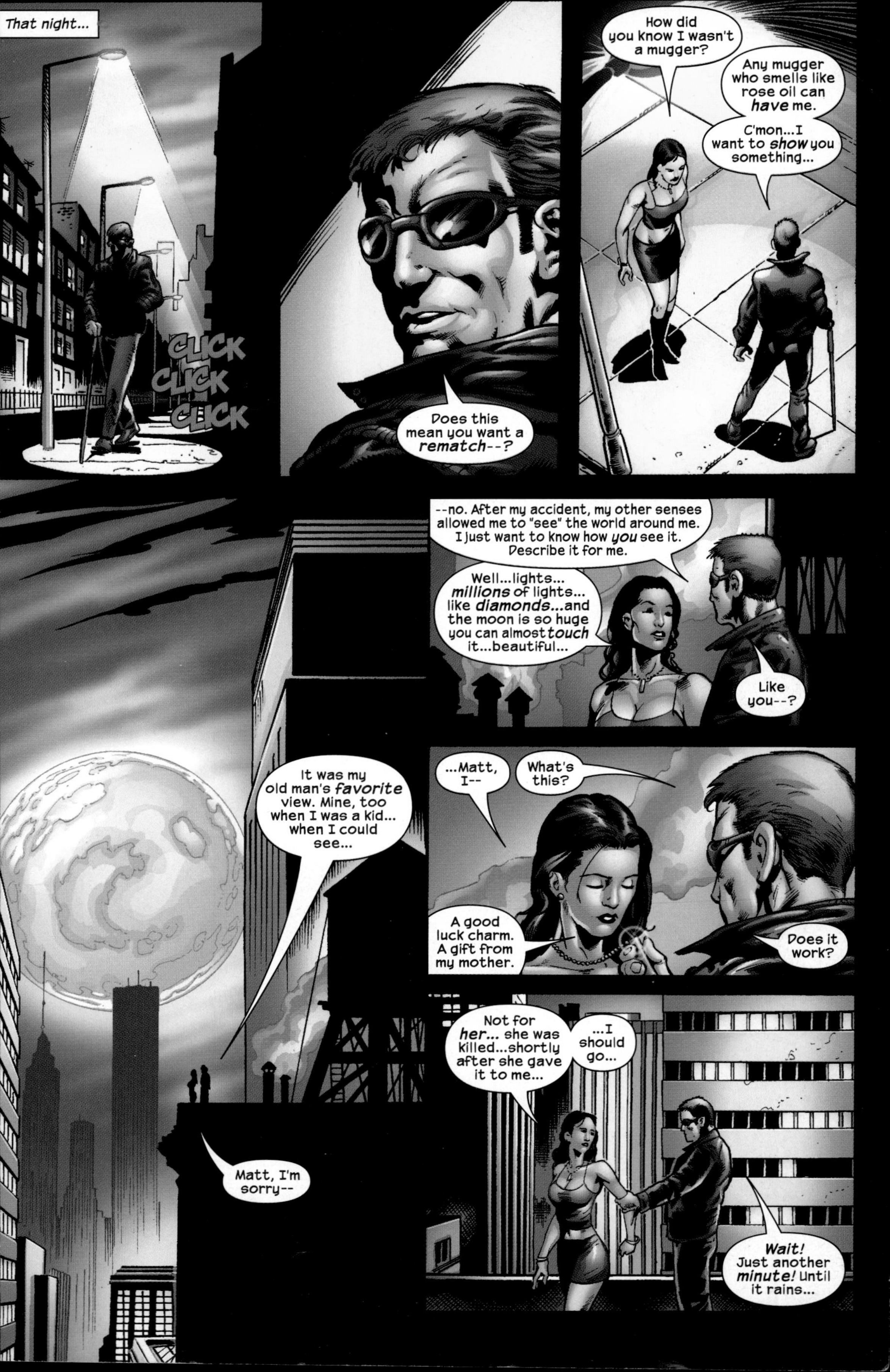
That night...
CLICK CLICK CLICK
Does this mean you want a *rematch*--?
How did you know I wasn't a mugger?
Any mugger who smells like rose oil can *have* me.
C'mon...I want to *show* you something...
It was my old man's *favorite* view. Mine, too when I was a kid... when I could see...
Matt, I'm sorry--
--no. After my accident, my other senses allowed me to "see" the world around me. I just want to know how *you* see it. Describe it for me.
Well...lights... *millions* of lights... like *diamonds*...and the moon is so huge you can almost *touch* it...beautiful...
Like you--?
...Matt, I--
What's this?
A good luck charm. A gift from my mother.
Does it work?
Not for *her*... she was killed...shortly after she gave it to me...
...I should go...
Wait! Just another *minute!* Until it rains...

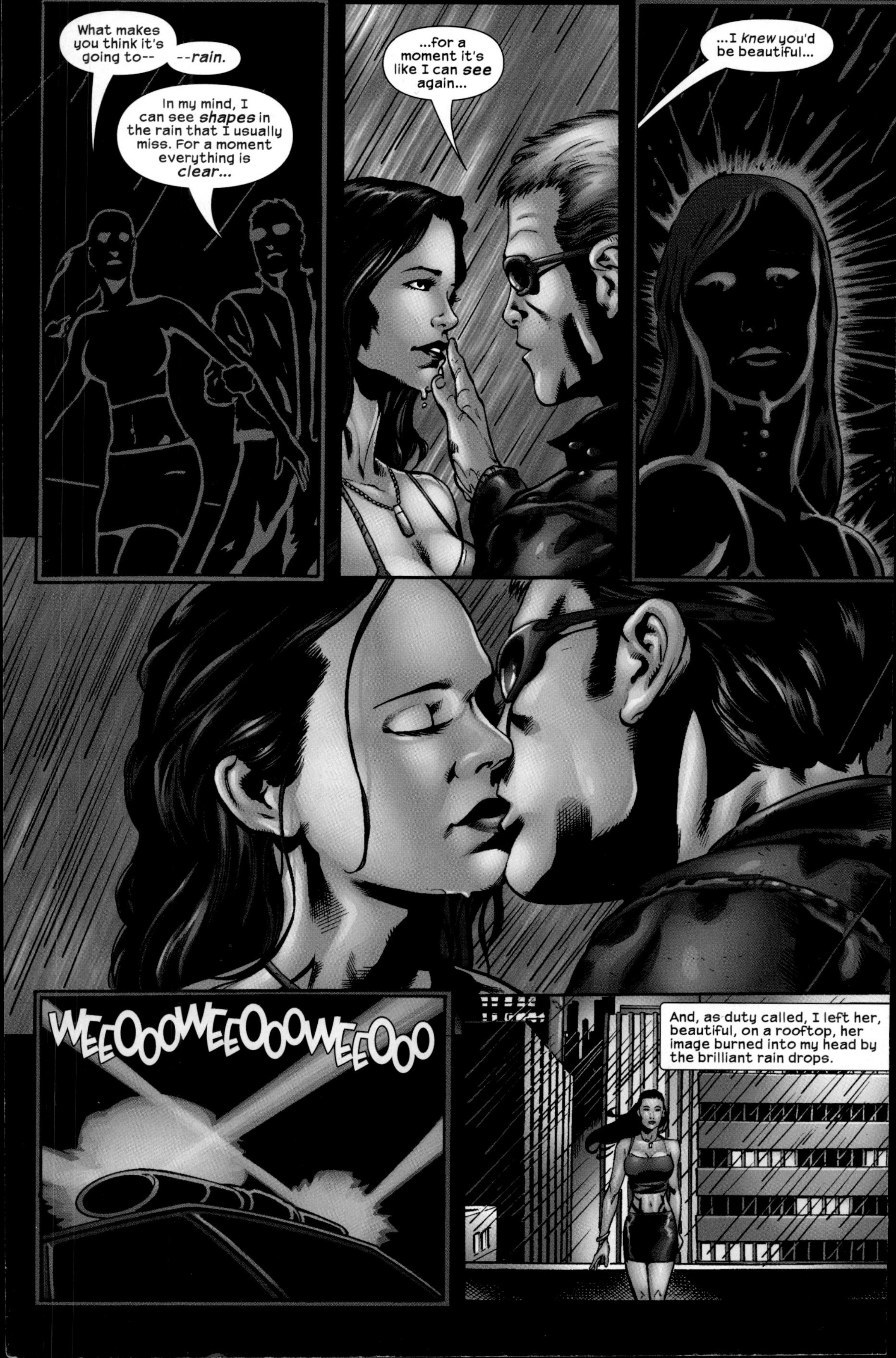

What makes you think it's going to--
--rain.
In my mind, I can see shapes in the rain that I usually miss. For a moment everything is clear...
...for a moment it's like I can see again...
...I knew you'd be beautiful...
WEEOOOWEEOOOWEEOOO
And, as duty called, I left her, beautiful, on a rooftop, her image burned into my head by the brilliant rain drops.

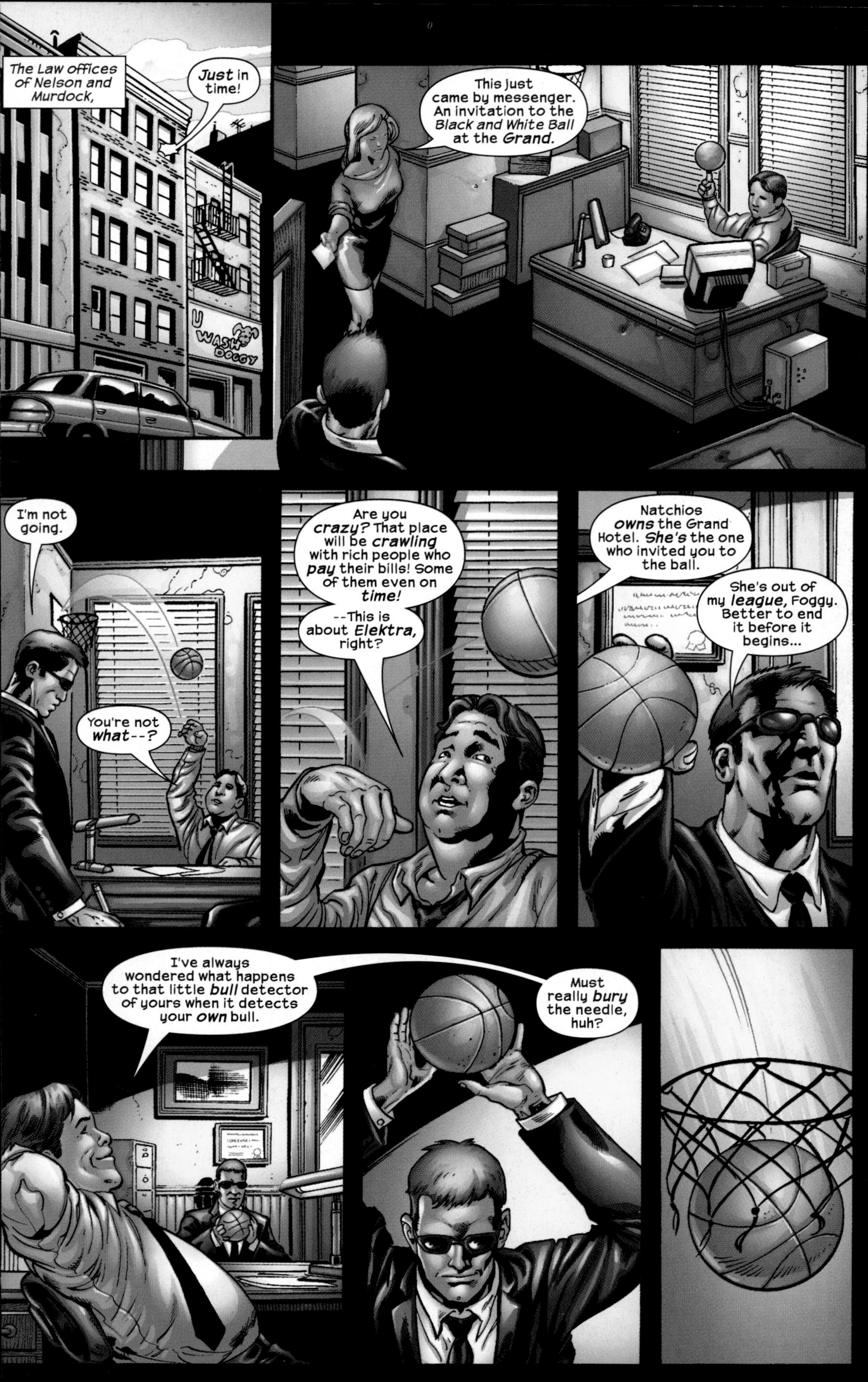
The Law offices of Nelson and Murdock,
Just in time!
This just came by messenger. An invitation to the Black and White Ball at the Grand.
I'm not going.
You're not what--?
Are you crazy? That place will be crawling with rich people who pay their bills! Some of them even on time!
--This is about Elektra, right?
Natchios owns the Grand Hotel. She's the one who invited you to the ball.
She's out of my league, Foggy. Better to end it before it begins...
I've always wondered what happens to that little bull detector of yours when it detects your own bull.
Must really bury the needle, huh?
U WASH DOGGY

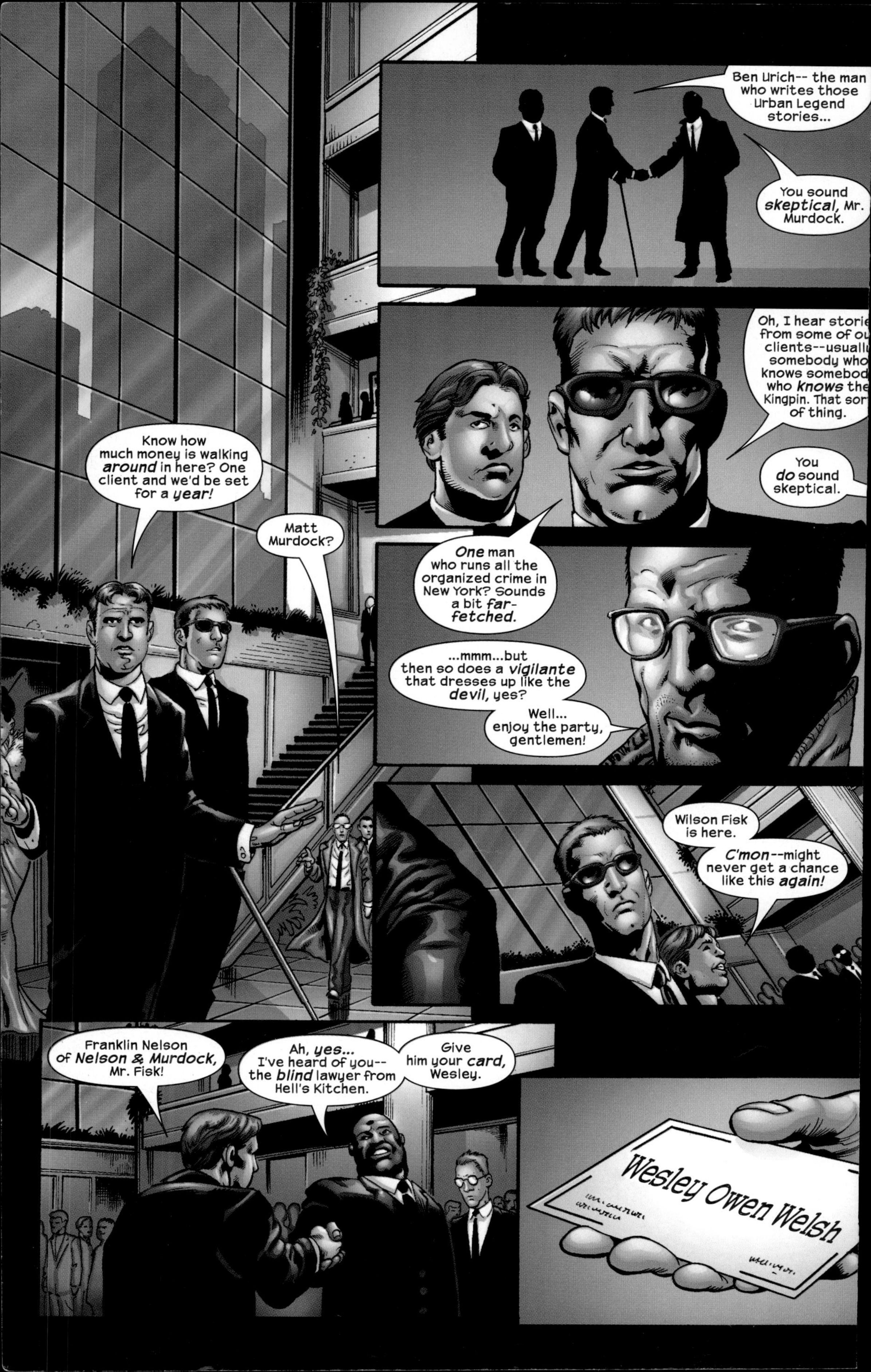
Ben Urich-- the man who writes those Urban Legend stories...
You sound skeptical, Mr. Murdock.
Oh, I hear storie from some of ou clients--usuall somebody who knows somebod who knows the Kingpin. That sor of thing.
You do sound skeptical.
Know how much money is walking around in here? One client and we'd be set for a year!
Matt Murdock?
One man who runs all the organized crime in New York? Sounds a bit far-fetched.
...mmm...but then so does a vigilante that dresses up like the devil, yes?
Well... enjoy the party, gentlemen!
Wilson Fisk is here.
C'mon--might never get a chance like this again!
Franklin Nelson of Nelson & Murdock, Mr. Fisk!
Ah, yes... I've heard of you-- the blind lawyer from Hell's Kitchen.
Give him your card, Wesley.
Wesley Owen Welsh

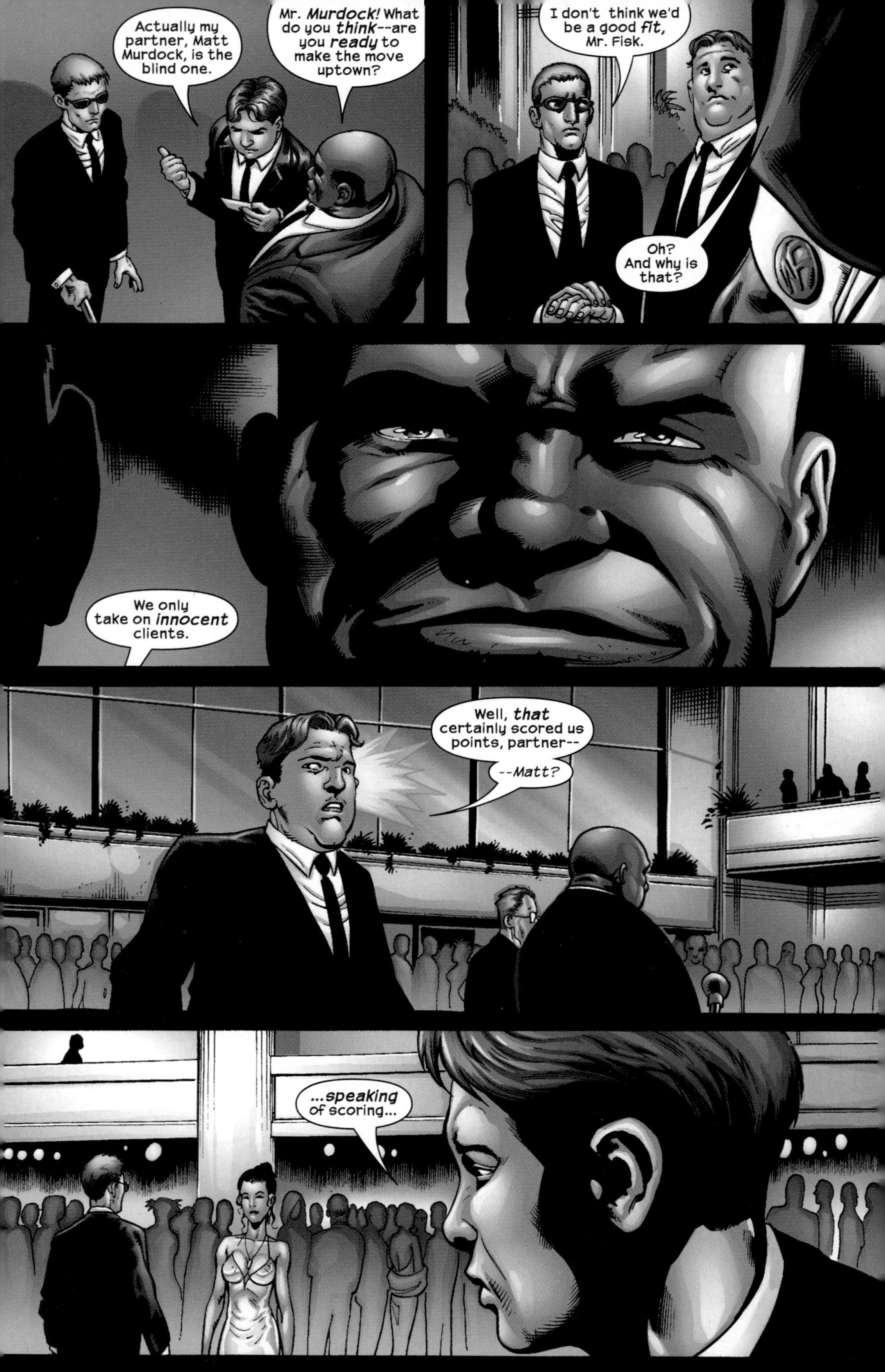
Actually my partner, Matt Murdock, is the blind one.
Mr. *Murdock!* What do you *think*--are you *ready* to make the move uptown?
I don't think we'd be a good *fit*, Mr. Fisk.
Oh? And why is that?
We only take on *innocent* clients.
Well, *that* certainly scored us points, partner--
--*Matt?*
...*speaking* of scoring...

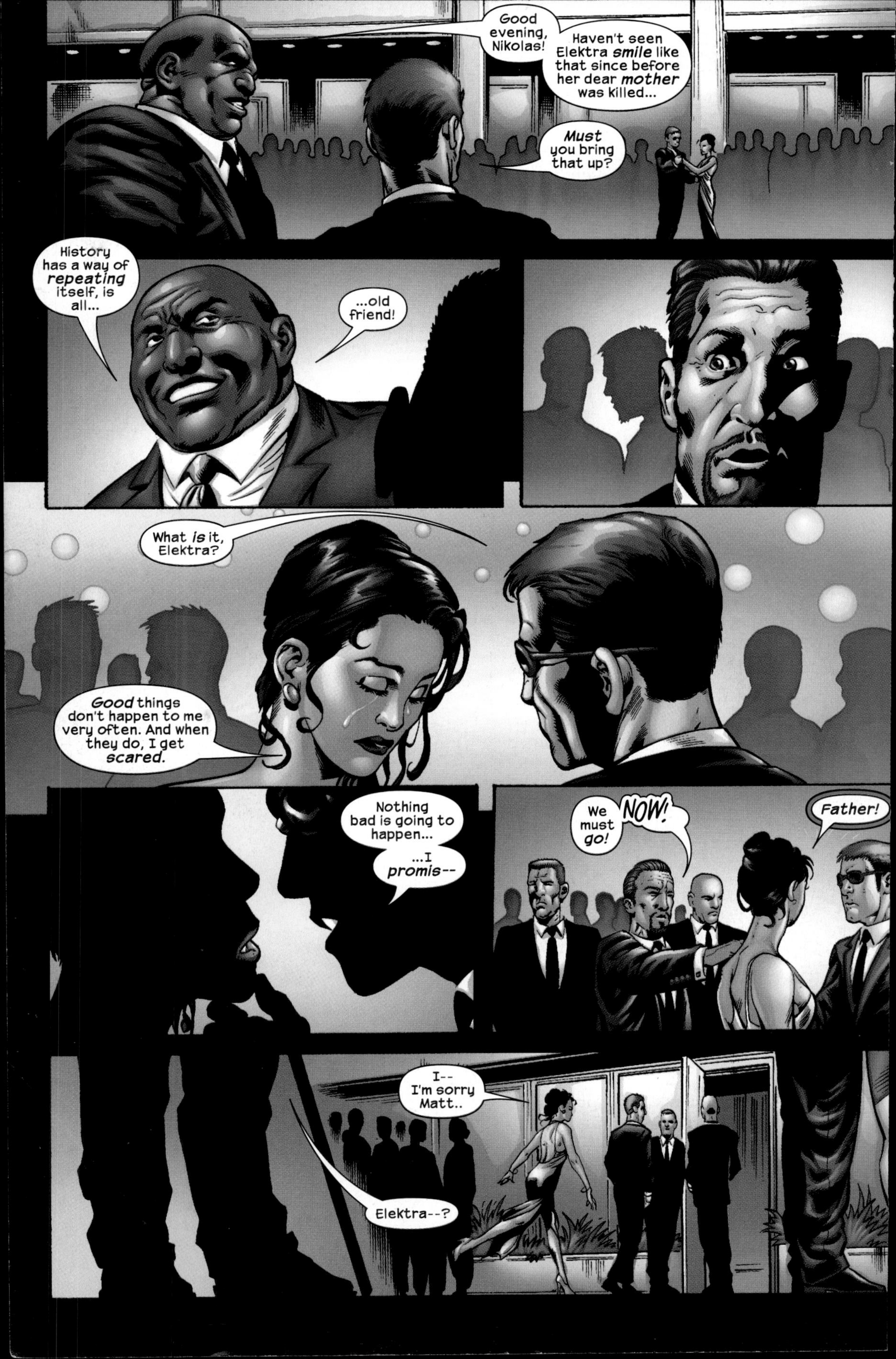
Good evening, Nikolas!
Haven't seen Elektra *smile* like that since before her dear *mother* was killed...
Must you bring that up?
History has a way of *repeating* itself, is all...
...old friend!
What *is* it, Elektra?
Good things don't happen to me very often. And when they do, I get *scared.*
Nothing bad is going to happen...
...I *promis--*
We must *go!*
NOW!
Father!
I-- I'm sorry Matt..
Elektra--?

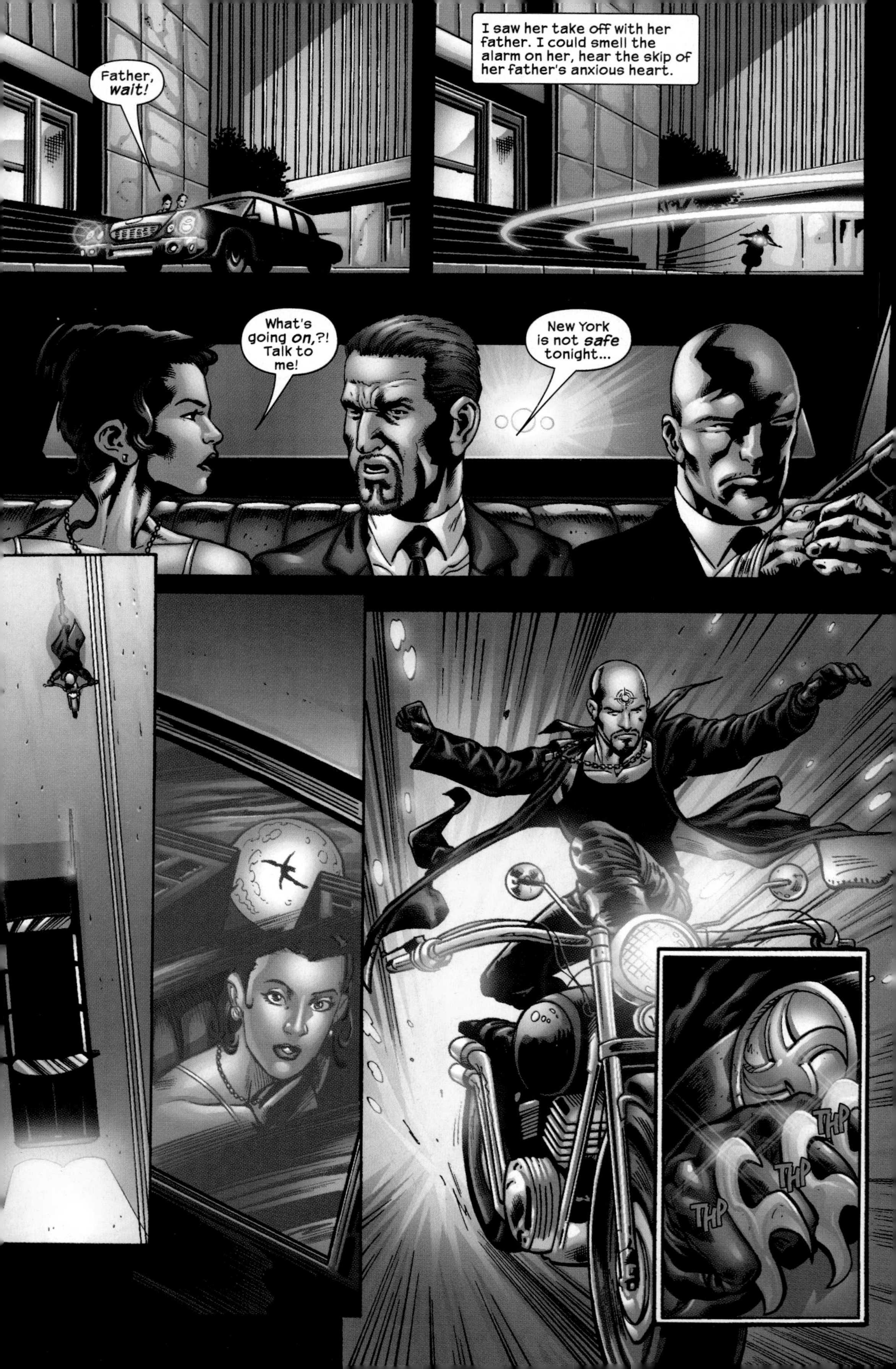

Father, wait!
I saw her take off with her father. I could smell the alarm on her, hear the skip of her father's anxious heart.
What's going on,?! Talk to me!
New York is not safe tonight...
THP
THP
THP

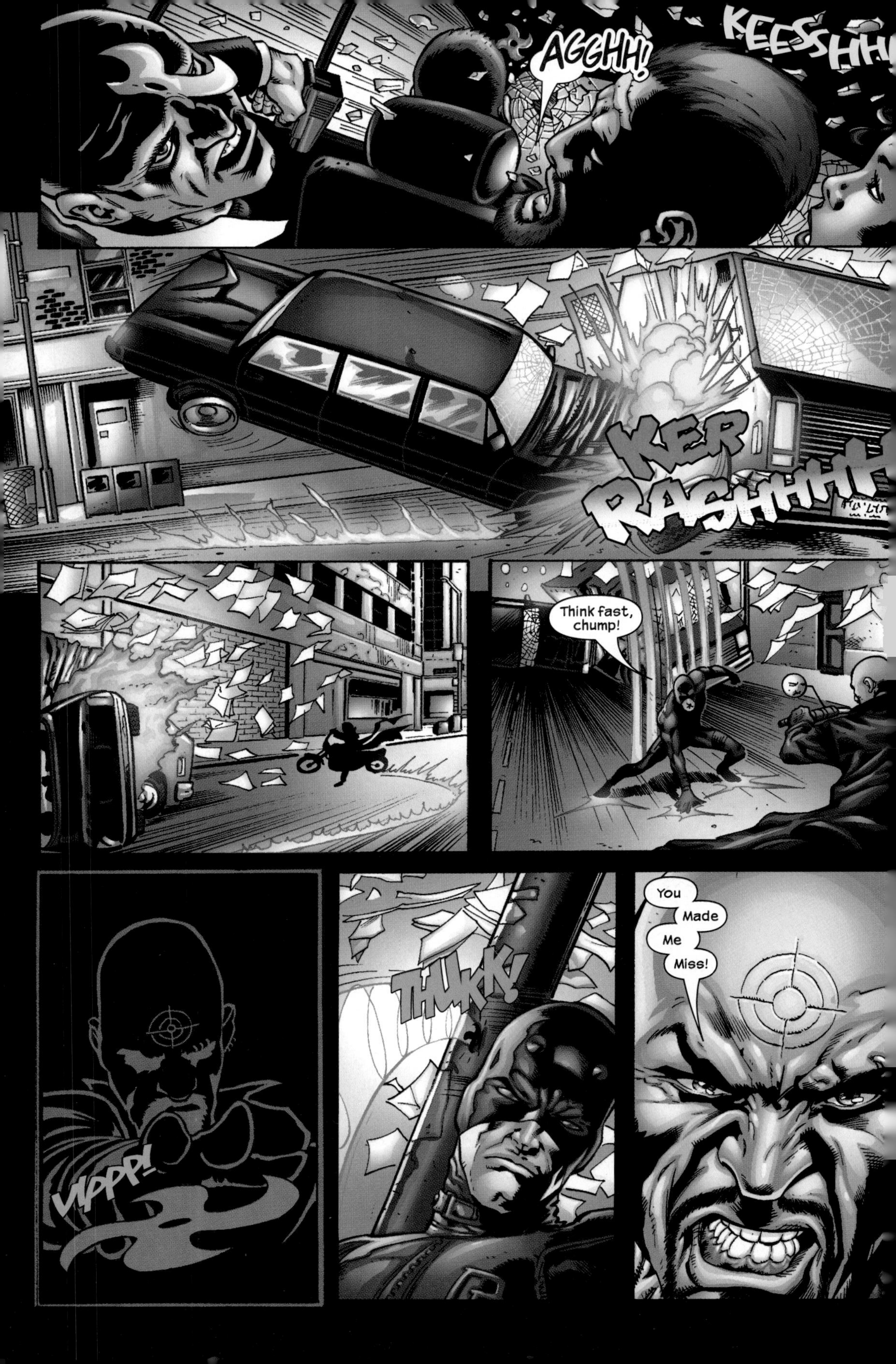
AGGHH!
KEESSHH
KER
RASHHH
Think fast, chump!
VIPPP!
THUKK!
You
Made
Me
Miss!

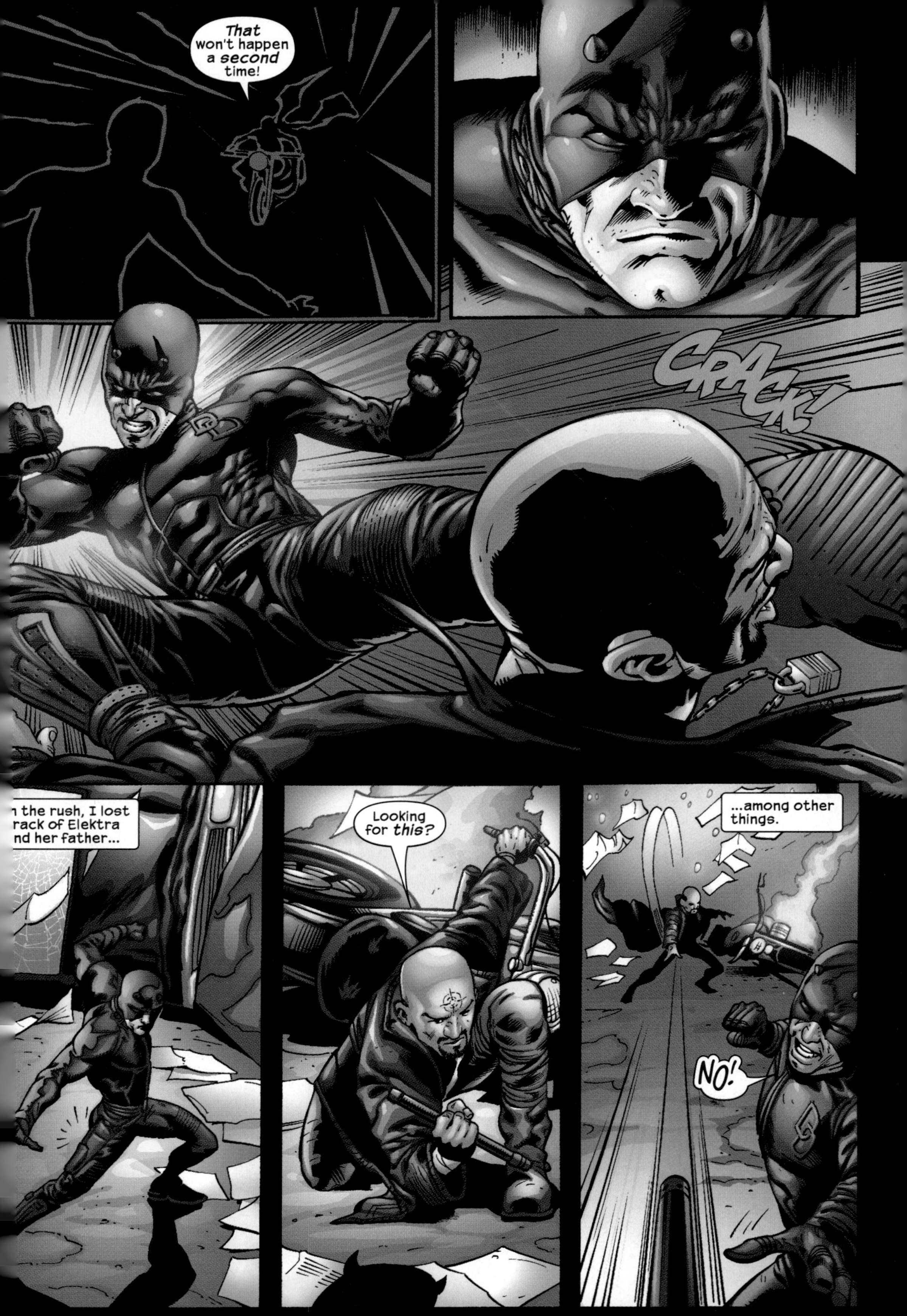
That won't happen a second time!
CRACK!
n the rush, I lost rack of Elektra nd her father...
Looking for this?
...among other things.
NO!

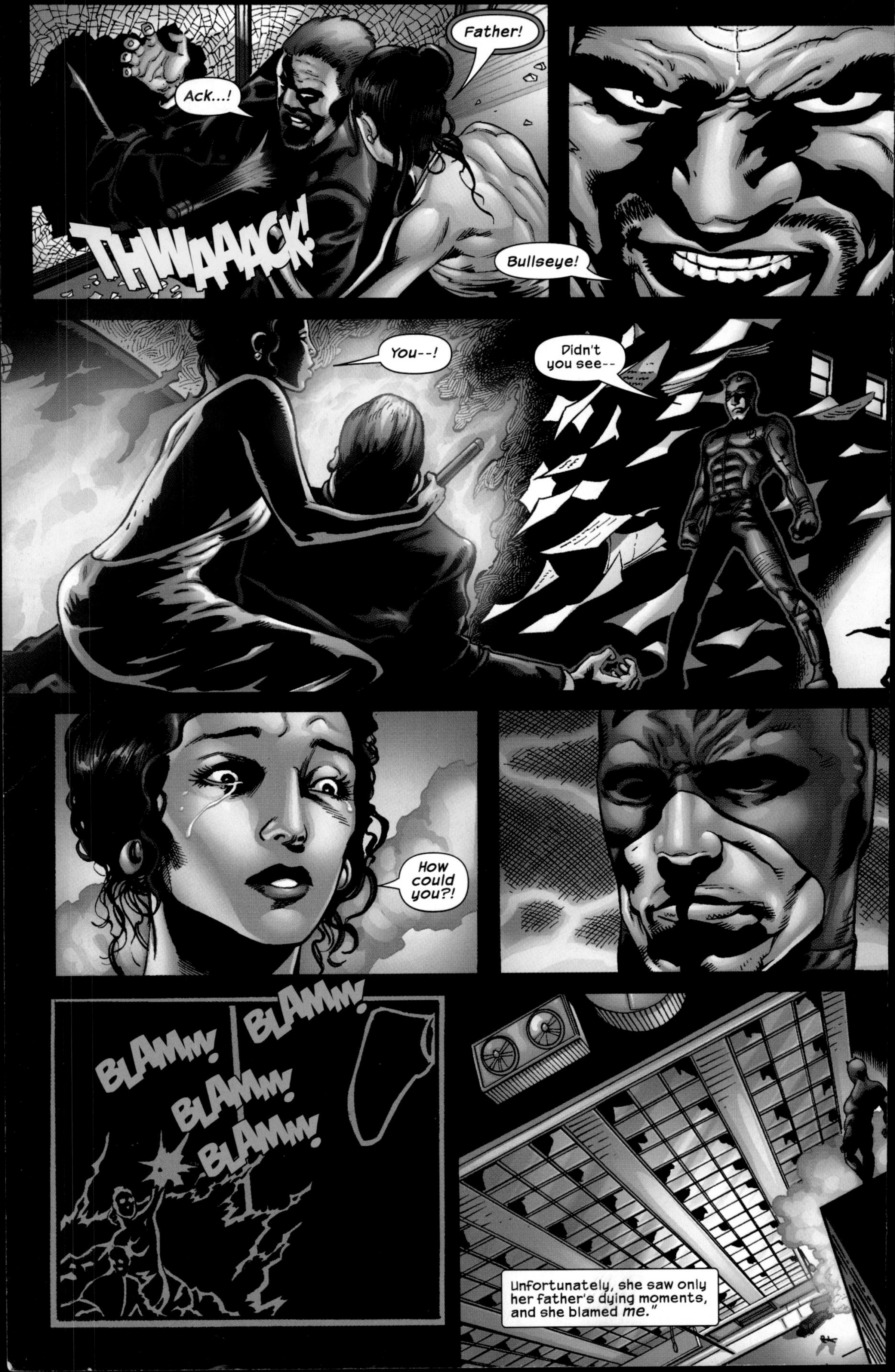
Father!
Ack...!
THWAAACK!
Bullseye!
You--!
Didn't you see--
How could you?!
BLAMM!
BLAMM!
BLAMM!
BLAMM!
Unfortunately, she saw only her father's dying moments, and she blamed *me*."

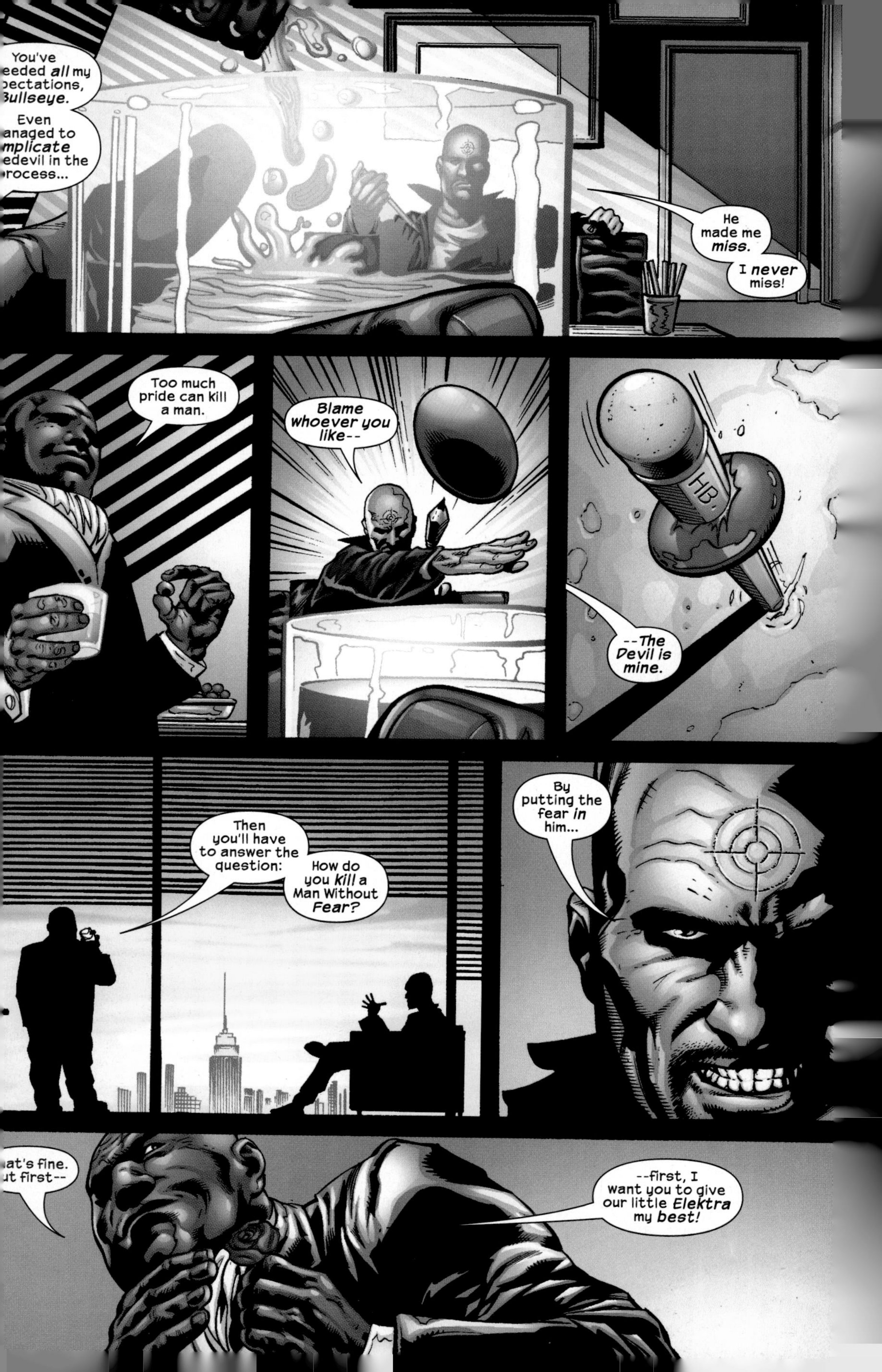
You've
eeded all my
pectations,
Bullseye.
Even
anaged to
mplicate
edevil in the
rocess...
He made me miss.
I never miss!
Too much pride can kill a man.
Blame whoever you like--
HB.
--The Devil is mine.
Then you'll have to answer the question:
How do you kill a Man Without Fear?
By putting the fear in him...
at's fine.
ut first--
--first, I want you to give our little Elektra my best!

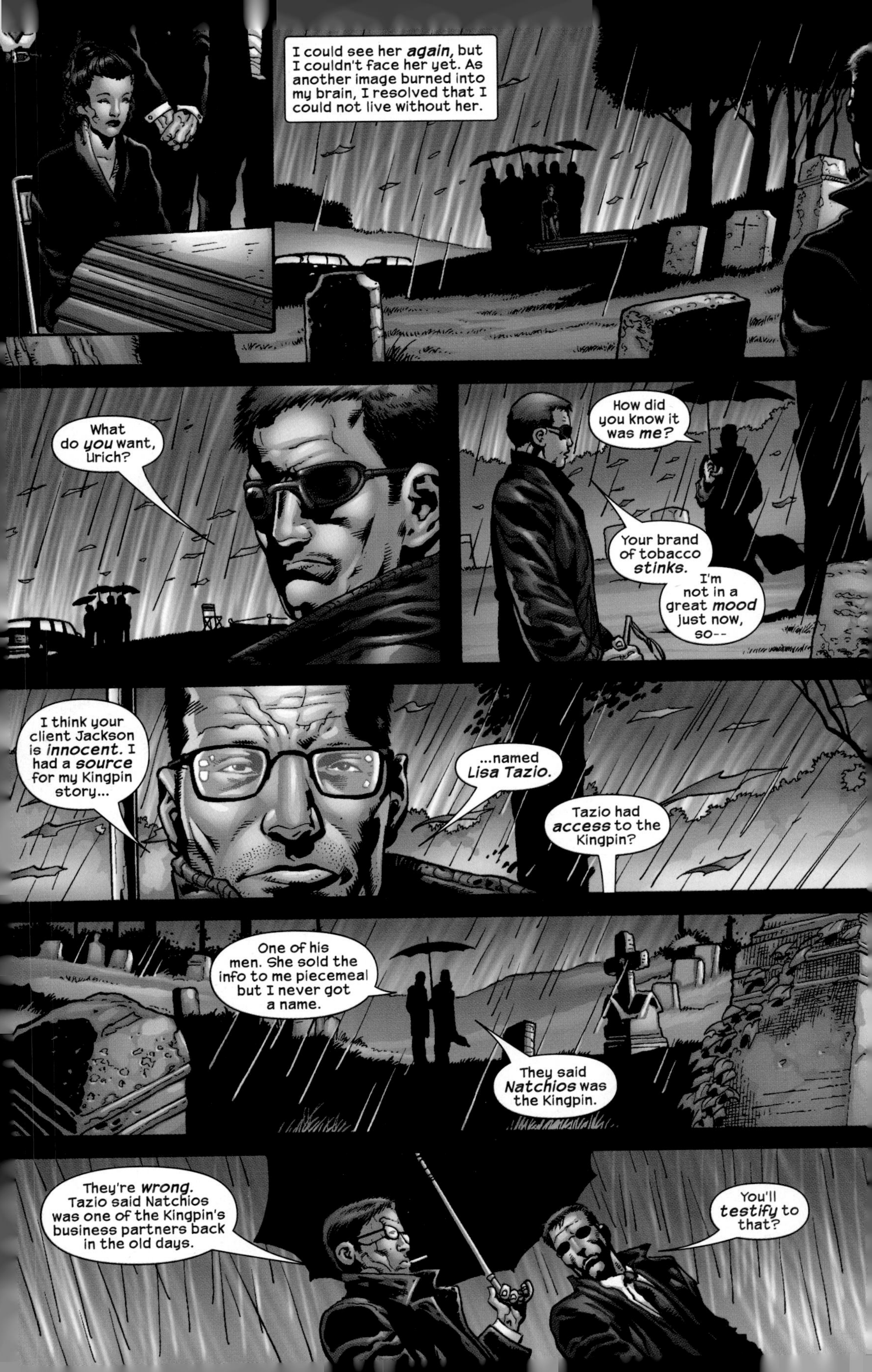
I could see her again, but I couldn't face her yet. As another image burned into my brain, I resolved that I could not live without her.
What do you want, Urich?
How did you know it was me?
Your brand of tobacco stinks.
I'm not in a great mood just now, so--
I think your client Jackson is innocent. I had a source for my Kingpin story...
...named Lisa Tazio.
Tazio had access to the Kingpin?
One of his men. She sold the info to me piecemeal but I never got a name.
They said Natchios was the Kingpin.
They're wrong. Tazio said Natchios was one of the Kingpin's business partners back in the old days.
You'll testify to that?

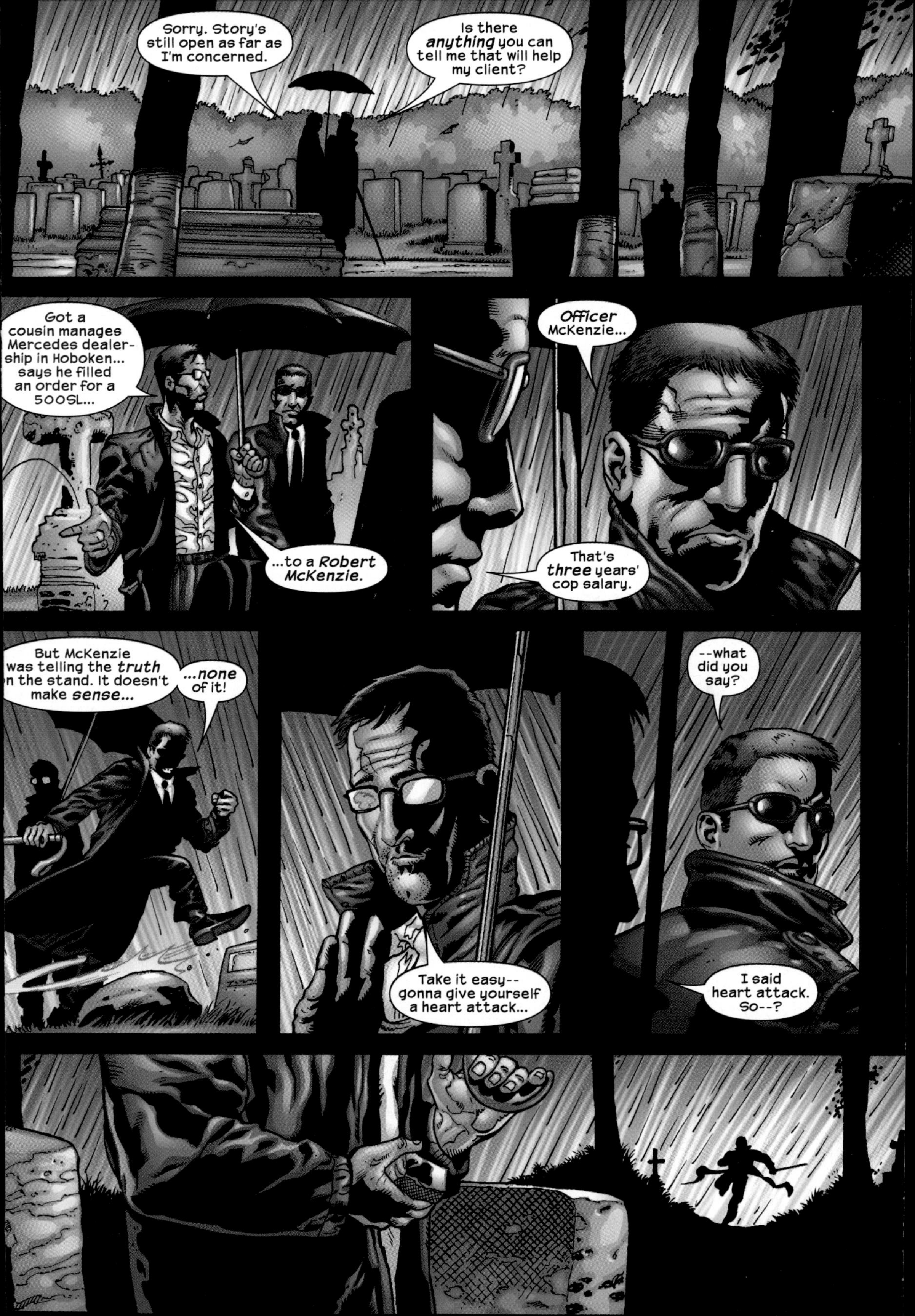
Sorry. Story's still open as far as I'm concerned.
Is there *anything* you can tell me that will help my client?
Got a cousin manages Mercedes dealer-ship in Hoboken... says he filled an order for a 500SL...
...to a *Robert McKenzie.*
Officer McKenzie...
That's *three* years' cop salary.
But McKenzie was telling the *truth* n the stand. It doesn't make *sense*...
...*none* of it!
Take it easy--gonna give yourself a heart attack...
--what did you say?
I said heart attack. So--?

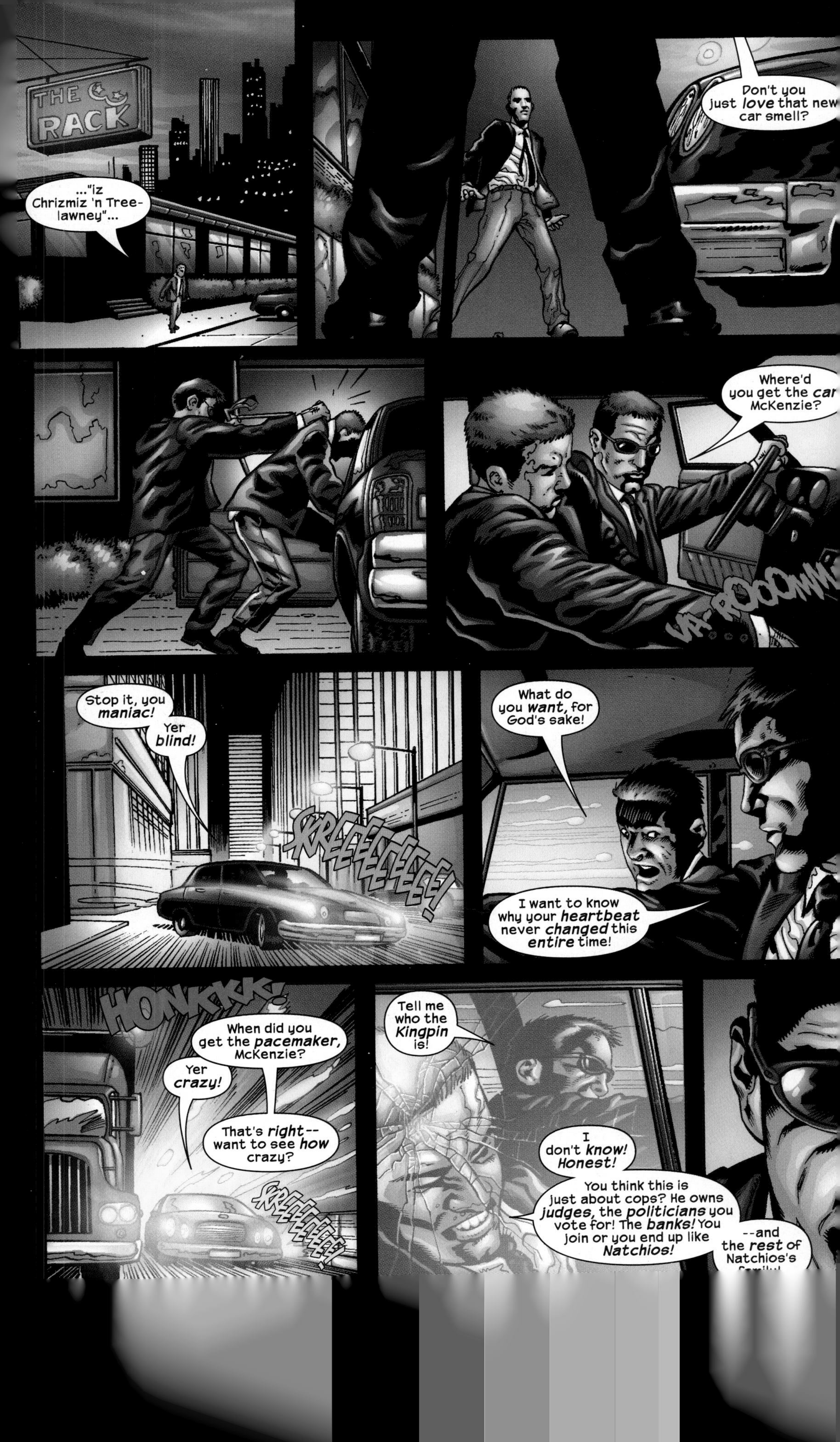
THE RACK
..."iz Chrizmiz 'n Tree-lawney"...
Don't you just love that new car smell?
Where'd you get the car McKenzie?
Stop it, you maniac!
Yer blind!
What do you want, for God's sake!
I want to know why your heartbeat never changed this entire time!
HONKKK!
When did you get the pacemaker, McKenzie?
Yer crazy!
That's right-- want to see how crazy?
Tell me who the Kingpin is!
I don't know! Honest!
You think this is just about cops? He owns judges, the politicians you vote for! The banks! You join or you end up like Natchios!
--and the rest of Natchios's

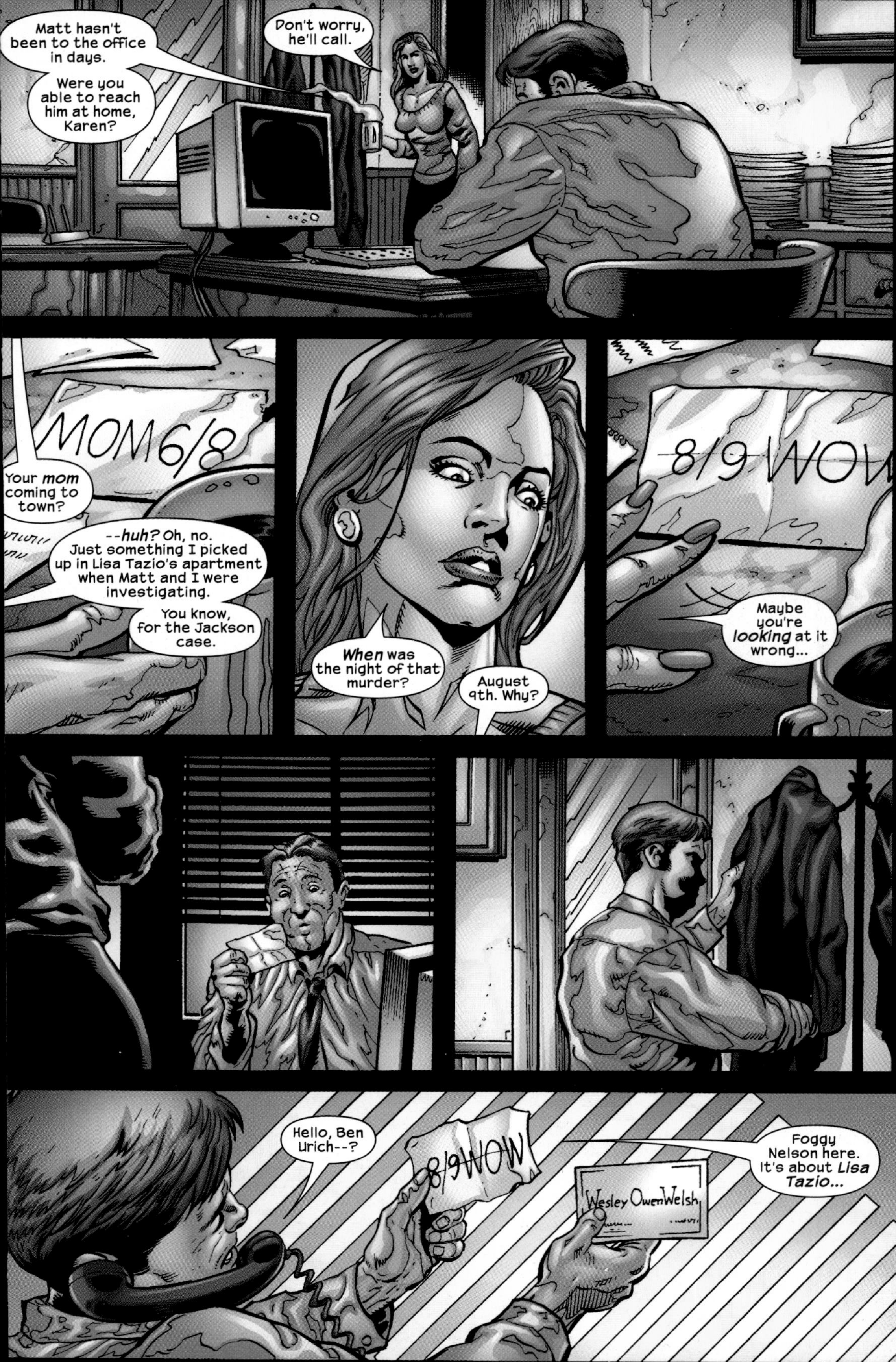

Matt hasn't been to the office in days.
Were you able to reach him at home, Karen?
Don't worry, he'll call.
MOM 6/8
Your *mom* coming to town?
--*huh?* Oh, no. Just something I picked up in Lisa Tazio's apartment when Matt and I were investigating.
You know, for the Jackson case.
When was the night of that murder?
August 9th. Why?
8/9 WOW
Maybe you're *looking* at it wrong...
Hello, Ben Urich--?
8/9 WOW
Wesley Owen Welsh
Foggy Nelson here. It's about *Lisa Tazio*...

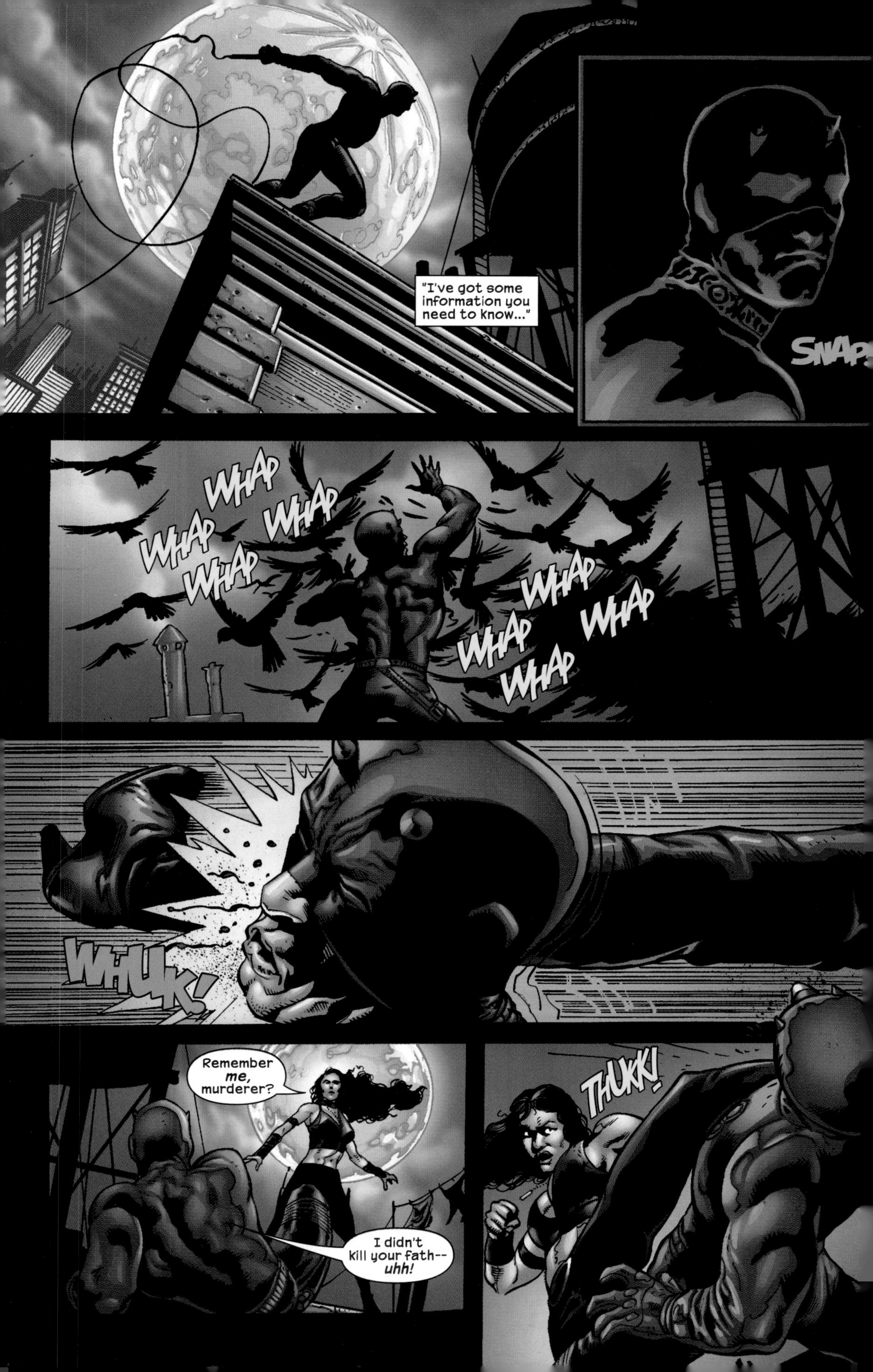
"I've got some information you need to know..."
SNAP!
WHAP
WHAP
WHAP
WHAP
WHAP
WHAP
WHAP
WHAP
WHUK!
Remember *me,* murderer?
I didn't kill your fath-- *uhh!*
THUKK!

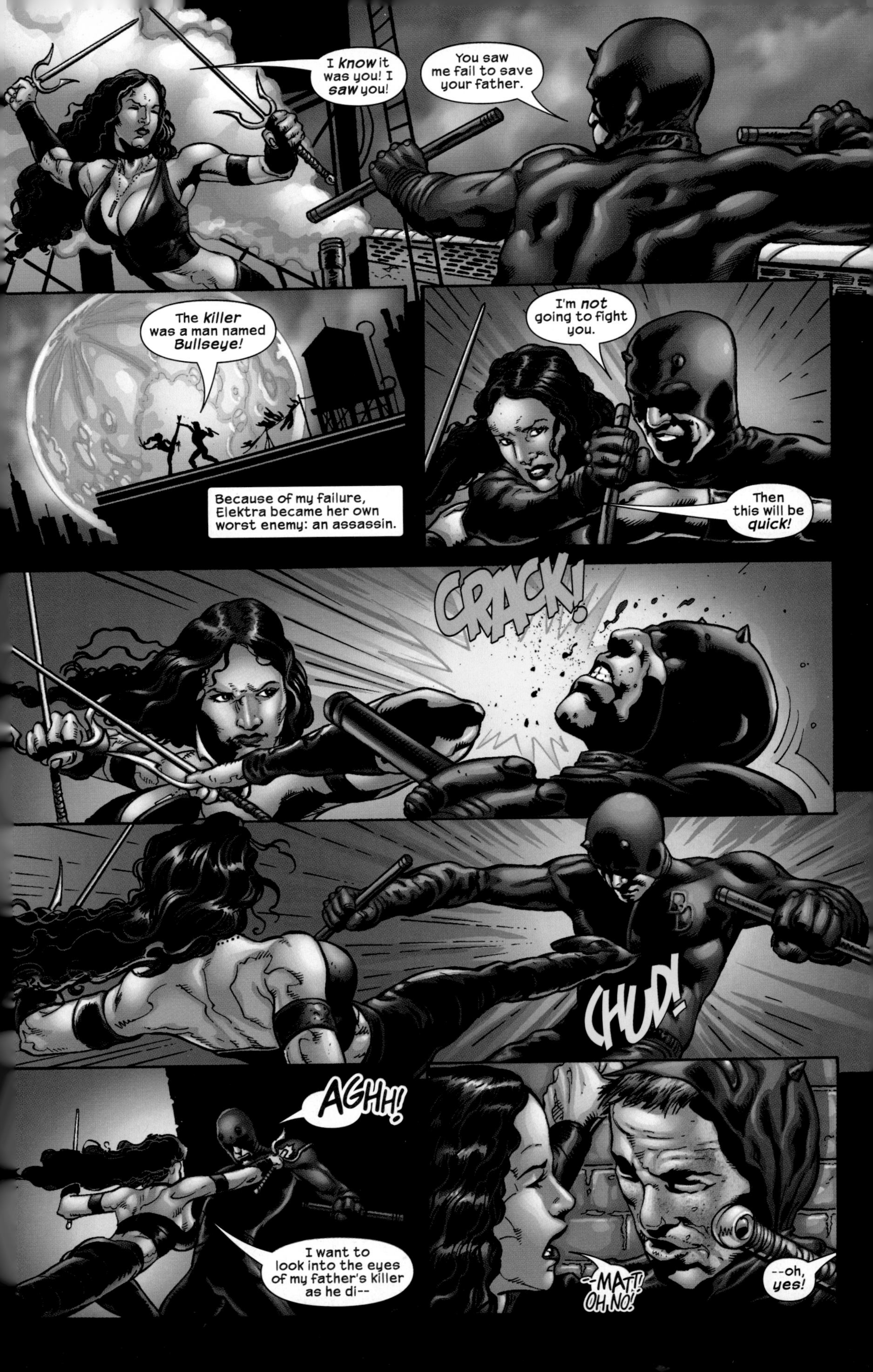
I know it was you! I saw you!
You saw me fail to save your father.
The killer was a man named Bullseye!
Because of my failure, Elektra became her own worst enemy: an assassin.
I'm not going to fight you.
Then this will be quick!
CRACK!
CHUD!
AGHH!
I want to look into the eyes of my father's killer as he di--
--MATT! OH, NO!
--oh, yes!

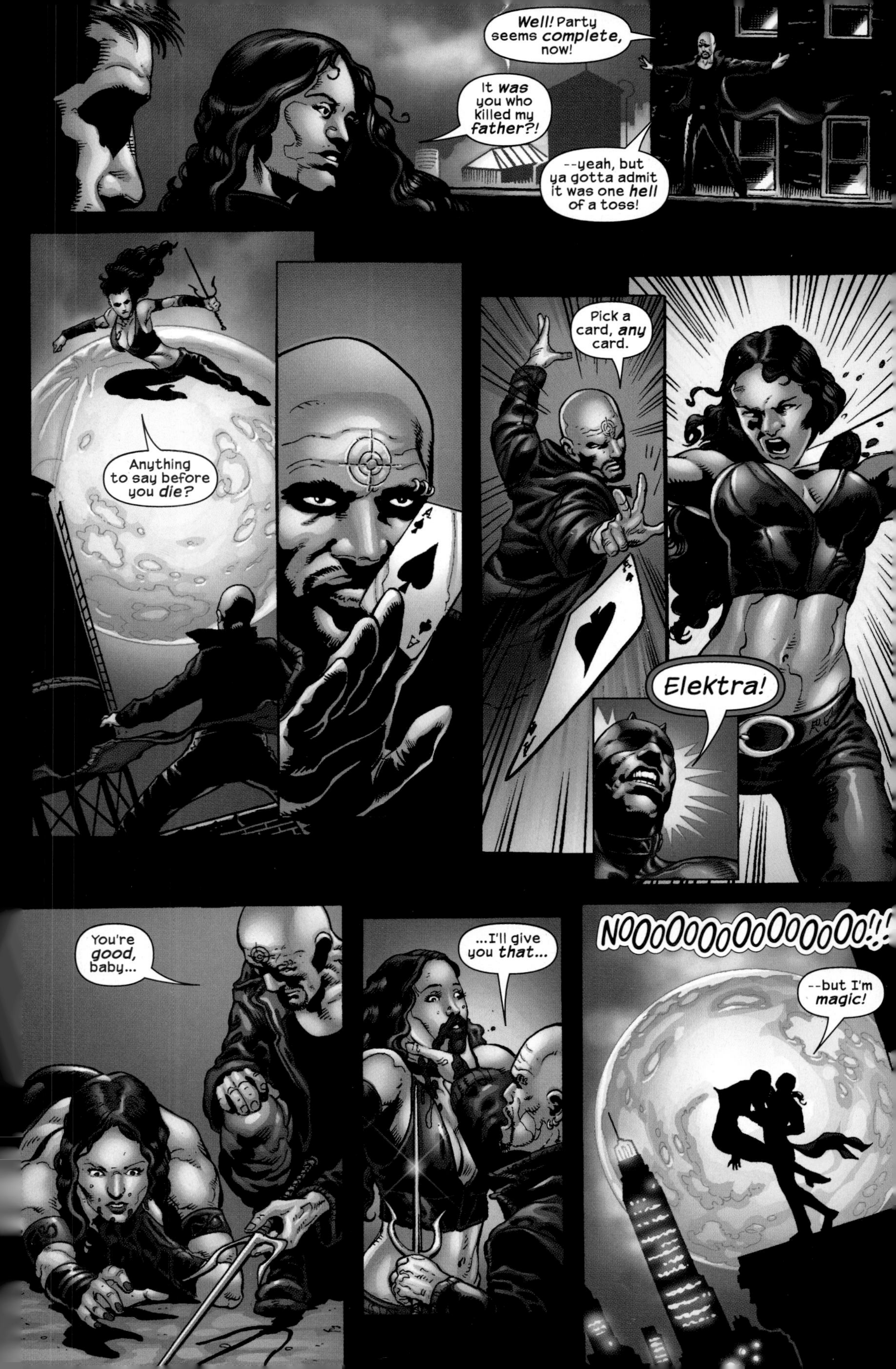
Well! Party seems complete, now!
It was you who killed my father?!
--yeah, but ya gotta admit it was one hell of a toss!
Anything to say before you die?
Pick a card, any card.
Elektra!
You're good, baby...
...I'll give you that...
NOOOOOOOOOOOOOOOO!!!
--but I'm magic!

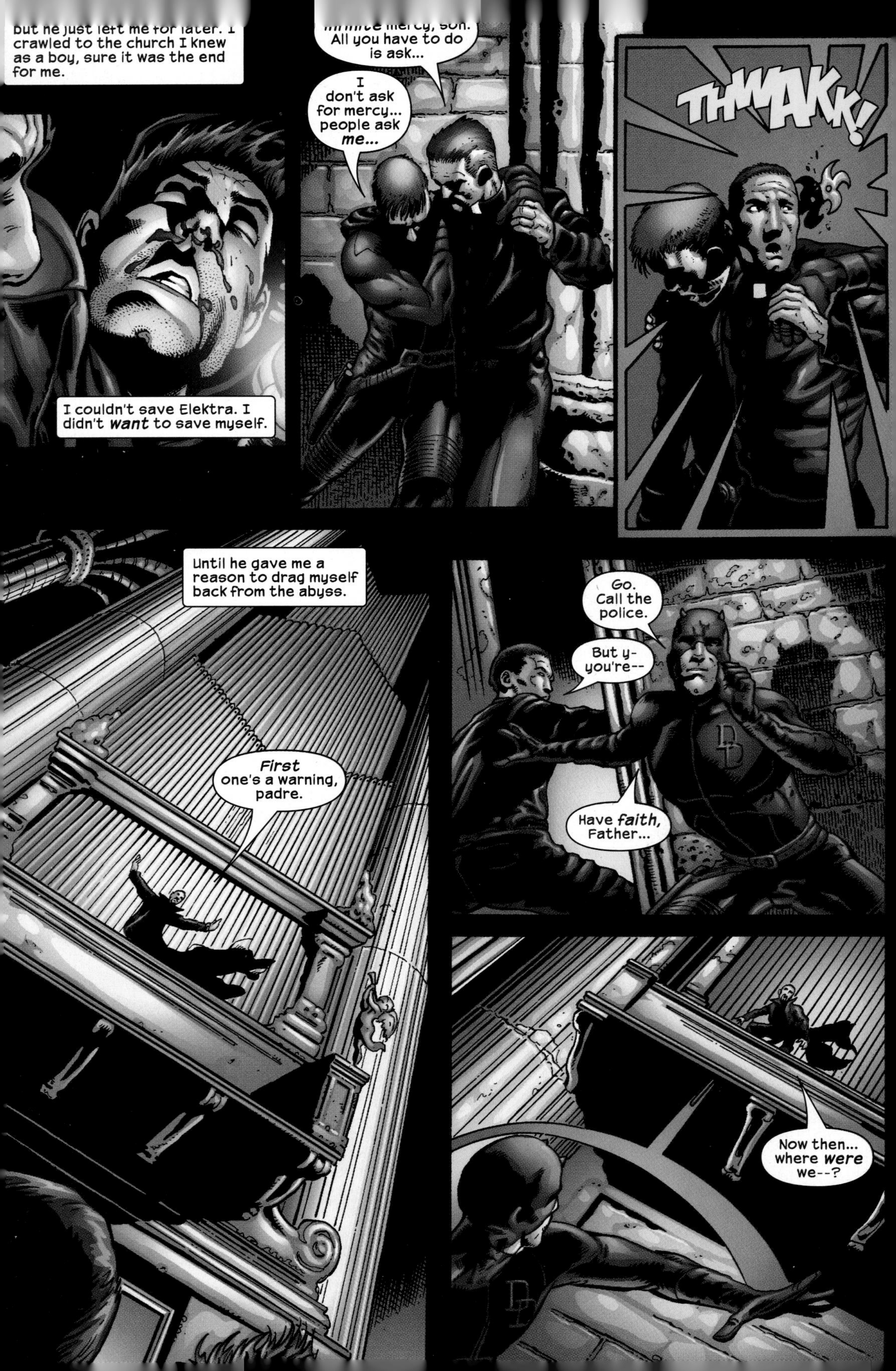

but he just left me for later. I crawled to the church I knew as a boy, sure it was the end for me.
I couldn't save Elektra. I didn't *want* to save myself.
mercy, son. All you have to do is ask...
I don't ask for mercy... people ask *me...*
THWAKK!
Until he gave me a reason to drag myself back from the abyss.
First one's a warning, padre.
Go. Call the police.
But y-you're--
Have *faith,* Father...
Now then... where *were* we--?

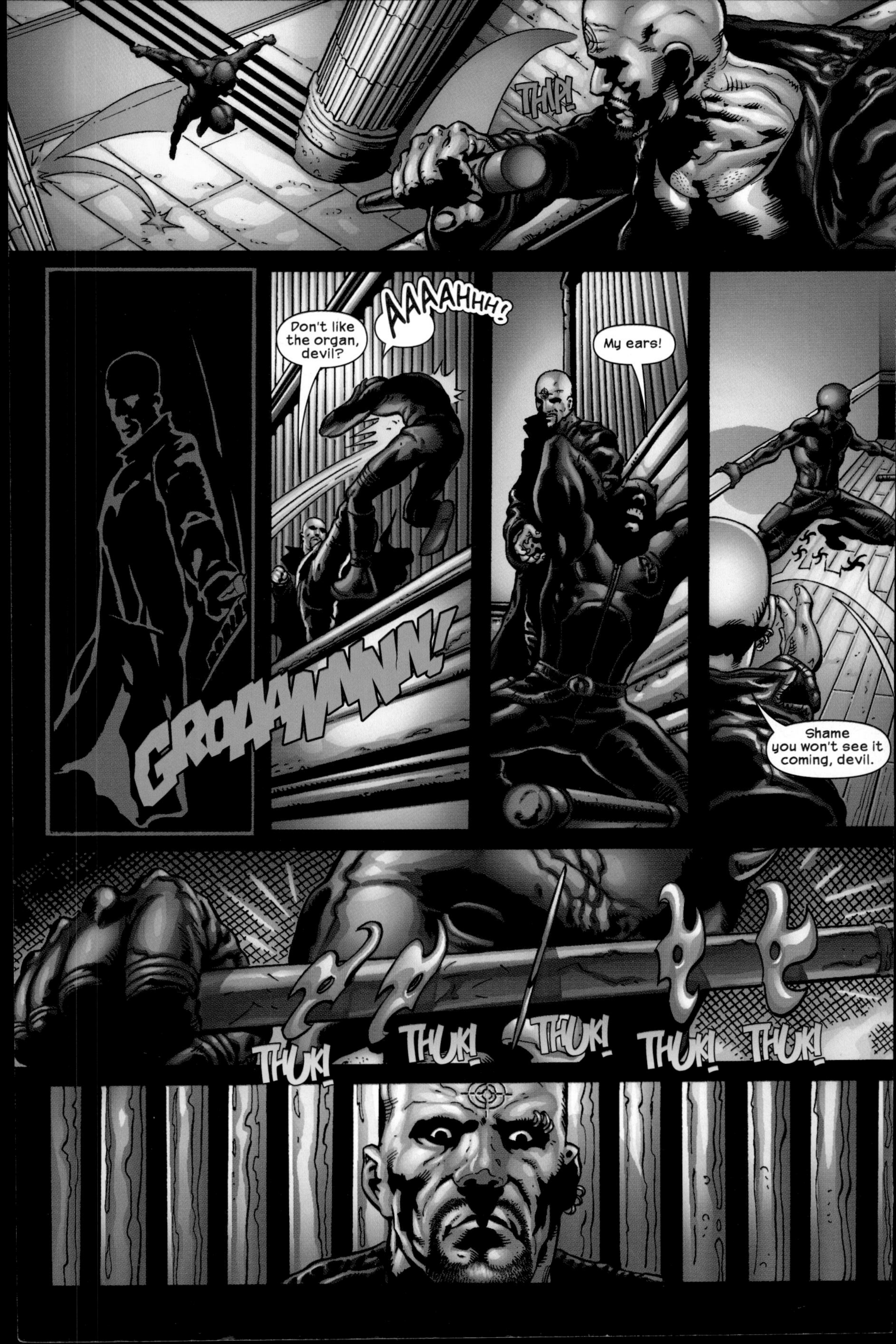
THWP!
Don't like the organ, devil?
AAAAHHH!
GROAAWWNNN!
My ears!
Shame you won't see it coming, devil.
THUK!
THUK!
THUK!
THUK!
THUK!

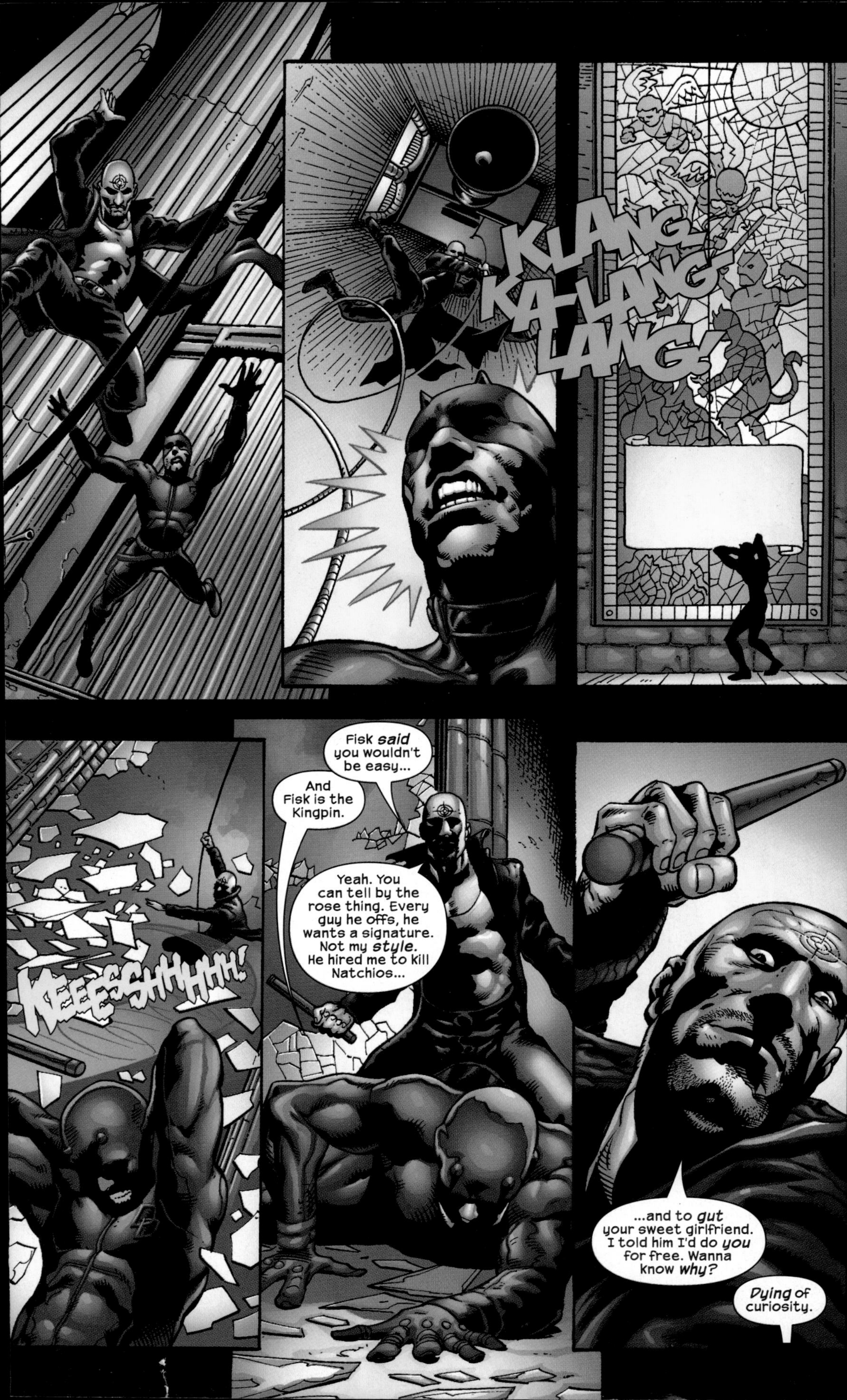
KLANG KA-LANG LANG!
KEEESHHHHH!
Fisk *said* you wouldn't be easy...
And Fisk is the Kingpin.
Yeah. You can tell by the rose thing. Every guy he offs, he wants a signature. Not my *style*. He hired me to kill Natchios...
...and to *gut* your sweet girlfriend. I told him I'd do *you* for free. Wanna know *why*?
Dying of curiosity.

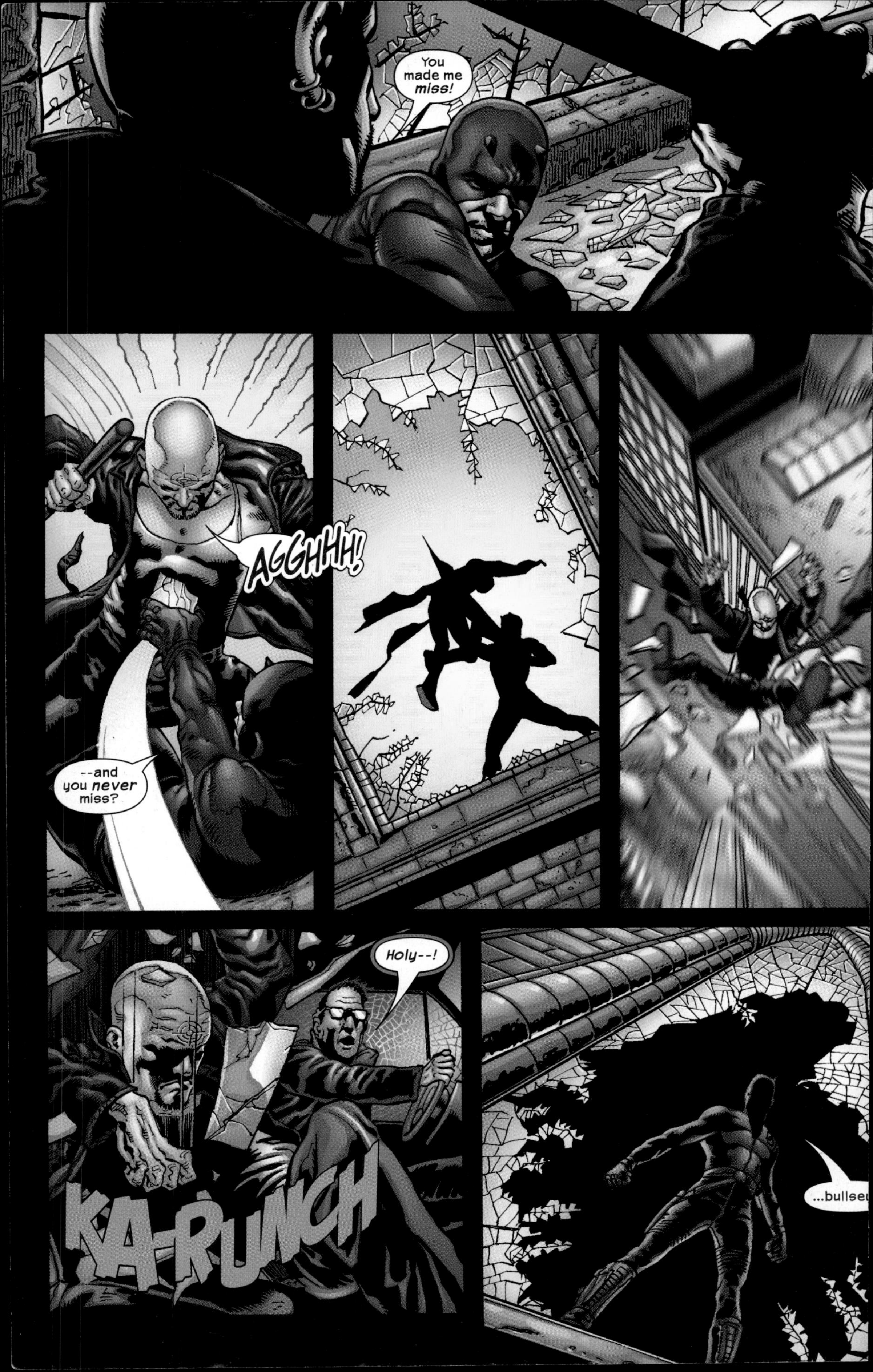
You made me miss!
AGGHHH!
--and you never miss?
Holy--!
KA-RUNCH
...bullse

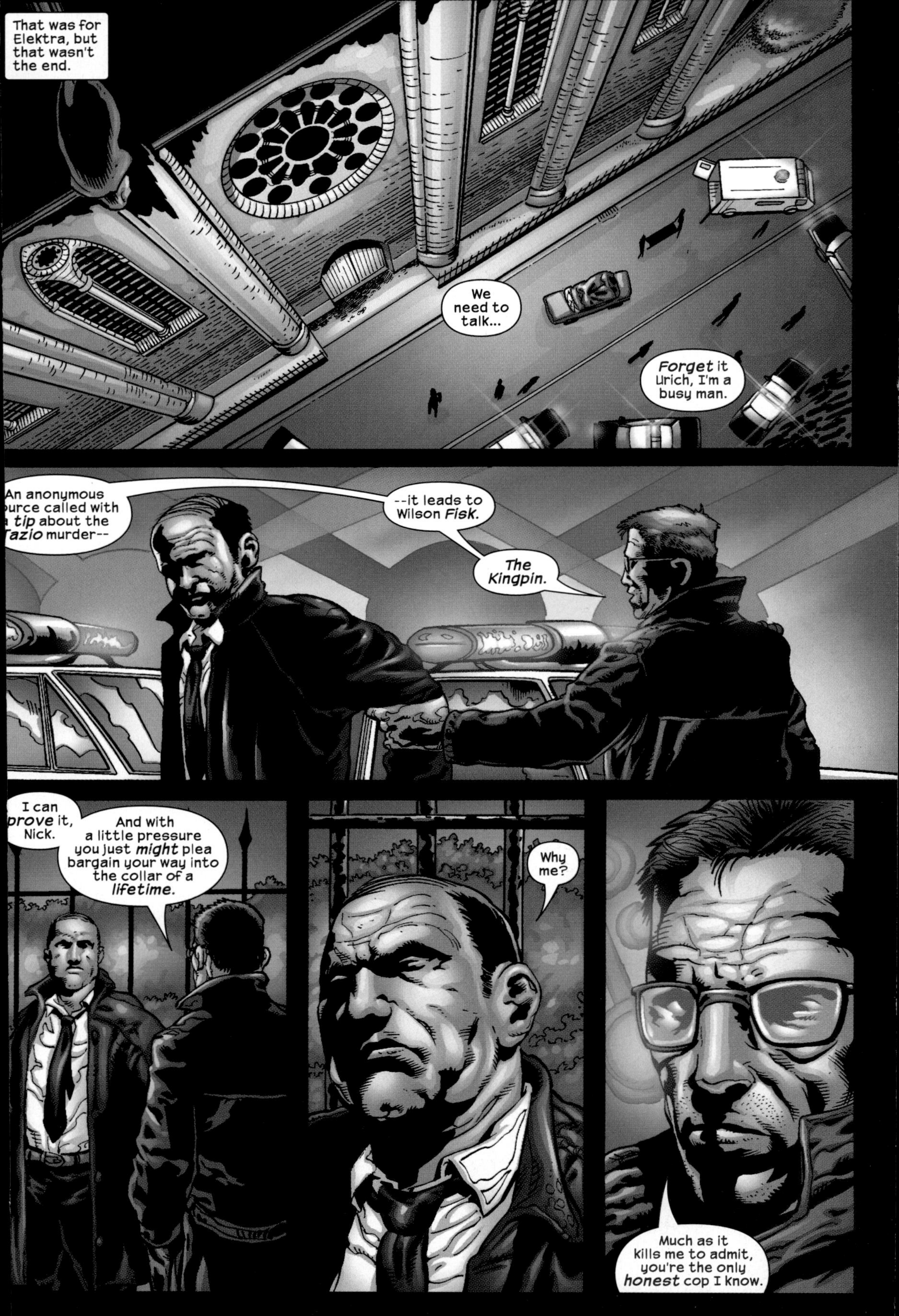
That was for Elektra, but that wasn't the end.
We need to talk...
Forget it Urich, I'm a busy man.
An anonymous source called with a tip about the Tazio murder--
--it leads to Wilson Fisk.
The Kingpin.
I can prove it, Nick.
And with a little pressure you just might plea bargain your way into the collar of a lifetime.
Why me?
Much as it kills me to admit, you're the only honest cop I know.

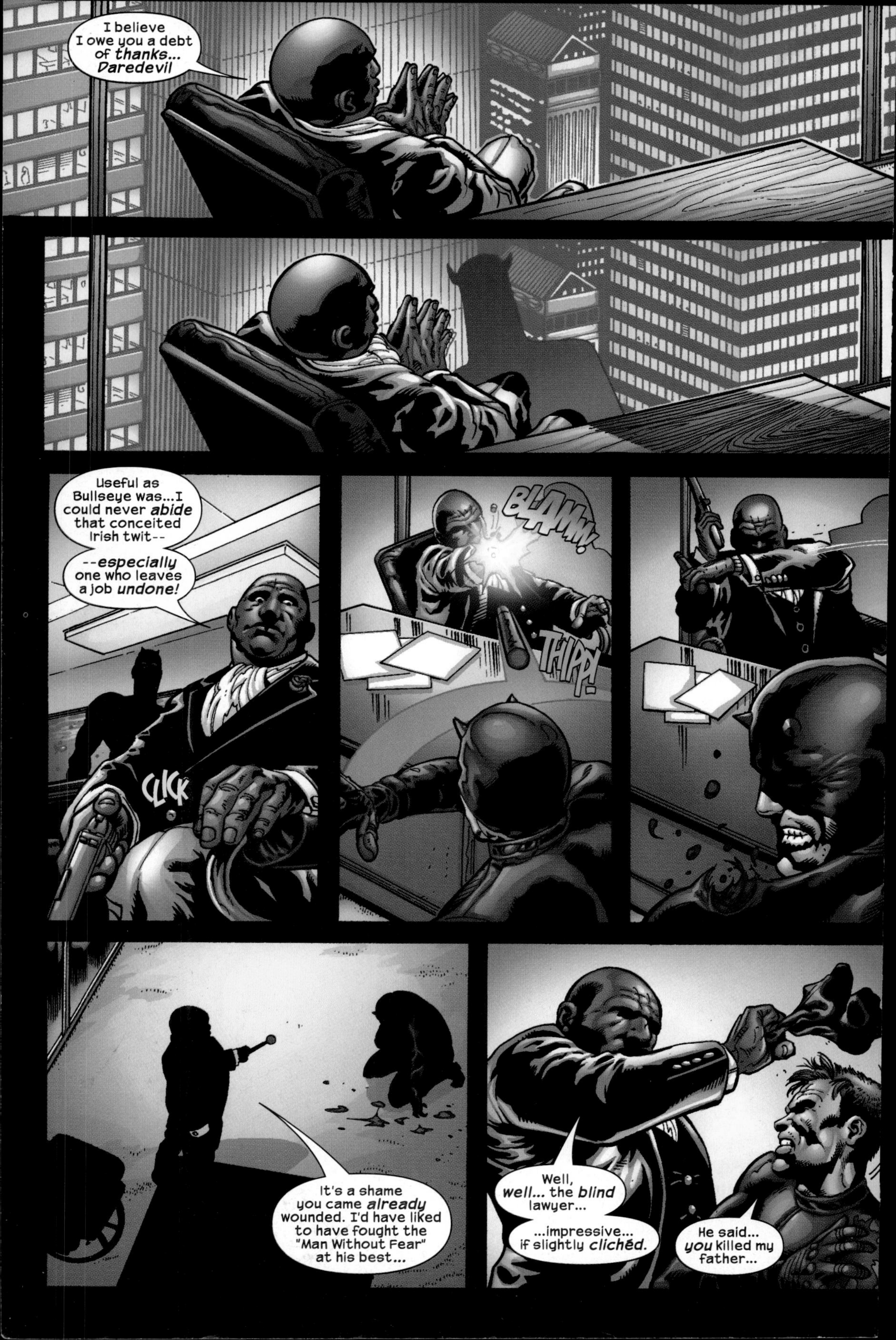
I believe I owe you a debt of thanks... Daredevil
Useful as Bullseye was...I could never abide that conceited Irish twit--
--especially one who leaves a job undone!
CLICK
BLAMM!
THIPP!
It's a shame you came already wounded. I'd have liked to have fought the "Man Without Fear" at his best...
Well, well... the blind lawyer...
...impressive... if slightly clichéd.
He said... you killed my father...

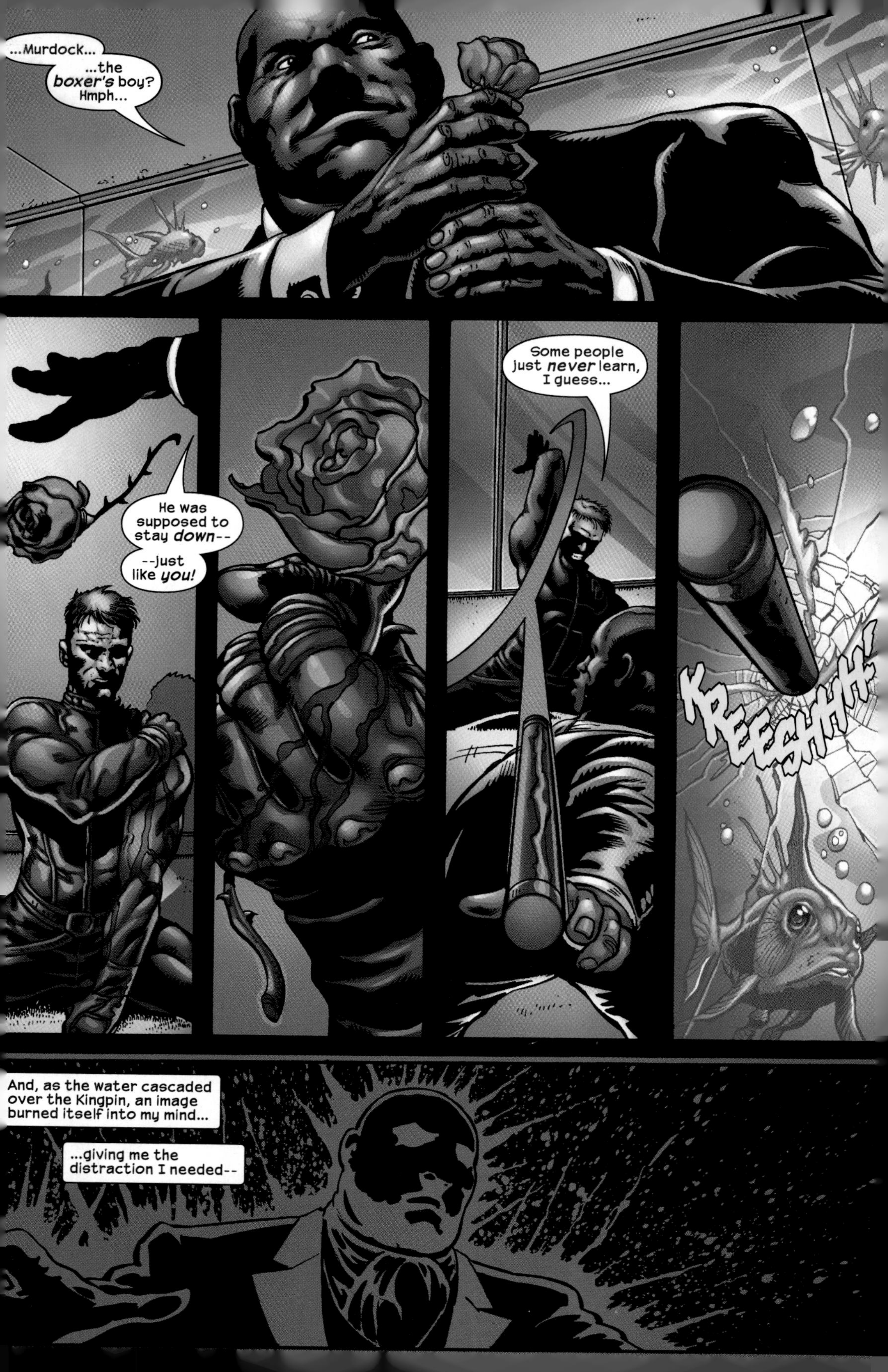
...Murdock...
...the *boxer's* boy? Hmph...
He was supposed to stay *down*--
--just like *you!*
Some people just *never* learn, I guess...
KREESHHH!
And, as the water cascaded over the Kingpin, an image burned itself into my mind...
...giving me the distraction I needed--

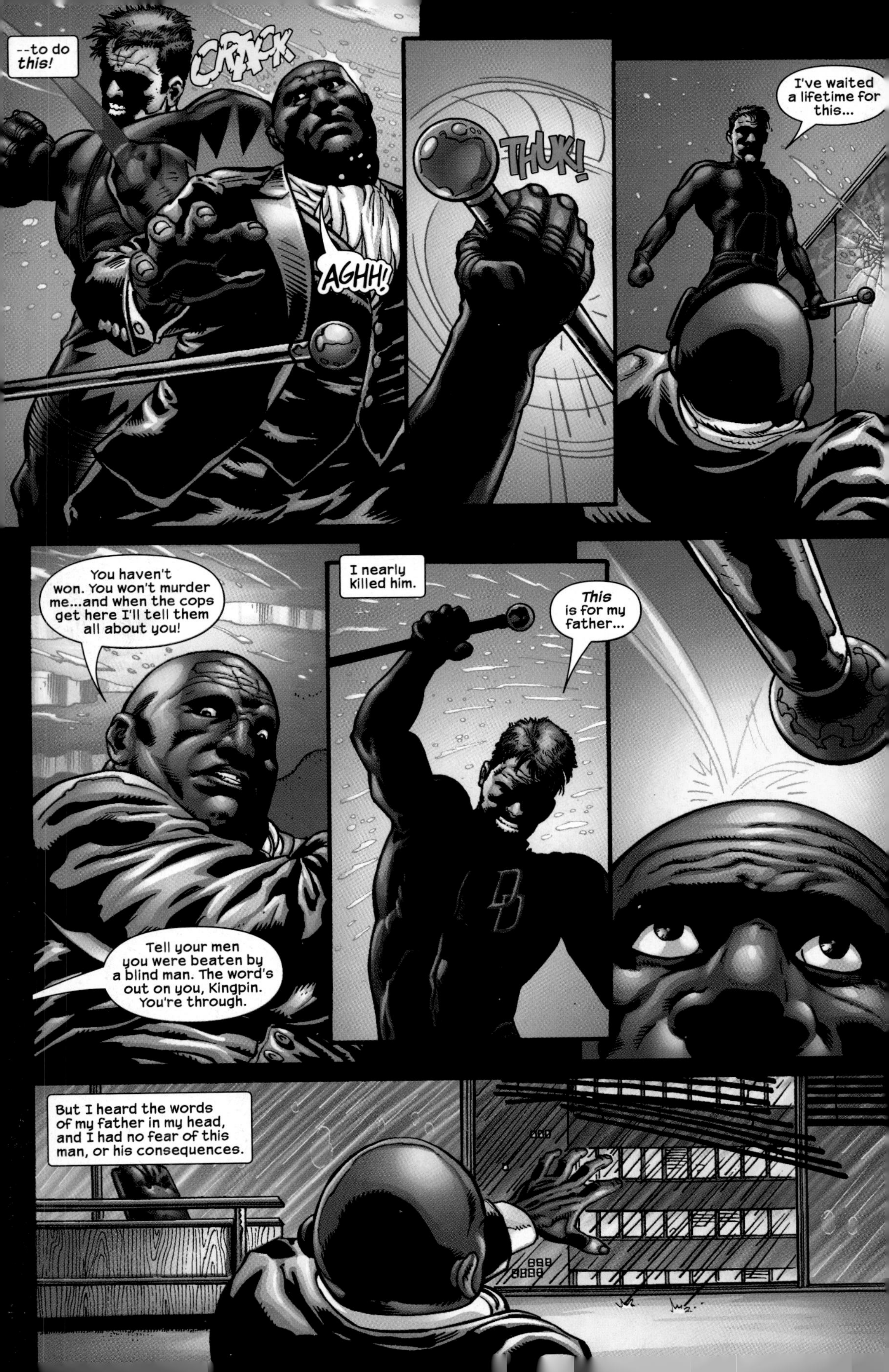
--to do *this!*
CRACK
AGHH!
THUK!
I've waited a lifetime for this...
You haven't won. You won't murder me...and when the cops get here I'll tell them all about you!
Tell your men you were beaten by a blind man. The word's out on you, Kingpin. You're through.
I nearly killed him.
This is for my father...
But I heard the words of my father in my head, and I had no fear of this man, or his consequences.

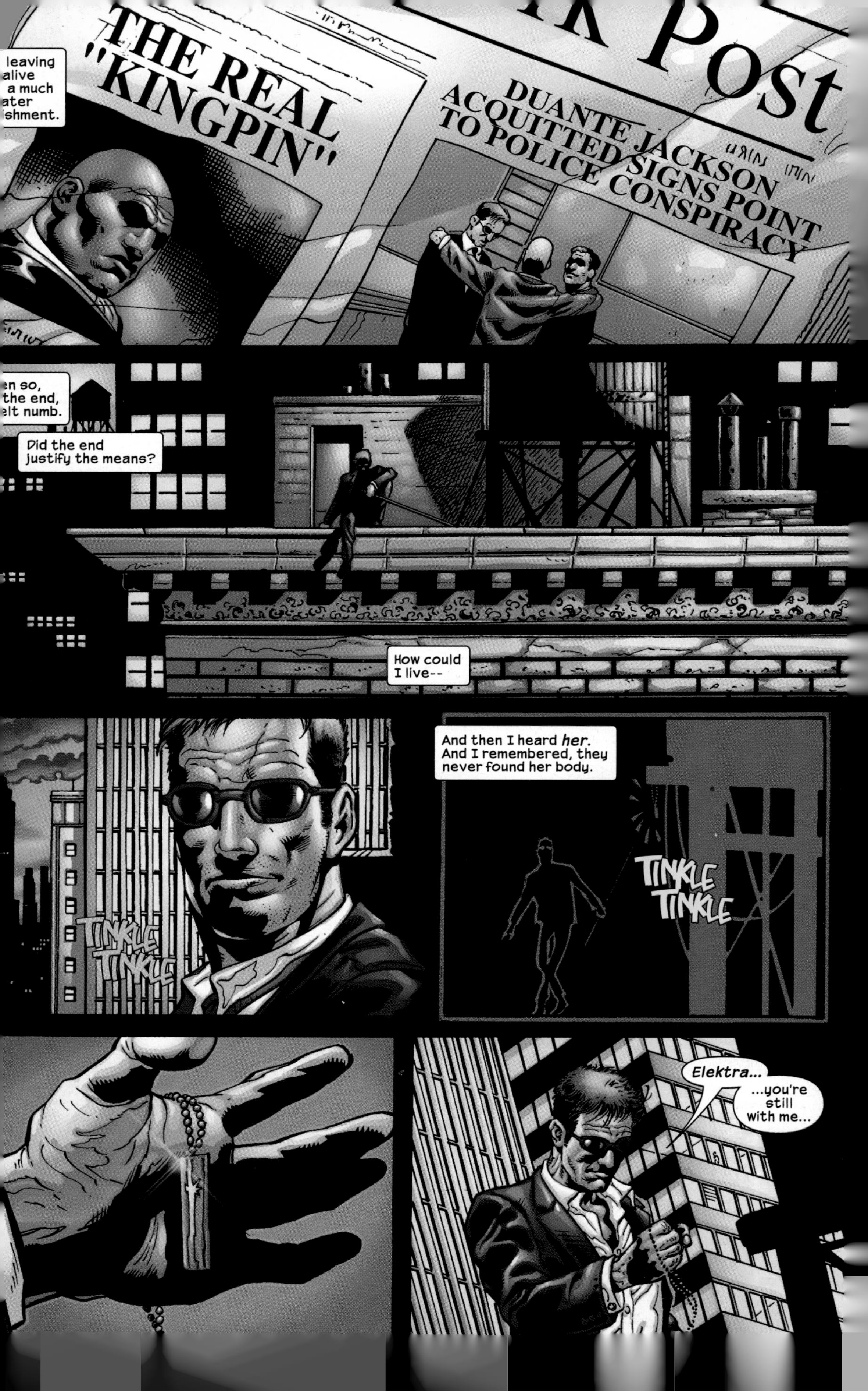

THE REAL "KINGPIN"
Post
DUANTE JACKSON ACQUITTED SIGNS POINT TO POLICE CONSPIRACY
leaving alive a much ater shment.
n so, the end, lt numb.
Did the end justify the means?
How could I live--
And then I heard her. And I remembered, they never found her body.
TINKLE TINKLE
TINKLE TINKLE
Elektra...
...you're still with me...

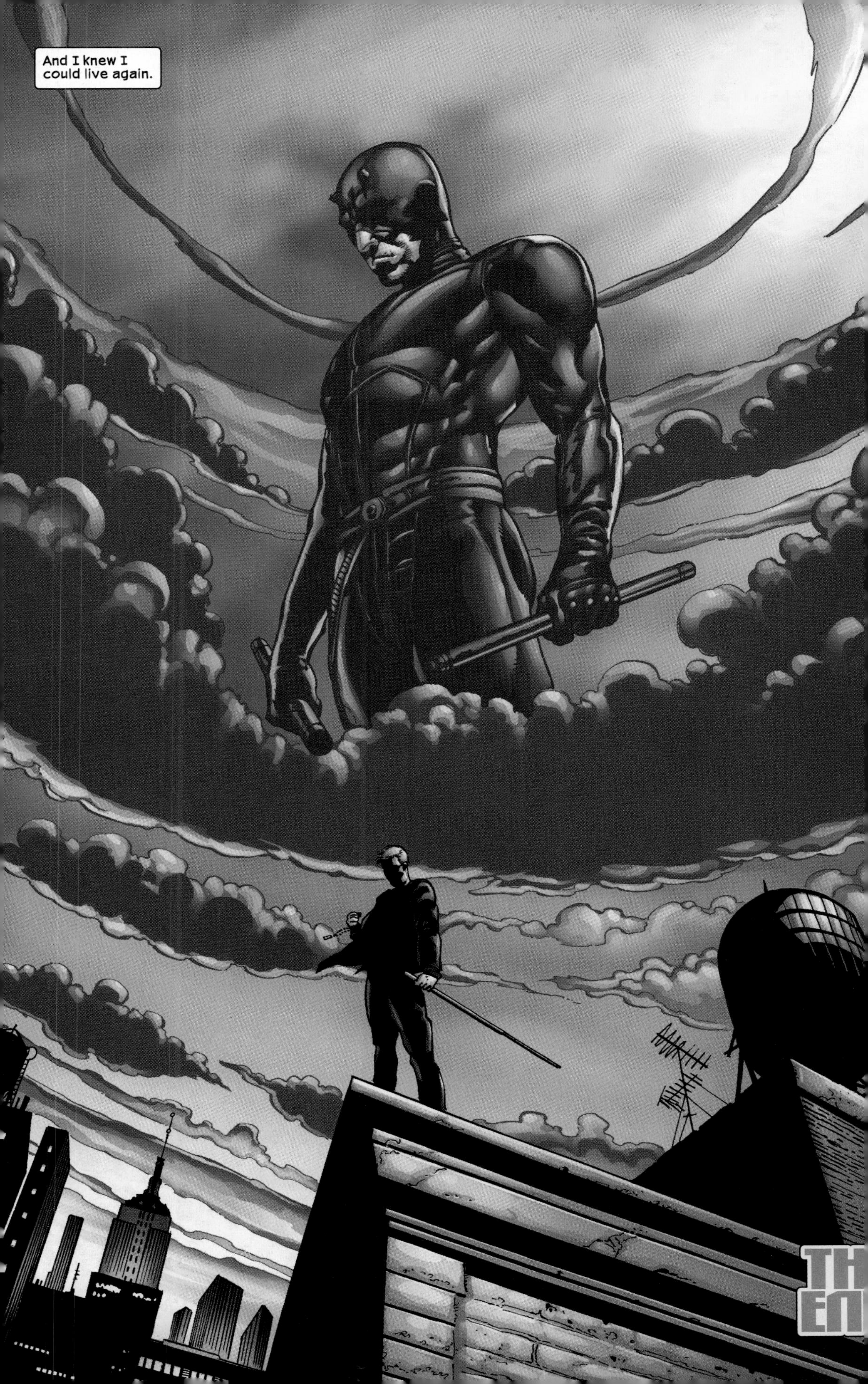
And I knew I could live again.

Now, the hottest creators in comics take on Marvel's Man Without Fear, the enigmatic Elektra and the Kingpin of Crime ...

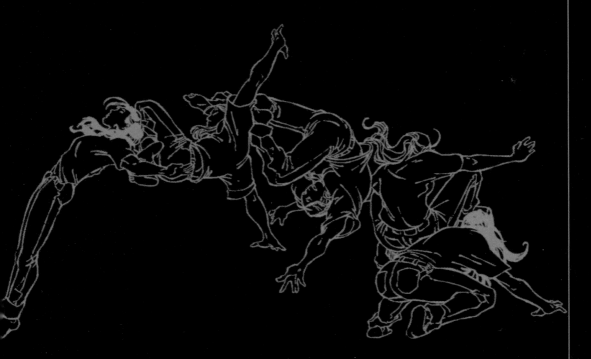

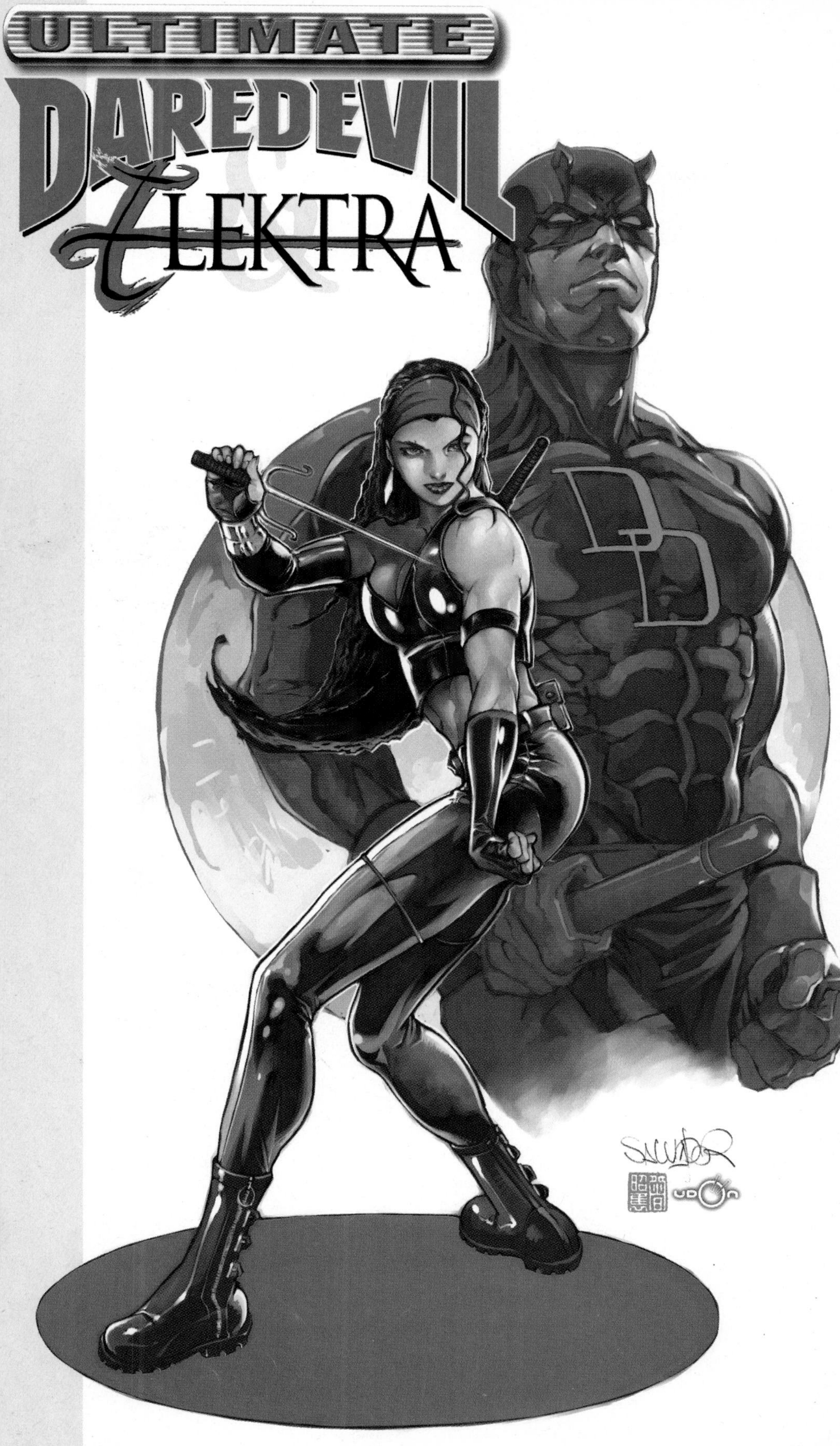
ULTIMATE
DAREDEVIL
ELEKTRA
SALVADOR
UDON

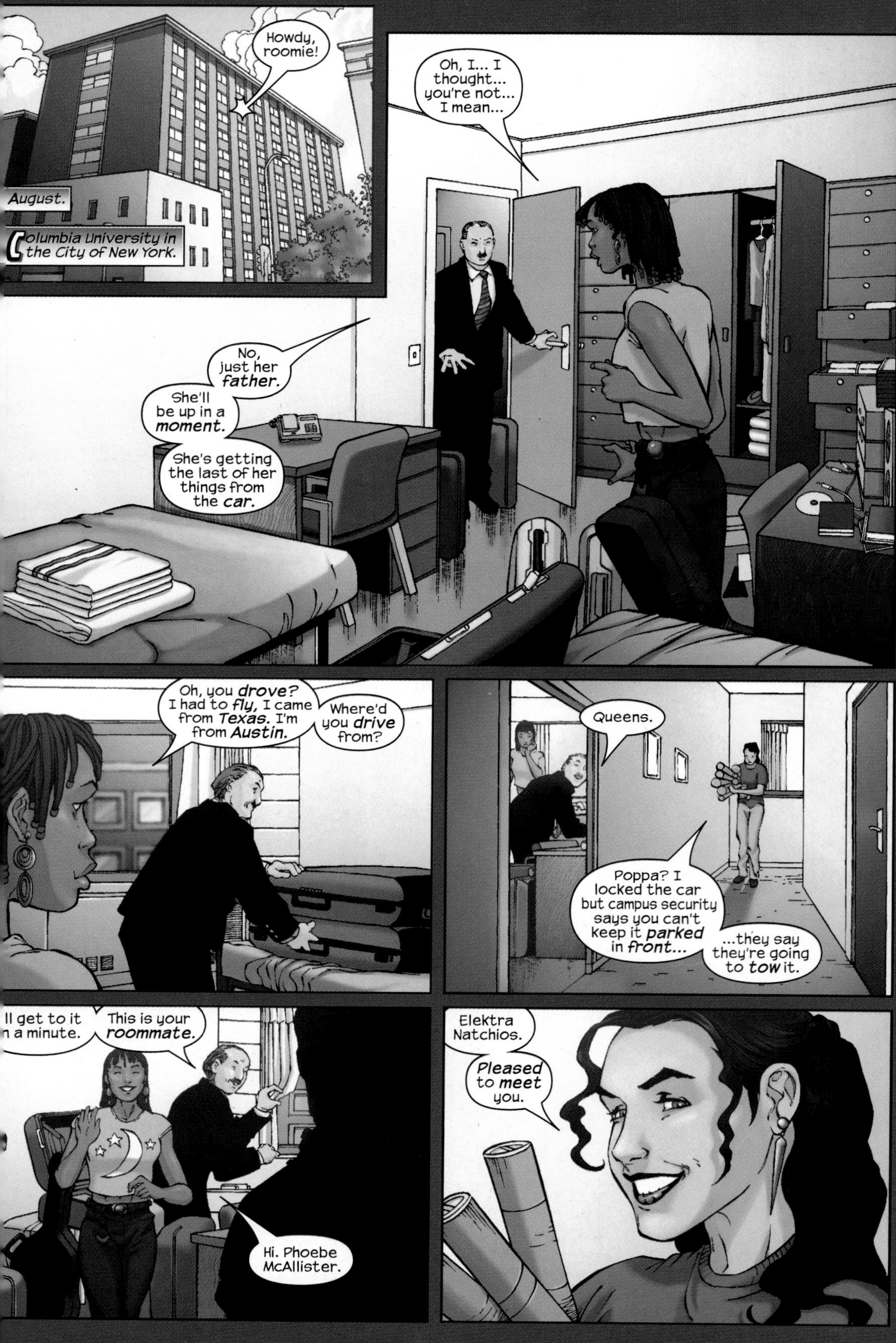
Howdy, roomie!
August.
Columbia University in the City of New York.
Oh, I... I thought... you're not... I mean...
No, just her father.
She'll be up in a moment.
She's getting the last of her things from the car.
Oh, you drove? I had to fly, I came from Texas. I'm from Austin.
Where'd you drive from?
Queens.
Poppa? I locked the car but campus security says you can't keep it parked in front...
...they say they're going to tow it.
ll get to it n a minute.
This is your roommate.
Hi. Phoebe McAllister.
Elektra Natchios.
Pleased to meet you.

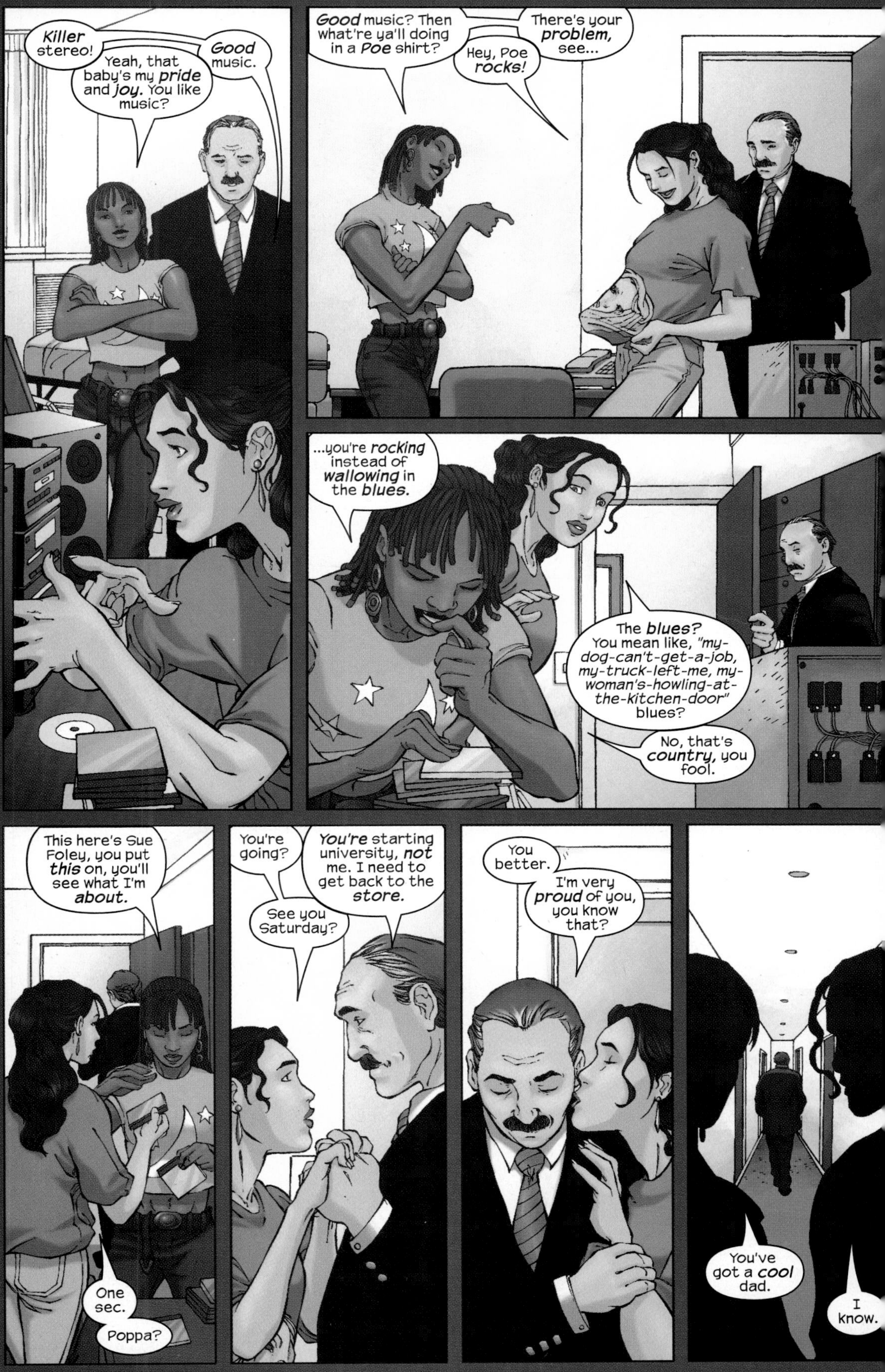

Killer stereo!
Good music.
Yeah, that baby's my pride and joy. You like music?
Good music? Then what're ya'll doing in a Poe shirt?
Hey, Poe rocks!
There's your problem, see...
...you're rocking instead of wallowing in the blues.
The blues? You mean like, "my-dog-can't-get-a-job, my-truck-left-me, my-woman's-howling-at-the-kitchen-door" blues?
No, that's country, you fool.
This here's Sue Foley, you put this on, you'll see what I'm about.
One sec.
Poppa?
You're going?
You're starting university, not me. I need to get back to the store.
See you Saturday?
You better.
I'm very proud of you, you know that?
You've got a cool dad.
I know.

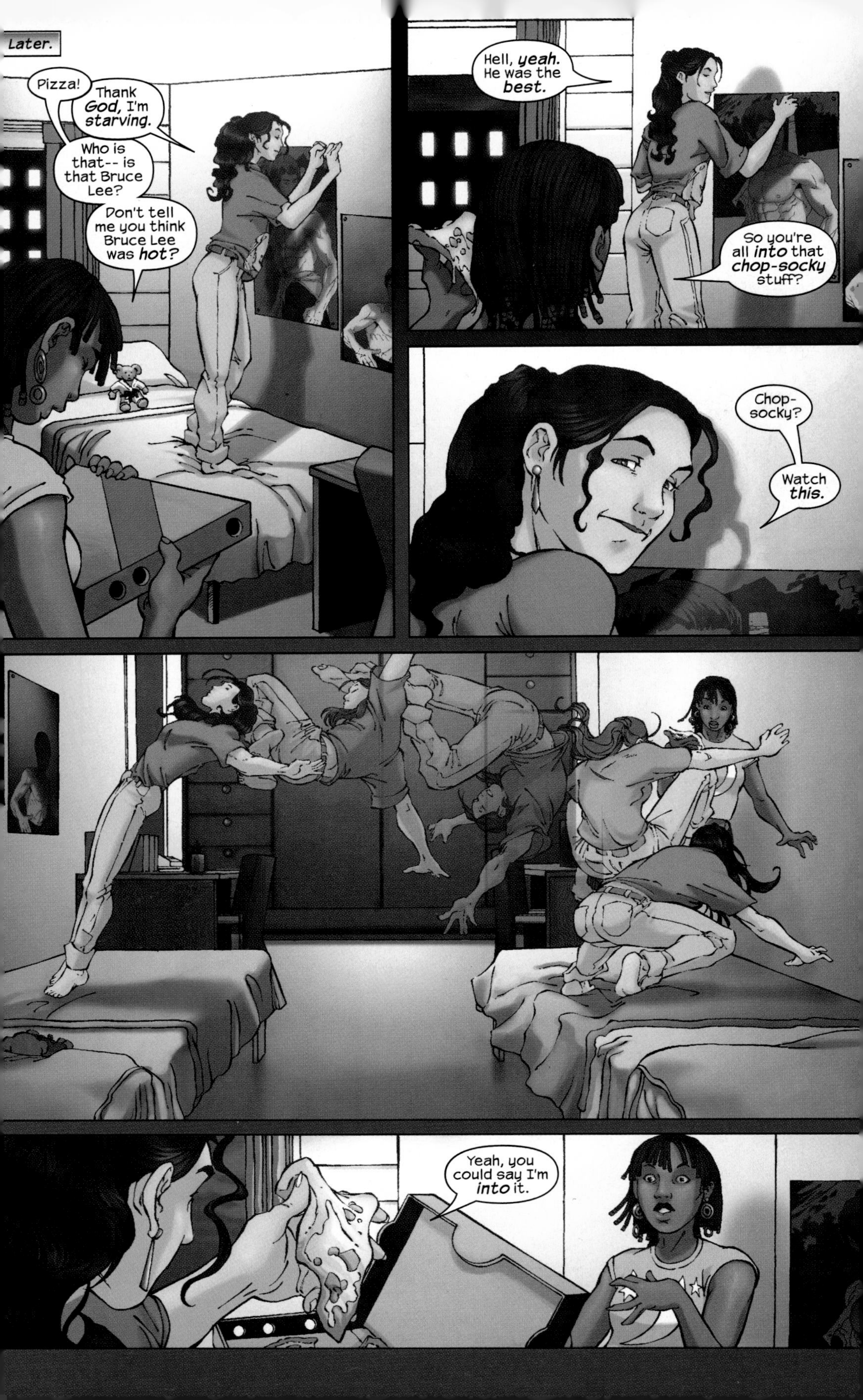
Later.
Pizza!
Thank God, I'm starving.
Who is that-- is that Bruce Lee?
Don't tell me you think Bruce Lee was hot?
Hell, yeah. He was the best.
So you're all into that chop-socky stuff?
Chop-socky?
Watch this.
Yeah, you could say I'm into it.

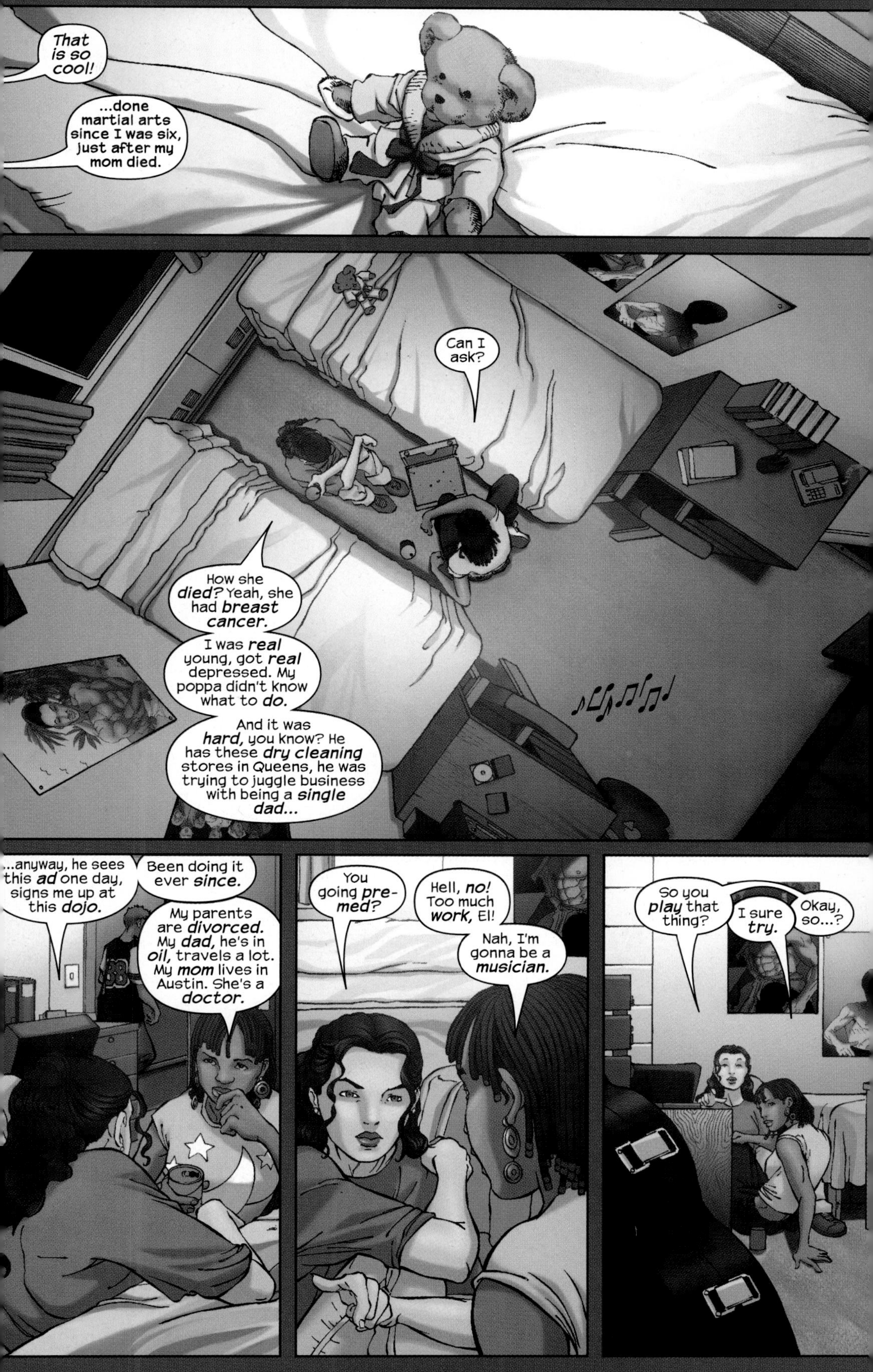

That is so cool!
...done martial arts since I was six, just after my mom died.
Can I ask?
How she died? Yeah, she had breast cancer.
I was real young, got real depressed. My poppa didn't know what to do.
And it was hard, you know? He has these dry cleaning stores in Queens, he was trying to juggle business with being a single dad...
...anyway, he sees this ad one day, signs me up at this dojo.
Been doing it ever since.
My parents are divorced. My dad, he's in oil, travels a lot. My mom lives in Austin. She's a doctor.
You going pre-med?
Hell, no! Too much work, El!
Nah, I'm gonna be a musician.
So you play that thing?
I sure try.
Okay, so...?

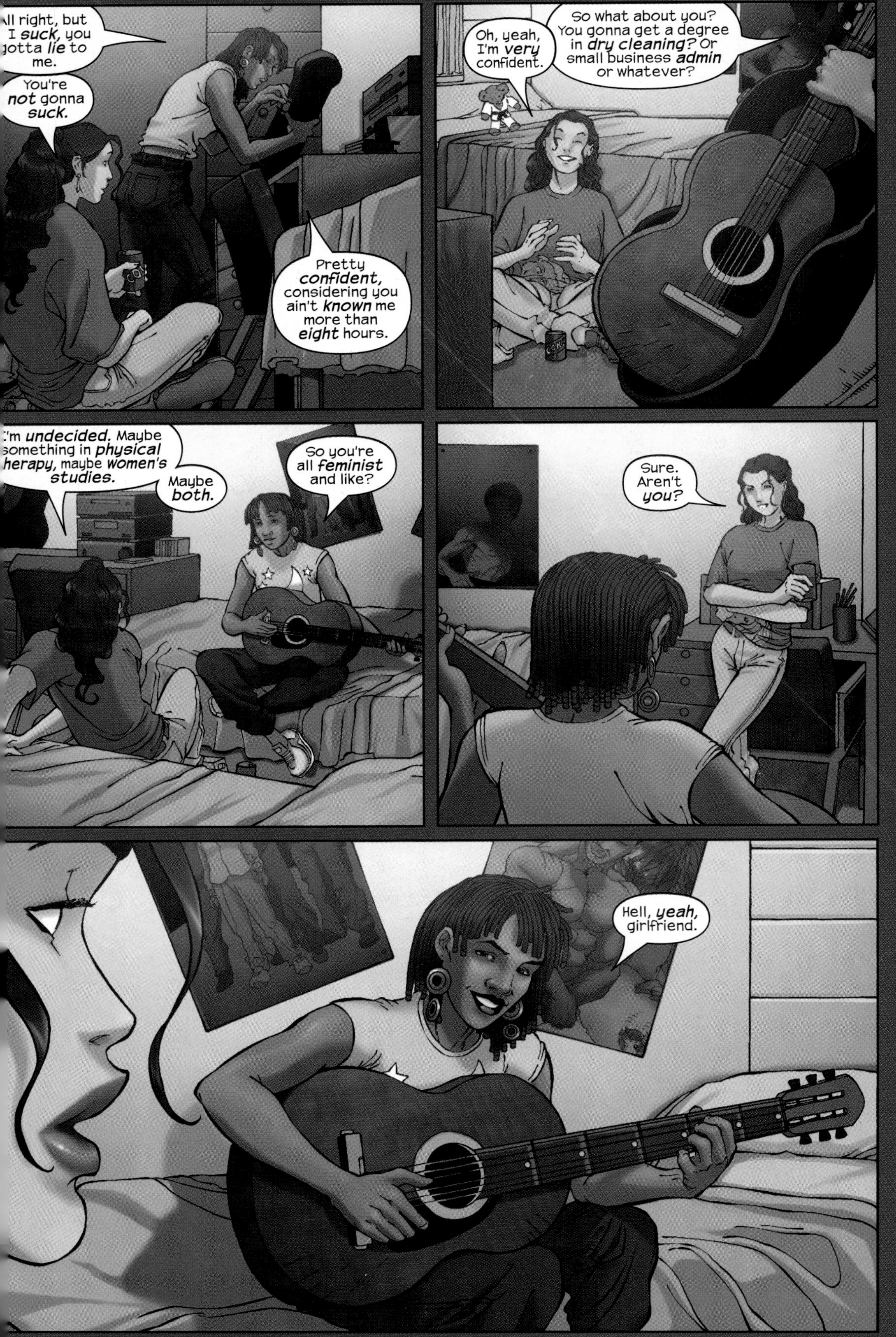
All right, but I suck, you gotta lie to me.
You're not gonna suck.
Pretty confident, considering you ain't known me more than eight hours.
Oh, yeah, I'm very confident.
So what about you? You gonna get a degree in dry cleaning? Or small business admin or whatever?
I'm undecided. Maybe something in physical therapy, maybe women's studies.
Maybe both.
So you're all feminist and like?
Sure. Aren't you?
Hell, yeah, girlfriend.

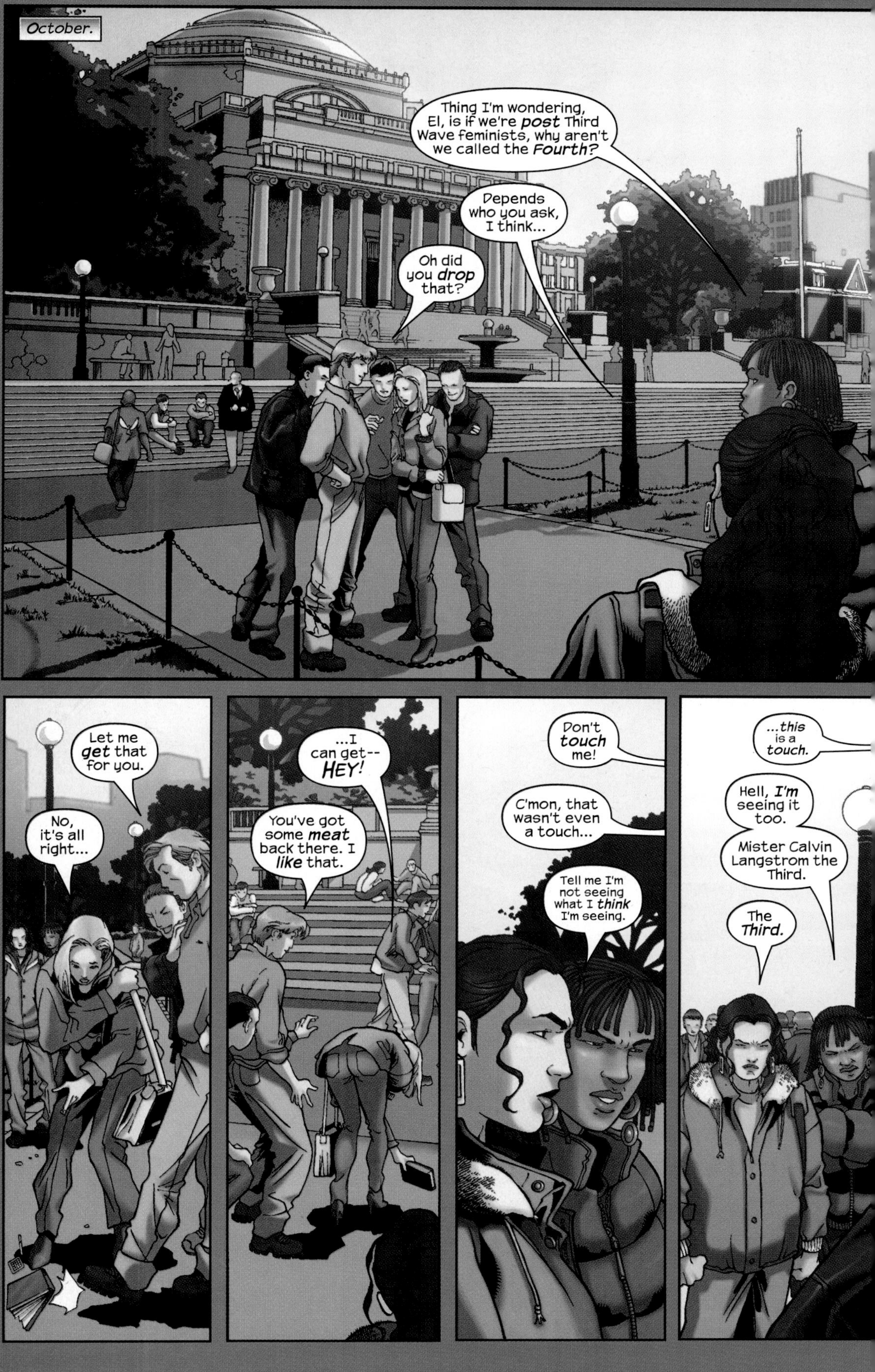
October.
Thing I'm wondering, El, is if we're post Third Wave feminists, why aren't we called the Fourth?
Depends who you ask, I think...
Oh did you drop that?
Let me get that for you.
No, it's all right...
...I can get-- HEY!
You've got some meat back there. I like that.
Don't touch me!
C'mon, that wasn't even a touch...
Tell me I'm not seeing what I think I'm seeing.
...this is a touch.
Hell, I'm seeing it too.
Mister Calvin Langstrom the Third.
The Third.

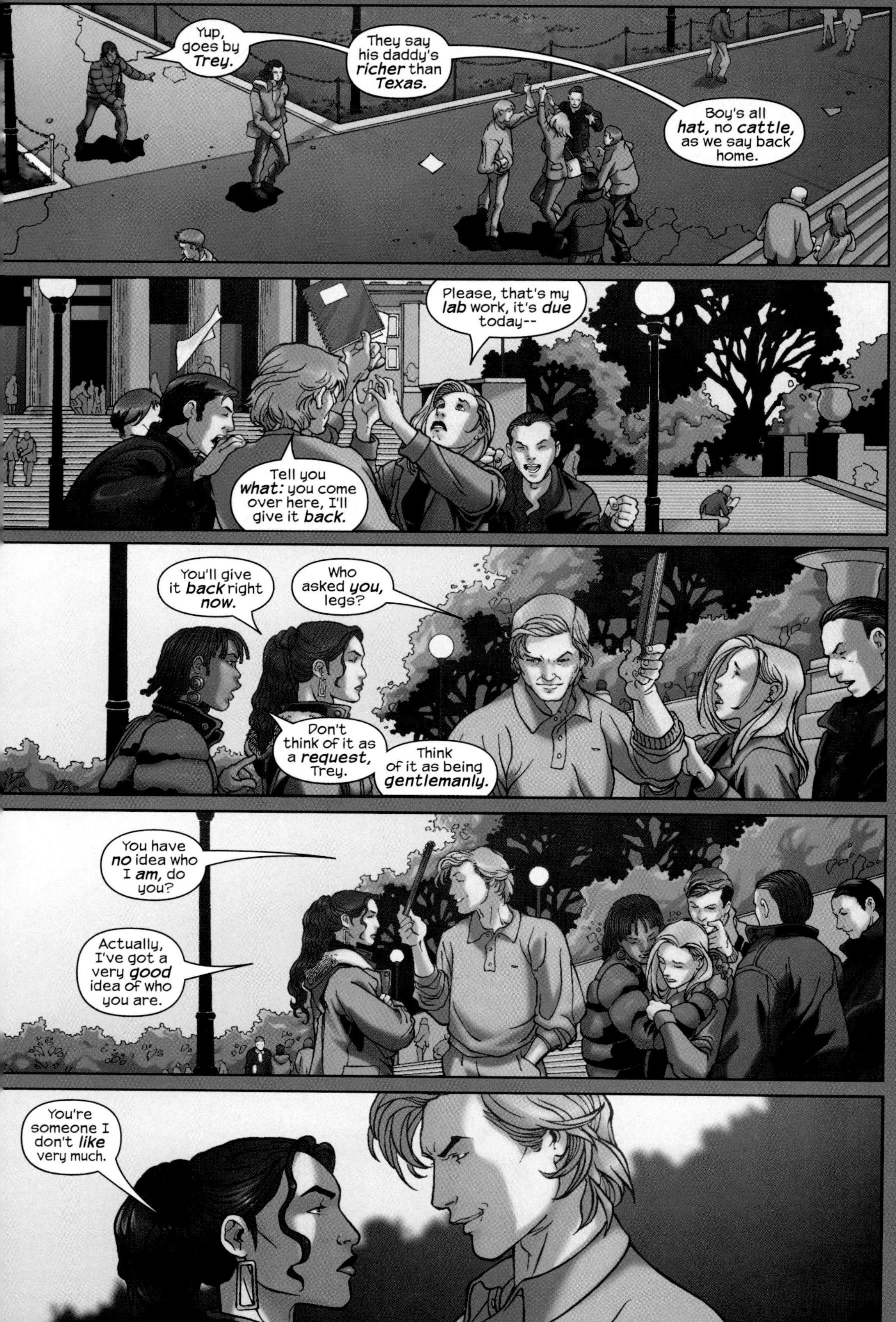
Yup, goes by *Trey.*
They say his daddy's *richer* than *Texas.*
Boy's all *hat,* no *cattle,* as we say back home.
Please, that's my *lab* work, it's *due* today--
Tell you *what:* you come over here, I'll give it *back.*
You'll give it *back* right *now.*
Who asked *you,* legs?
Don't think of it as a *request,* Trey.
Think of it as being *gentlemanly.*
You have *no* idea who I *am,* do you?
Actually, I've got a very *good* idea of who you are.
You're someone I don't *like* very much.

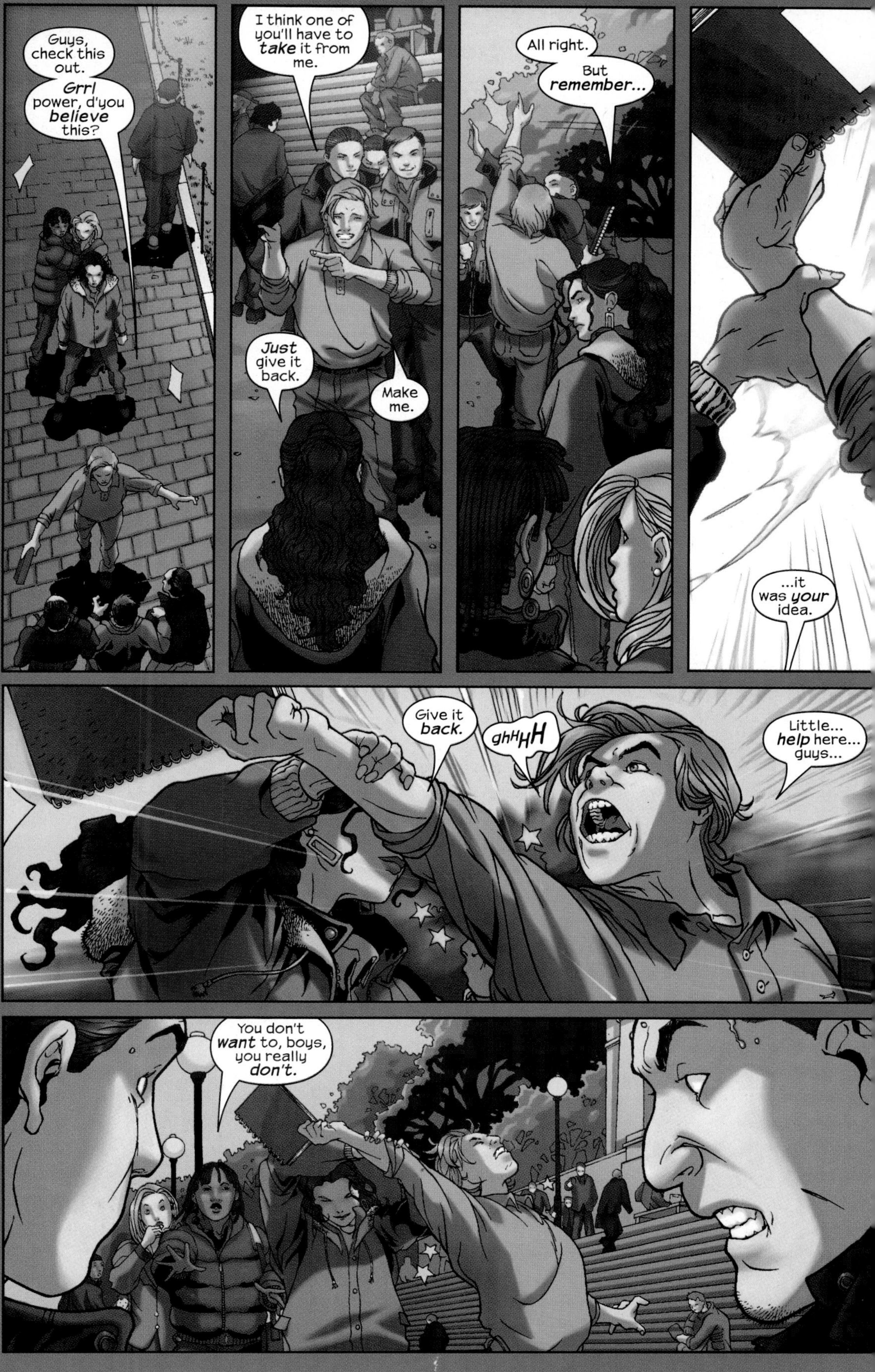

Guys, check this out.
Grrl power, d'you believe this?
I think one of you'll have to take it from me.
Just give it back.
Make me.
All right.
But remember...
...it was your idea.
Give it back.
ghHHH
Little... help here... guys...
You don't want to, boys, you really don't.

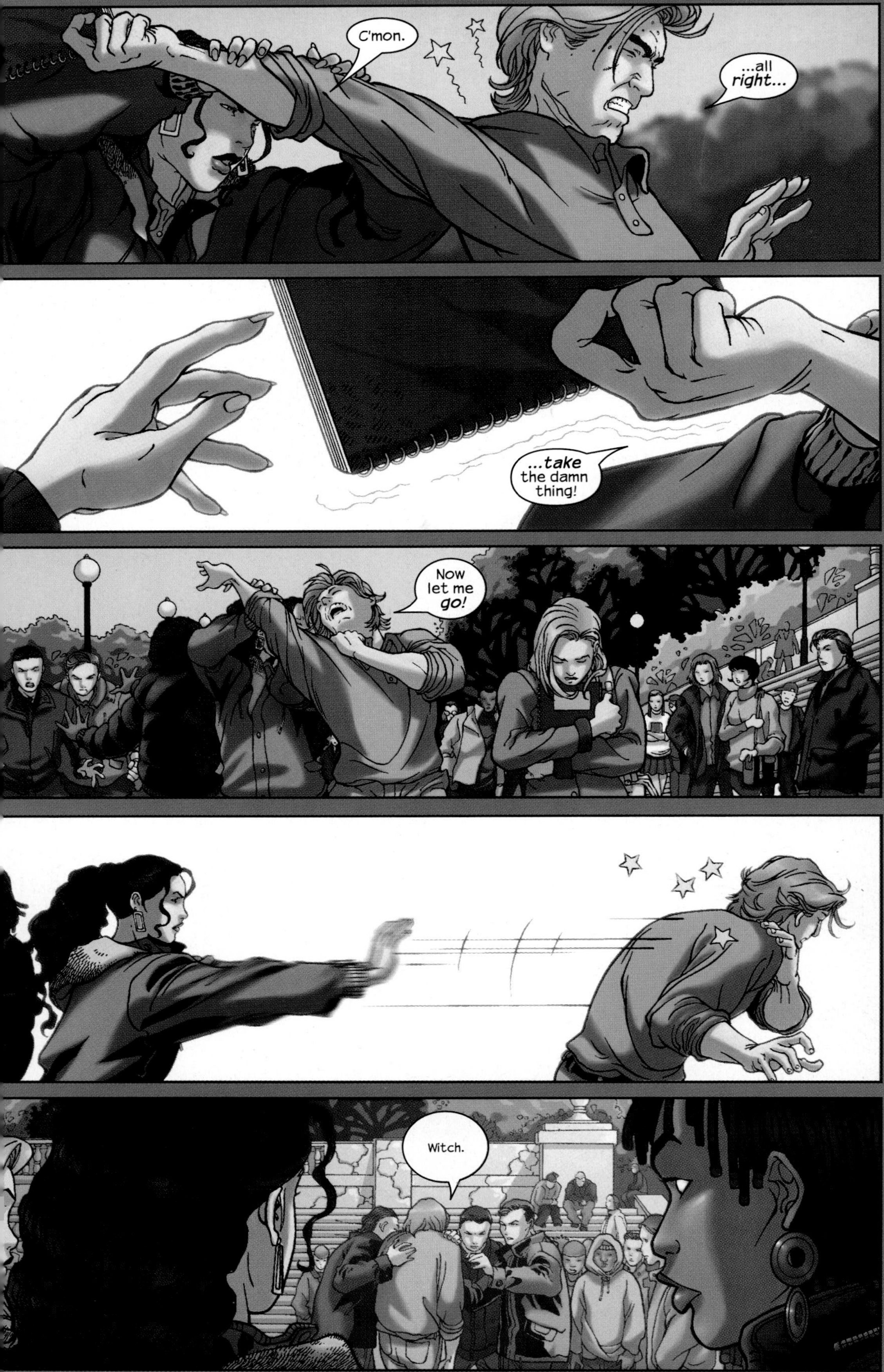
C'mon.
...all right...
...take the damn thing!
Now let me go!
Witch.

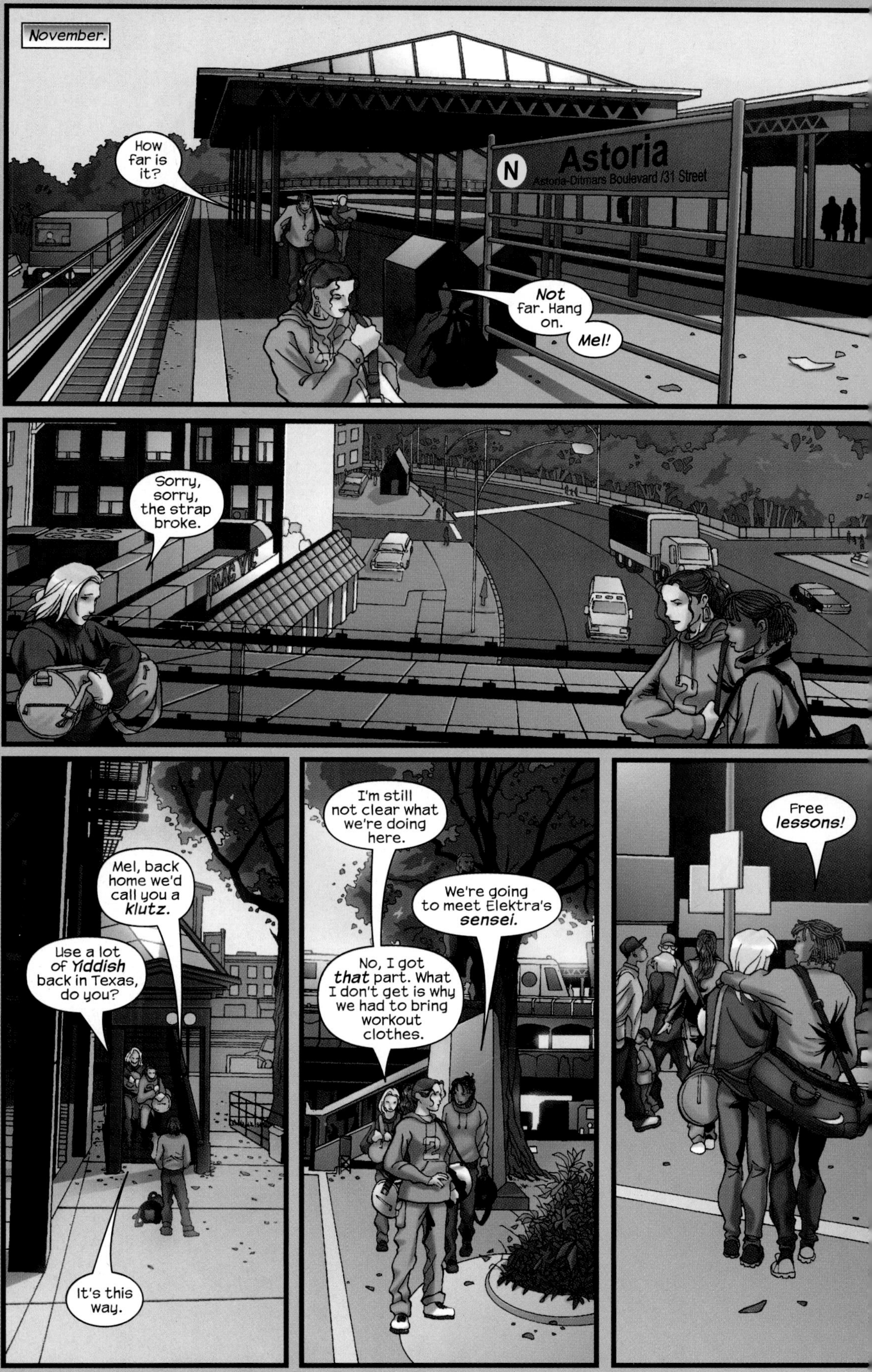
November.
How far is it?
Astoria
N
Astoria-Ditmars Boulevard /31 Street
Not far. Hang on.
Mel!
Sorry, sorry, the strap broke.
Mel, back home we'd call you a klutz.
Use a lot of Yiddish back in Texas, do you?
It's this way.
I'm still not clear what we're doing here.
We're going to meet Elektra's sensei.
No, I got that part. What I don't get is why we had to bring workout clothes.
Free lessons!

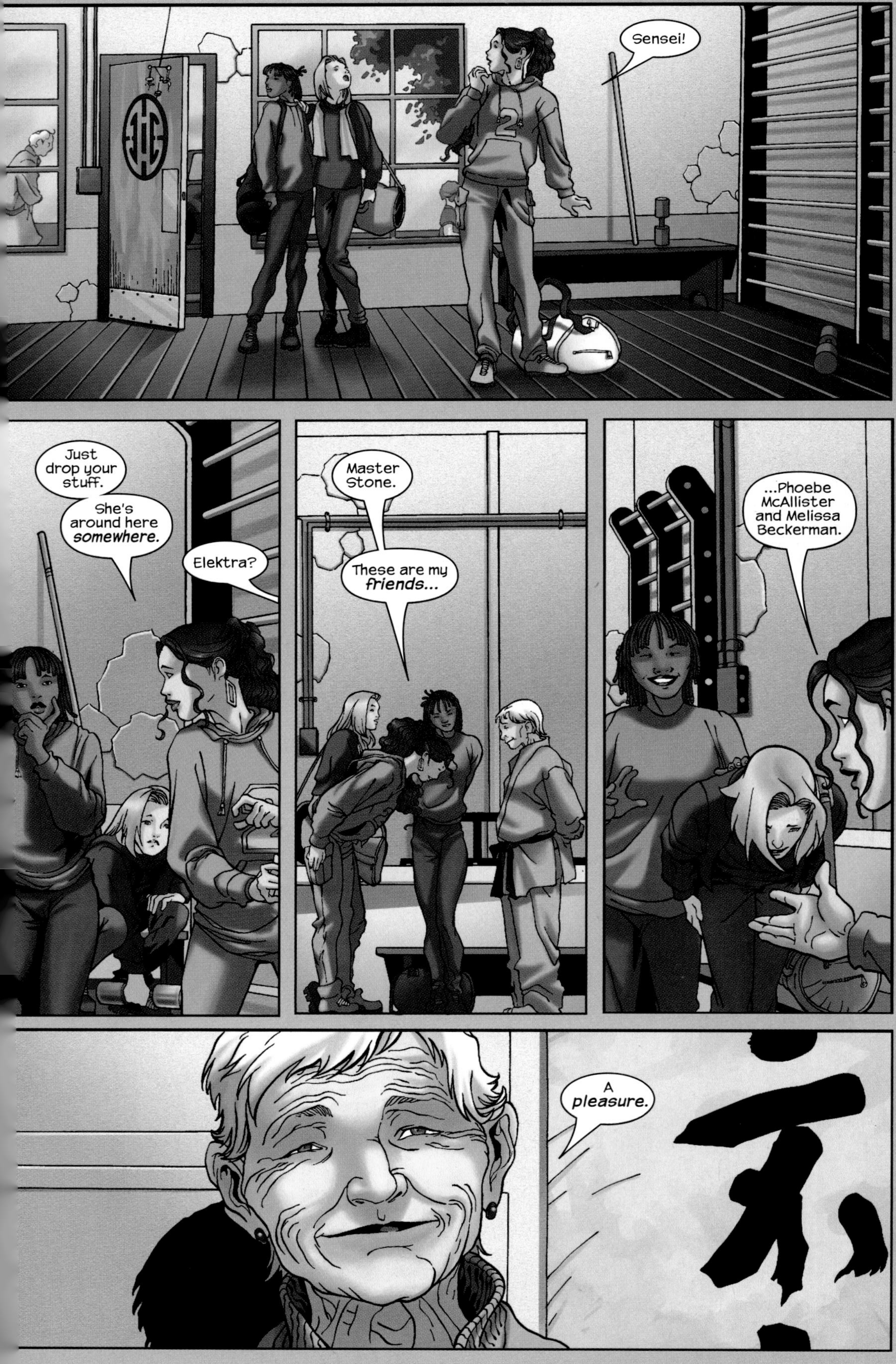
Sensei!
Just drop your stuff.
She's around here *somewhere.*
Elektra?
Master Stone.
These are my *friends...*
...Phoebe McAllister and Melissa Beckerman.
A *pleasure.*

No, too rigid. Hard *and* soft.

Flowing.

Flowing, *right.*

You *move* but with no *intention*, Phoebe.

Well, see, it's the *flowing* that kinda *loses* me.

Elektra.

Sensei?

Phoebe does not understand flow.

Demonstrate with me.

Hai, Sensei.

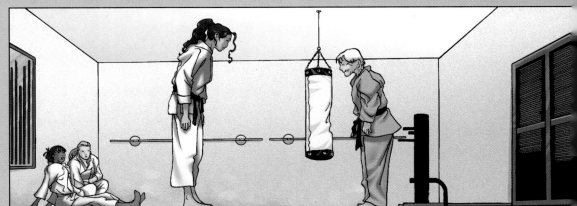

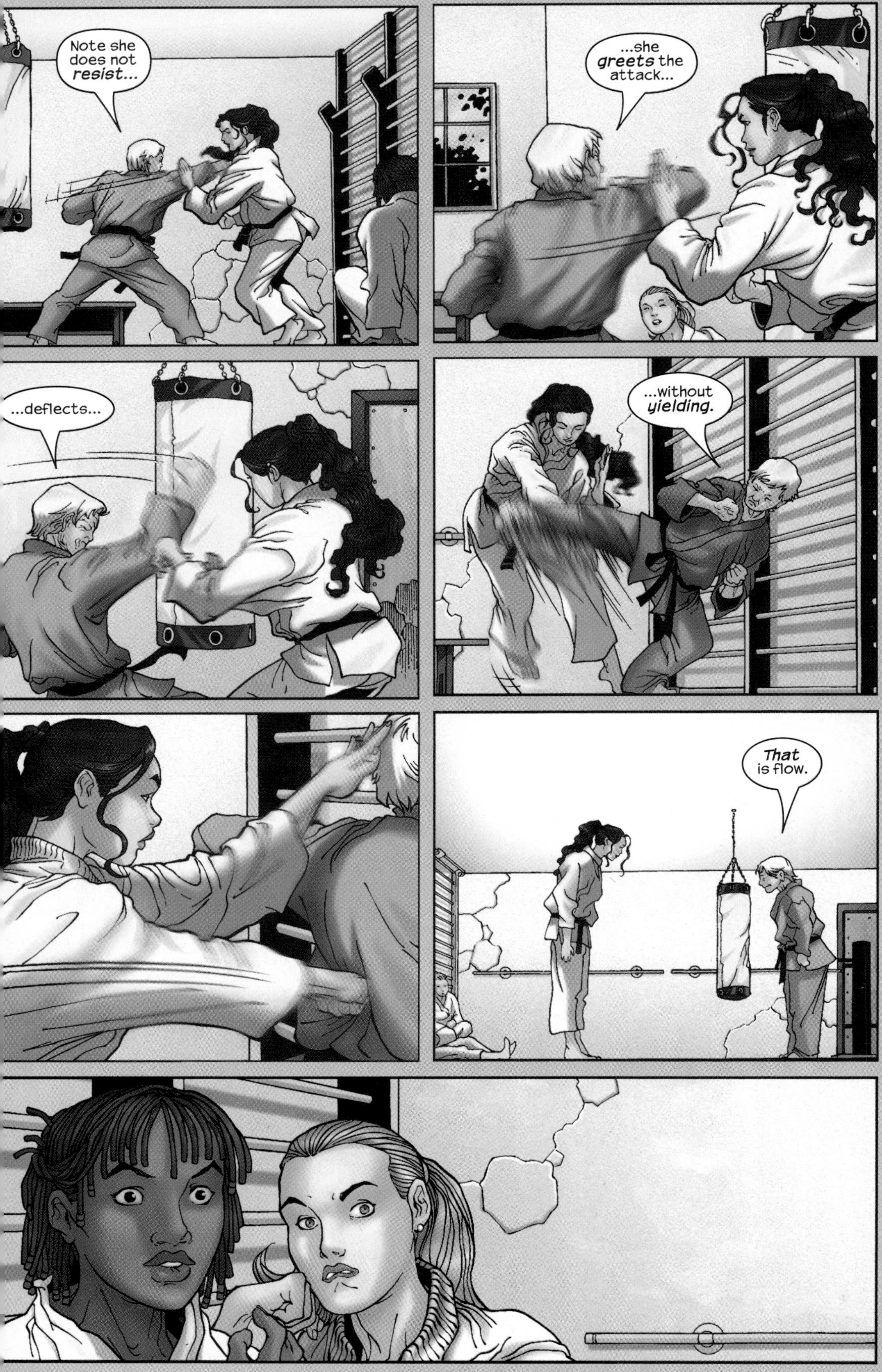
Note she does not *resist...*
...she *greets* the attack...
...deflects...
...without *yielding.*
That is flow.

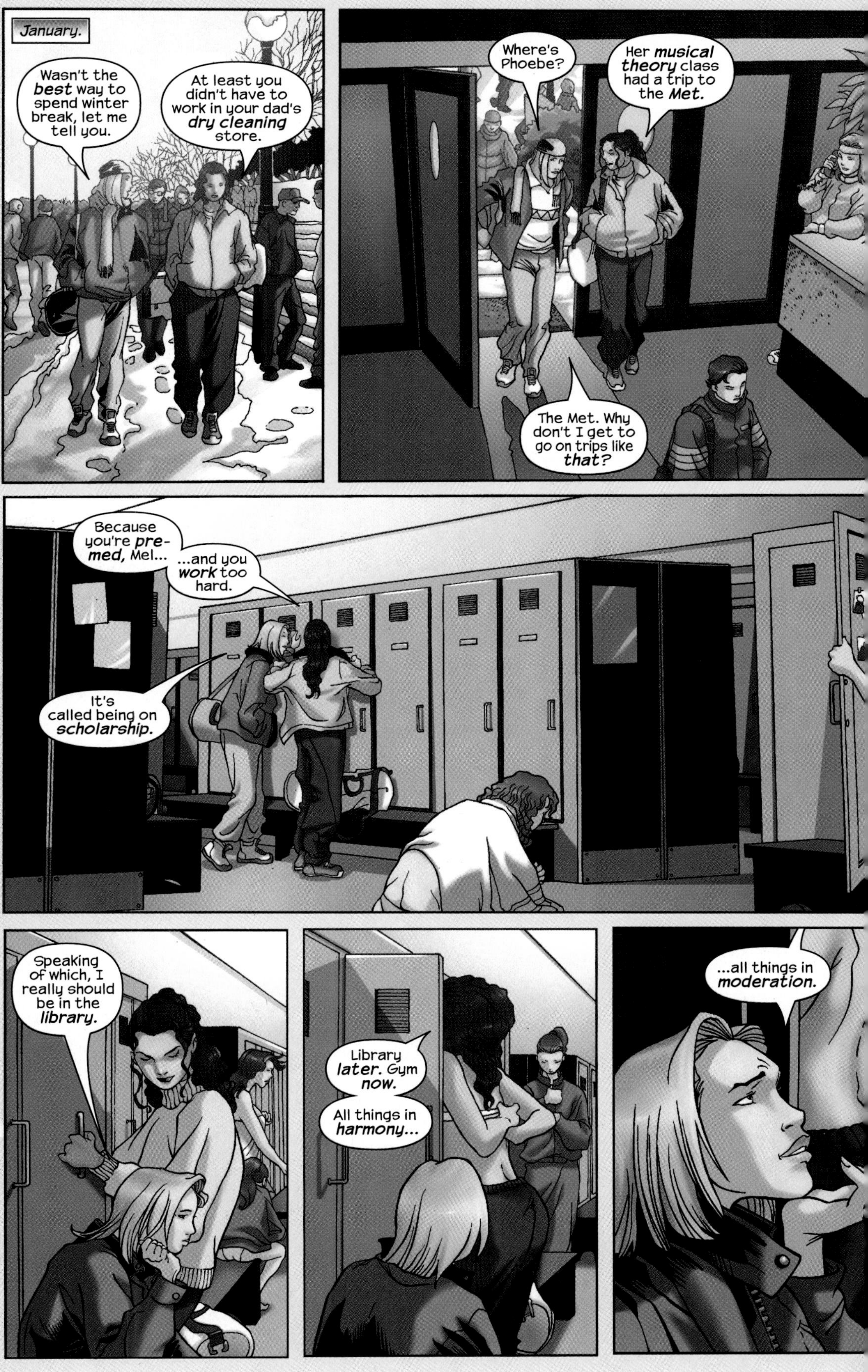
January.
Wasn't the best way to spend winter break, let me tell you.
At least you didn't have to work in your dad's dry cleaning store.
Where's Phoebe?
Her musical theory class had a trip to the Met.
The Met. Why don't I get to go on trips like that?
Because you're pre-med, Mel...
...and you work too hard.
It's called being on scholarship.
Speaking of which, I really should be in the library.
Library later. Gym now.
All things in harmony...
...all things in moderation.

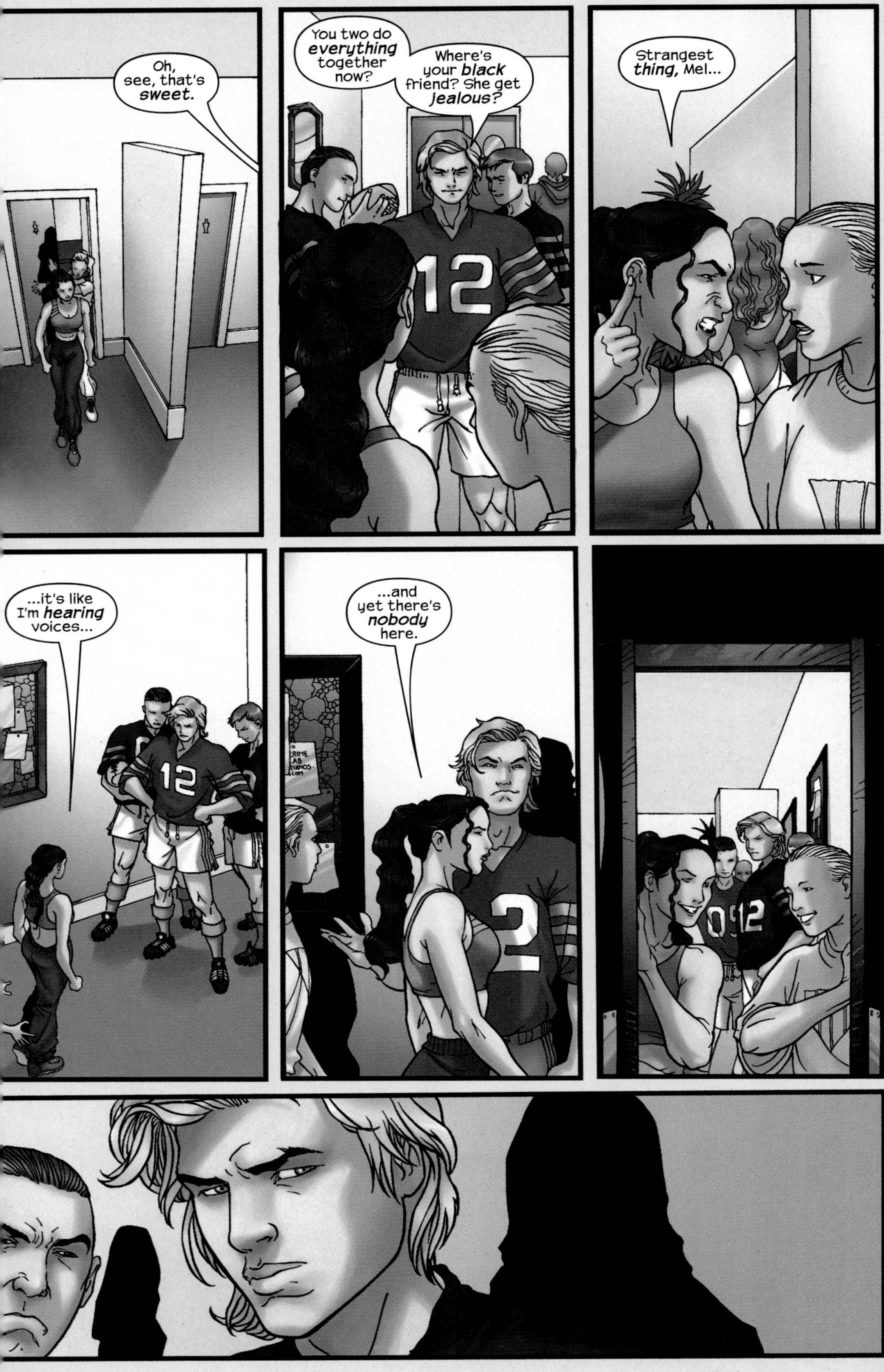
Oh, see, that's *sweet.*
You two do *everything* together now?
Where's your *black* friend? She get *jealous?*
Strangest *thing,* Mel...
...it's like I'm *hearing* voices...
...and yet there's *nobody* here.

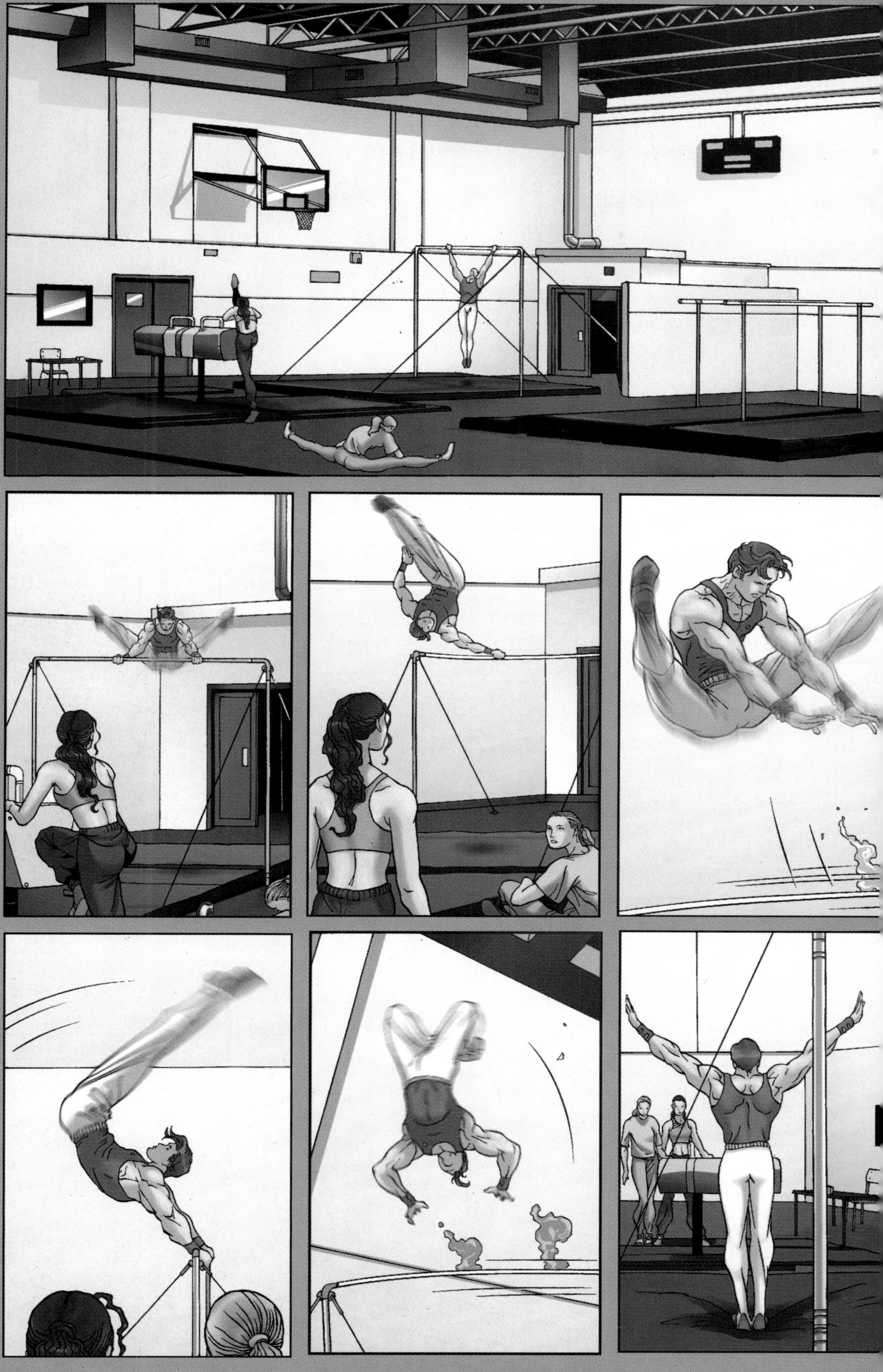

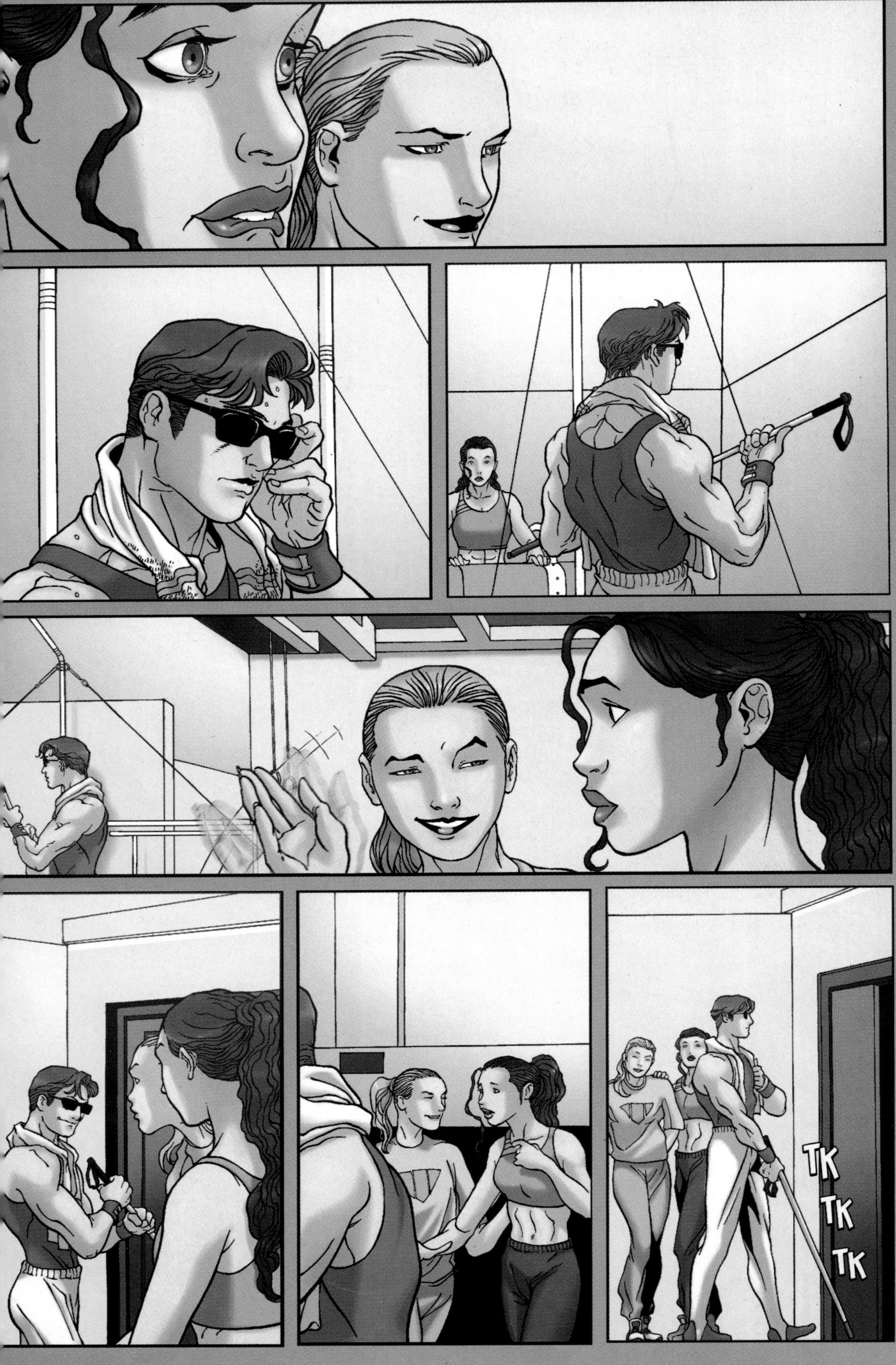
TK
TK
TK

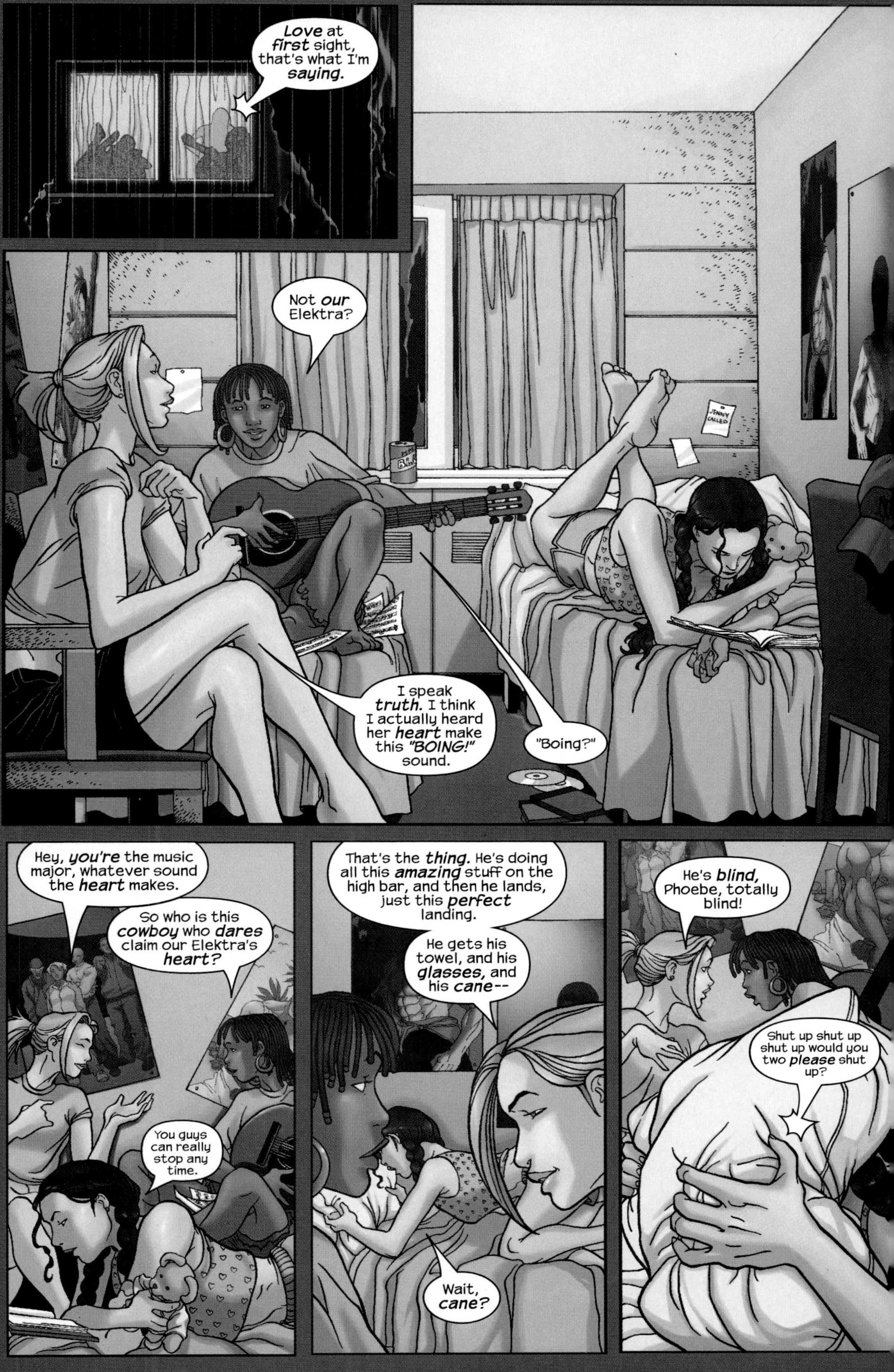
Love at first sight, that's what I'm saying.
Not our Elektra?
I speak truth. I think I actually heard her heart make this "BOING!" sound.
"Boing?"
JENNY CALLED
Hey, you're the music major, whatever sound the heart makes.
So who is this cowboy who dares claim our Elektra's heart?
You guys can really stop any time.
That's the thing. He's doing all this amazing stuff on the high bar, and then he lands, just this perfect landing.
He gets his towel, and his glasses, and his cane--
Wait, cane?
He's blind, Phoebe, totally blind!
Shut up shut up shut up would you two please shut up?

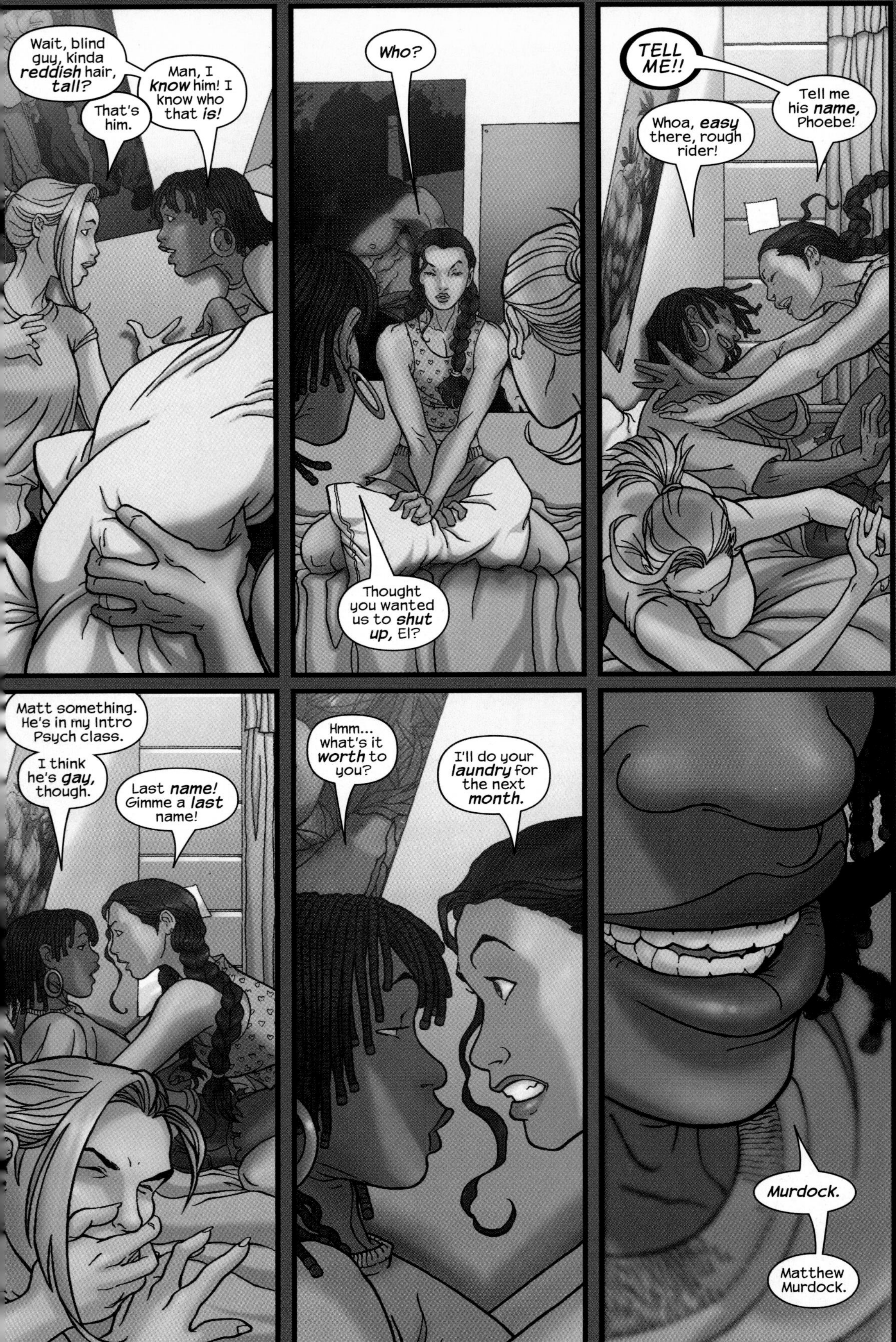
Wait, blind guy, kinda reddish hair, tall?
That's him.
Man, I know him! I know who that is!
Who?
Thought you wanted us to shut up, El?
TELL ME!!
Tell me his name, Phoebe!
Whoa, easy there, rough rider!
Matt something. He's in my Intro Psych class.
I think he's gay, though.
Last name! Gimme a last name!
Hmm... what's it worth to you?
I'll do your laundry for the next month.
Murdock.
Matthew Murdock.

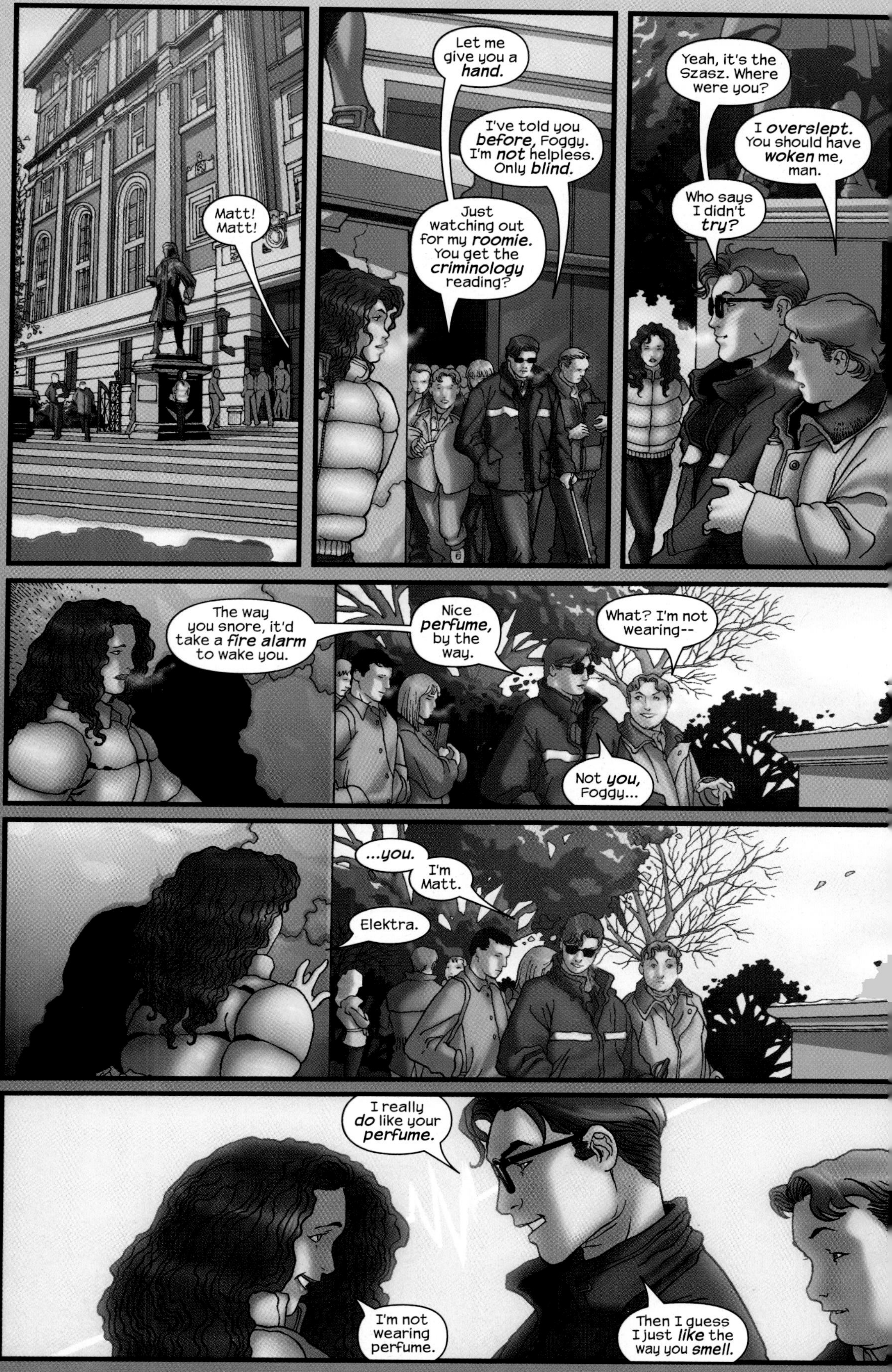
Matt! Matt!
Let me give you a hand.
I've told you before, Foggy. I'm not helpless. Only blind.
Just watching out for my roomie. You get the criminology reading?
Yeah, it's the Szasz. Where were you?
I overslept. You should have woken me, man.
Who says I didn't try?
The way you snore, it'd take a fire alarm to wake you.
Nice perfume, by the way.
What? I'm not wearing--
Not you, Foggy...
...you.
I'm Matt.
Elektra.
I really do like your perfume.
I'm not wearing perfume.
Then I guess I just like the way you smell.

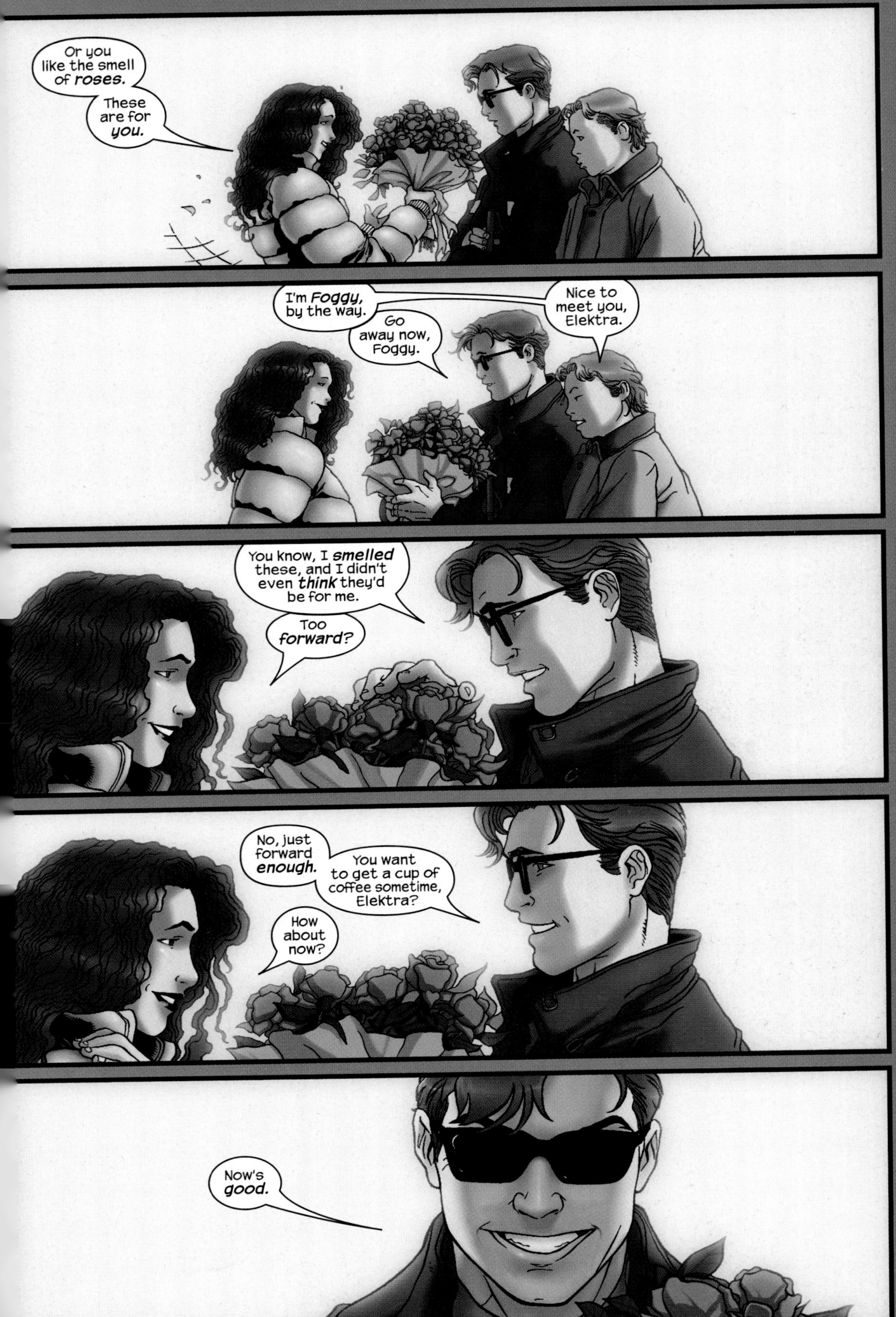
Or you like the smell of *roses.*
These are for *you.*
I'm *Foggy,* by the way.
Nice to meet you, Elektra.
Go away now, Foggy.
You know, I *smelled* these, and I didn't even *think* they'd be for me.
Too *forward?*
No, just forward *enough.*
You want to get a cup of coffee sometime, Elektra?
How about now?
Now's *good.*

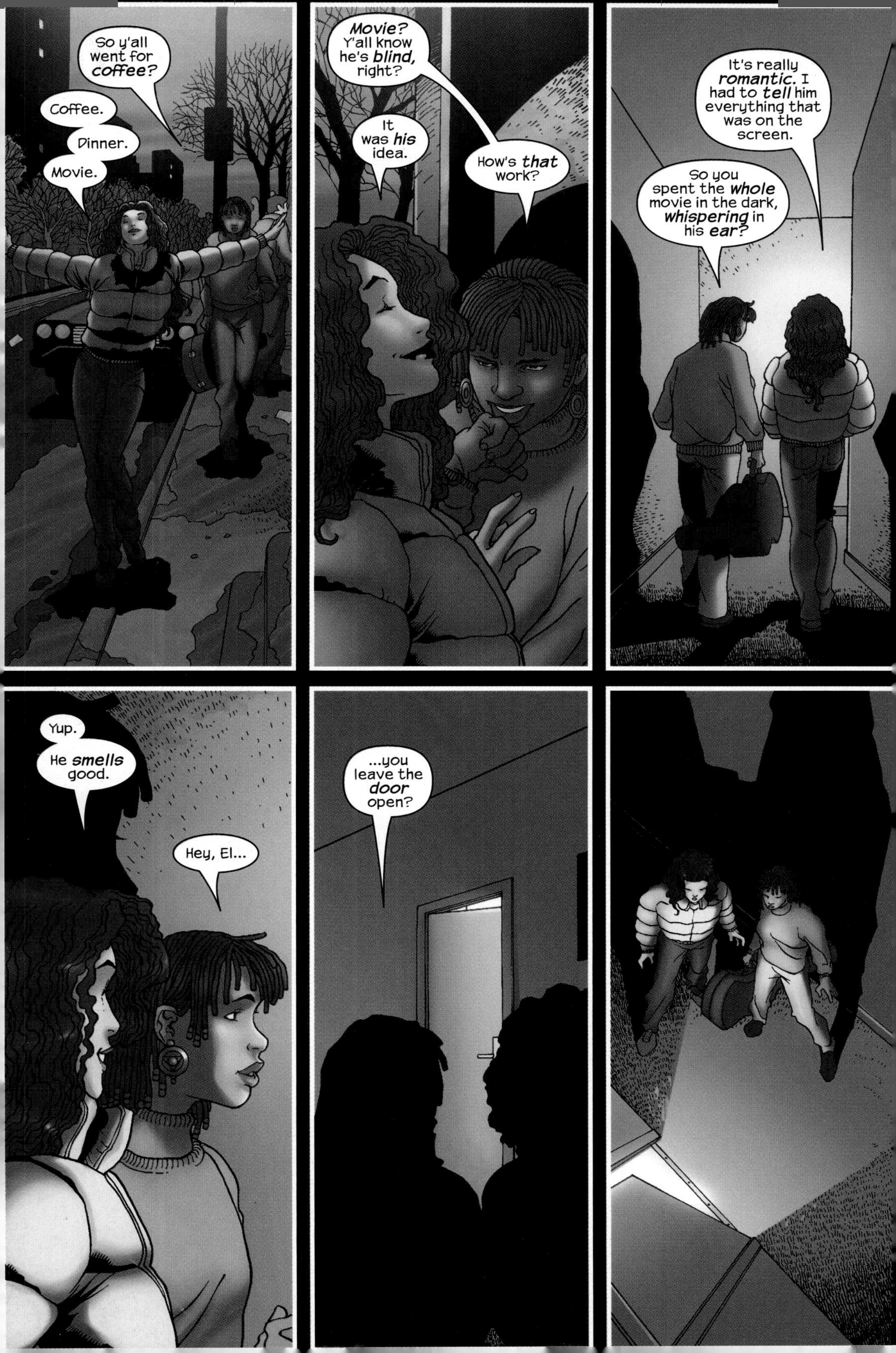
So y'all went for *coffee?*
Coffee.
Dinner.
Movie.
Movie? Y'all know he's *blind,* right?
It was *his* idea.
How's *that* work?
It's really *romantic.* I had to *tell* him everything that was on the screen.
So you spent the *whole* movie in the dark, *whispering* in his *ear?*
Yup.
He *smells* good.
Hey, El...
...you leave the *door* open?

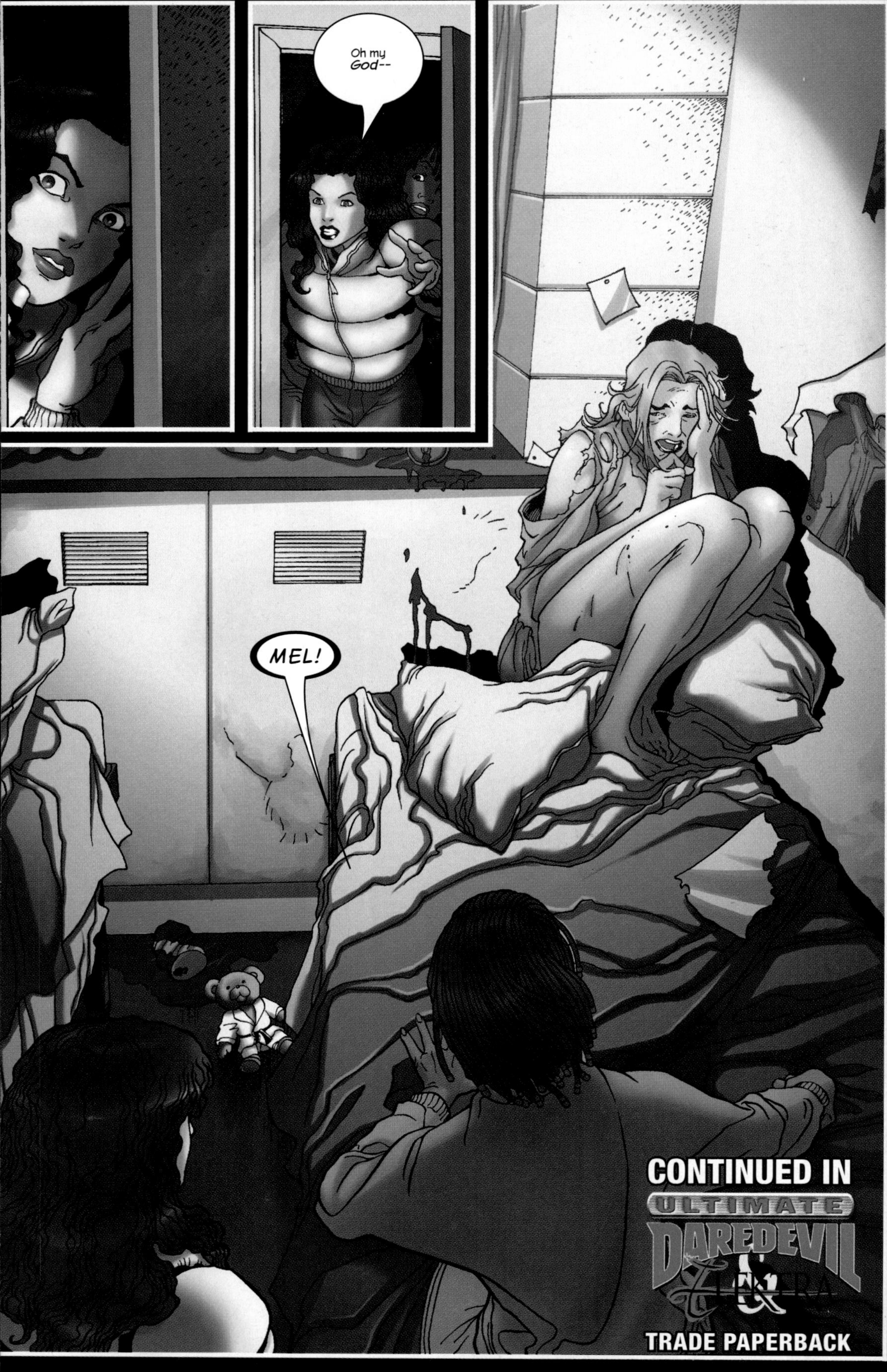

Oh my God--
MEL!
CONTINUED IN
ULTIMATE DAREDEVIL & ELEKTRA
TRADE PAPERBACK

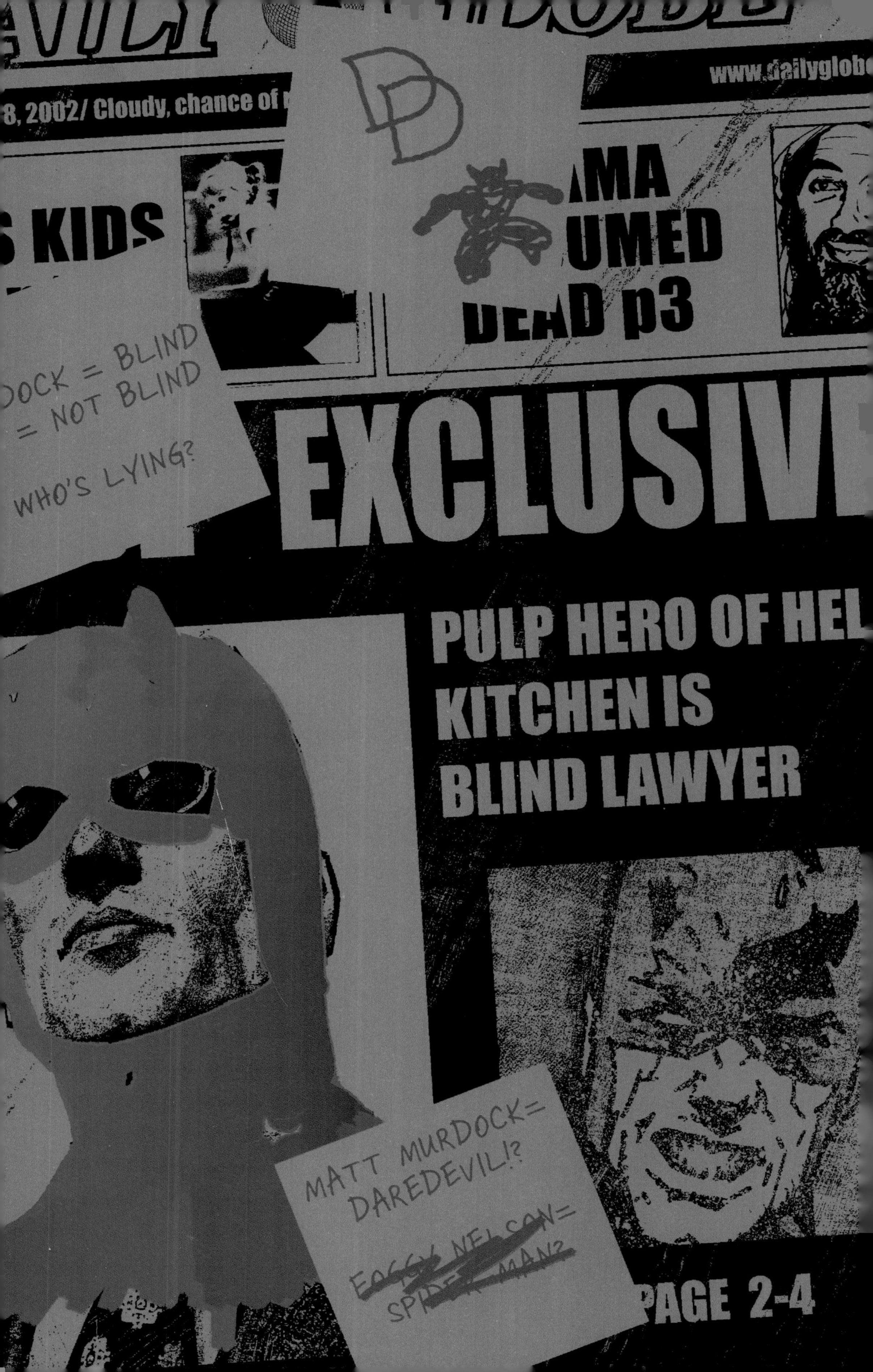

www.dailyglobe
8, 2002/ Cloudy, chance of
S KIDS
MA
UMED
DEAD p3
DOCK = BLIND
= NOT BLIND
WHO'S LYING?
EXCLUSIVE
PULP HERO OF HEL
KITCHEN IS
BLIND LAWYER
MATT MURDOCK=
DAREDEVIL!?
FOGGY NELSON=
SPIDER MAN?
PAGE 2-4

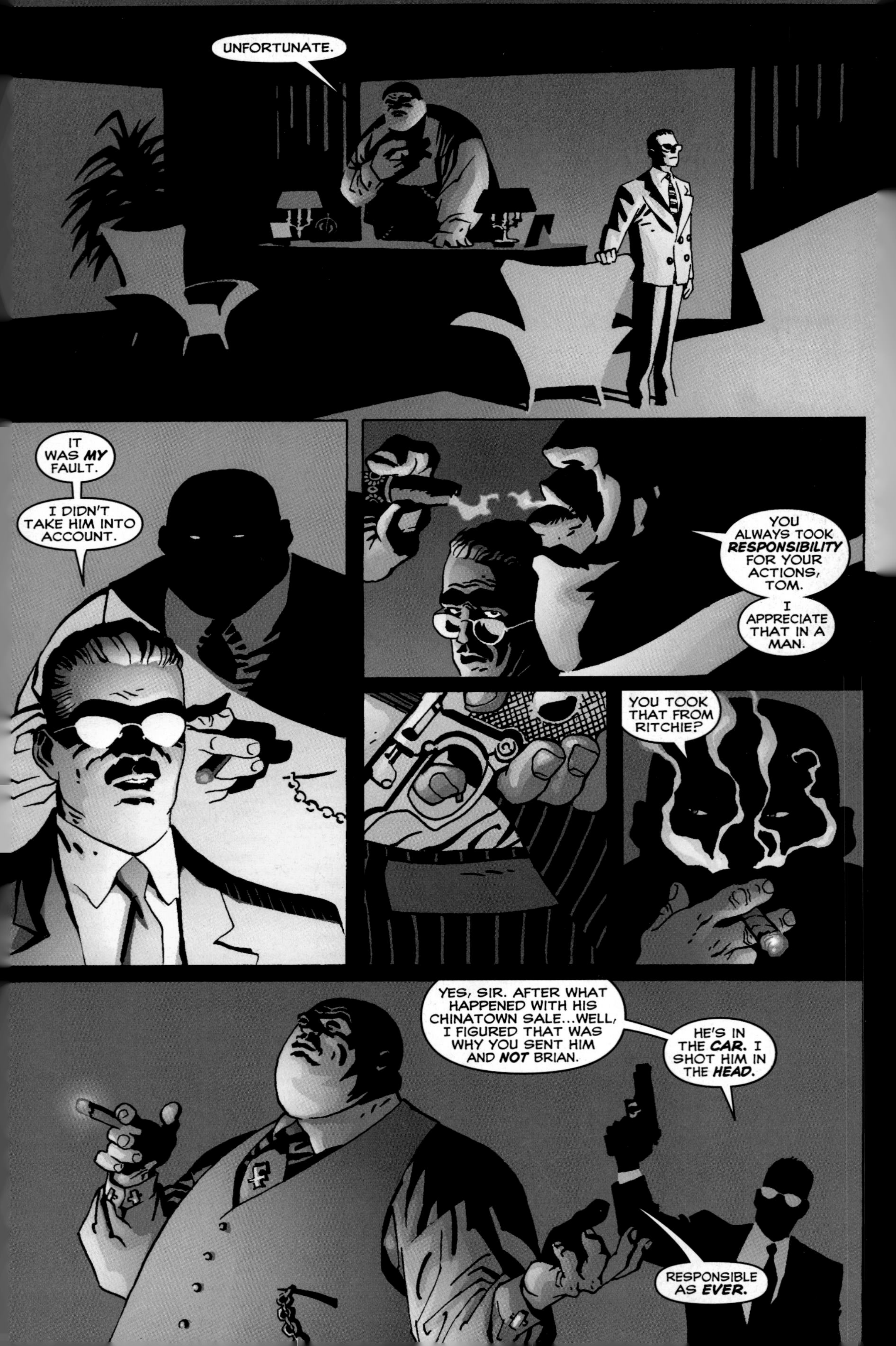
UNFORTUNATE.
IT WAS **MY** FAULT.
I DIDN'T TAKE HIM INTO ACCOUNT.
YOU ALWAYS TOOK **RESPONSIBILITY** FOR YOUR ACTIONS, TOM.
I APPRECIATE THAT IN A MAN.
YOU TOOK THAT FROM RITCHIE?
YES, SIR. AFTER WHAT HAPPENED WITH HIS CHINATOWN SALE...WELL, I FIGURED THAT WAS WHY YOU SENT HIM AND **NOT** BRIAN.
HE'S IN THE **CAR**. I SHOT HIM IN THE **HEAD**.
RESPONSIBLE AS **EVER**.

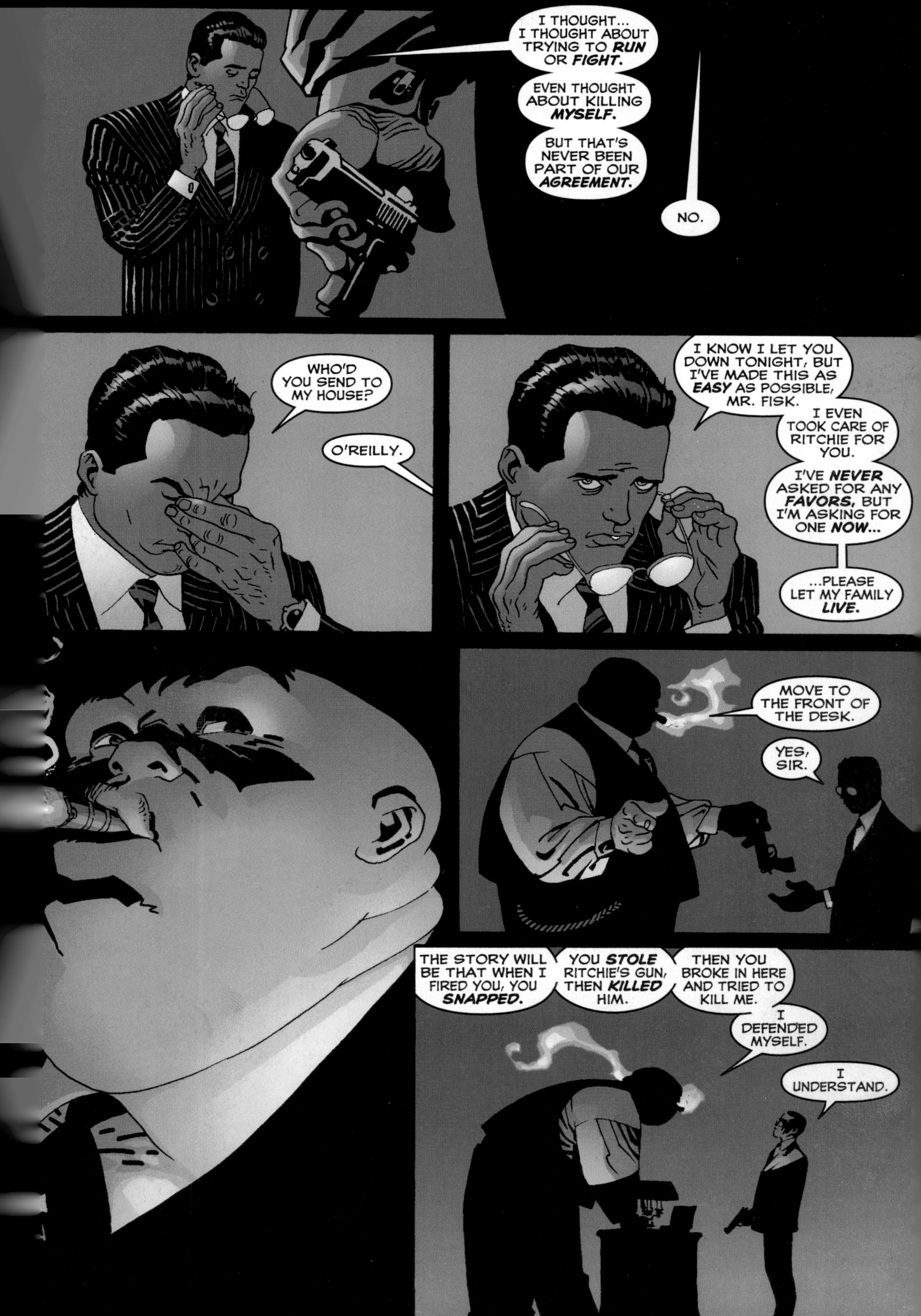
I THOUGHT... I THOUGHT ABOUT TRYING TO **RUN** OR **FIGHT**.
EVEN THOUGHT ABOUT KILLING **MYSELF**.
BUT THAT'S NEVER BEEN PART OF OUR **AGREEMENT**.
NO.
WHO'D YOU SEND TO MY HOUSE?
O'REILLY.
I KNOW I LET YOU DOWN TONIGHT, BUT I'VE MADE THIS AS **EASY** AS POSSIBLE, MR. FISK.
I EVEN TOOK CARE OF RITCHIE FOR YOU.
I'VE **NEVER** ASKED FOR ANY **FAVORS**, BUT I'M ASKING FOR ONE **NOW**...
...PLEASE LET MY FAMILY **LIVE**.
MOVE TO THE FRONT OF THE DESK.
YES, SIR.
THE STORY WILL BE THAT WHEN I FIRED YOU, YOU **SNAPPED**.
YOU **STOLE** RITCHIE'S GUN, THEN **KILLED** HIM.
THEN YOU BROKE IN HERE AND TRIED TO KILL ME.
I DEFENDED MYSELF.
I UNDERSTAND.

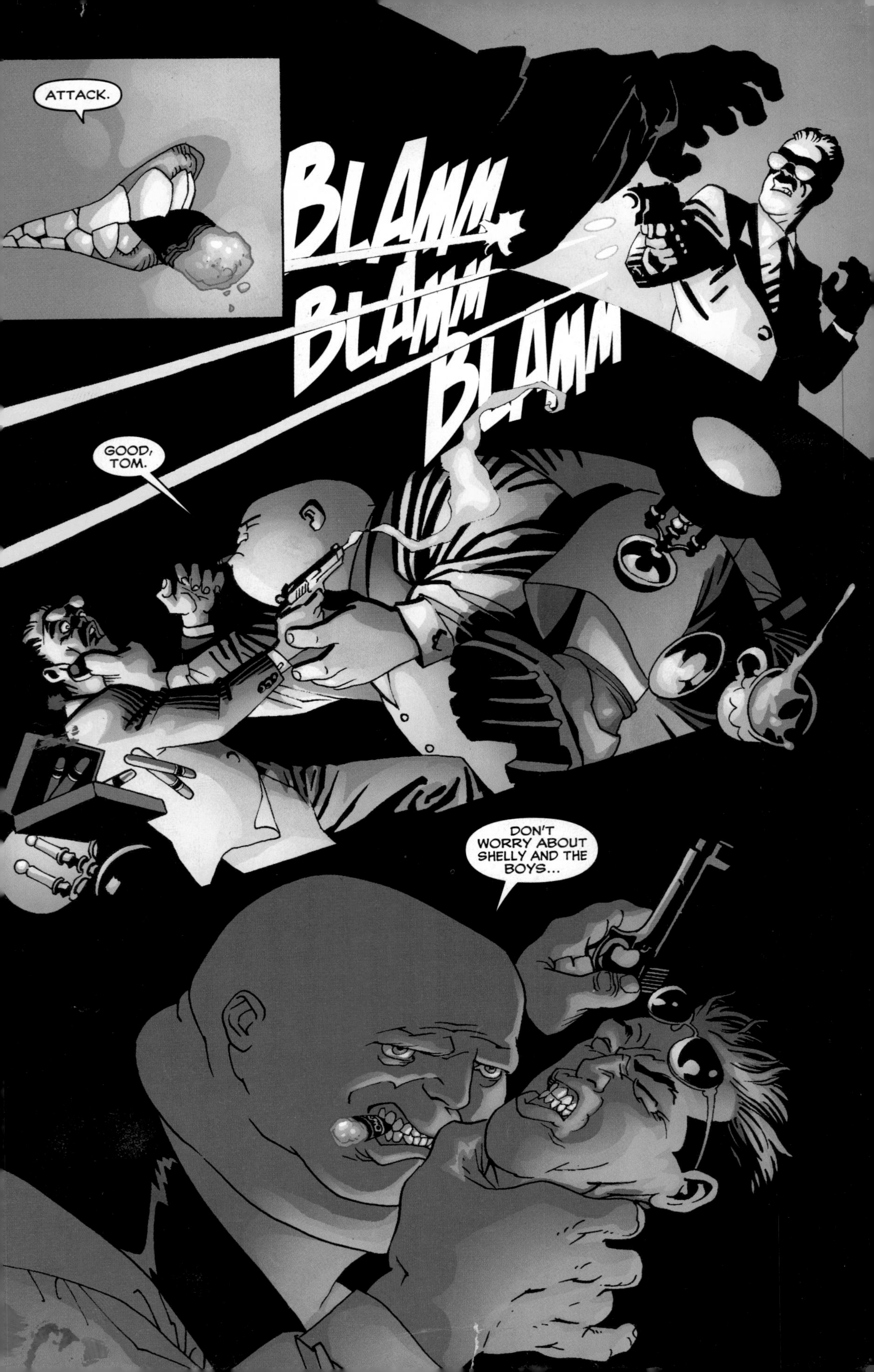
ATTACK.
BLAMM
BLAMM
BLAMM
GOOD, TOM.
DON'T WORRY ABOUT SHELLY AND THE BOYS...

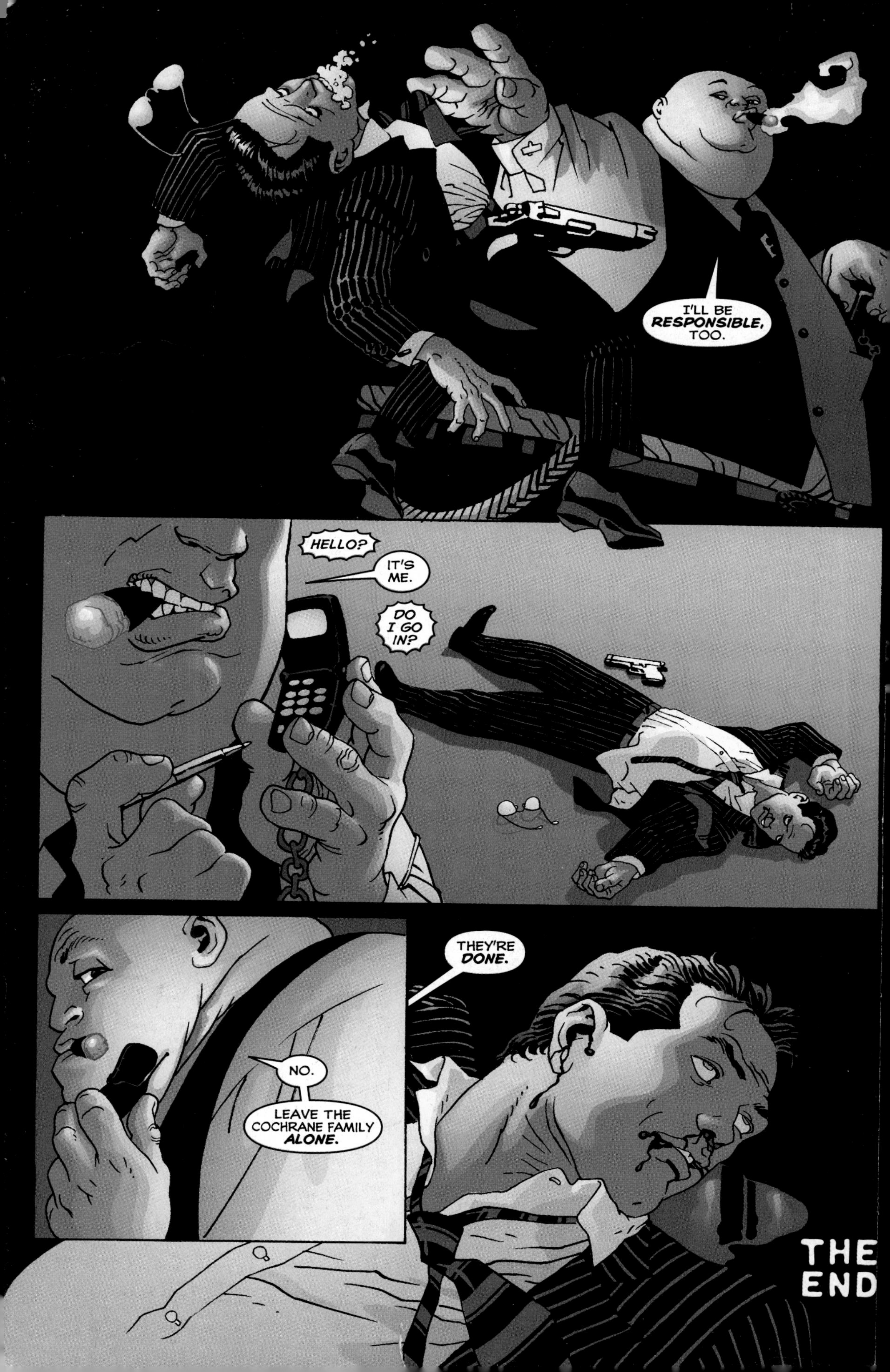
I'LL BE RESPONSIBLE, TOO.
HELLO?
IT'S ME.
DO I GO IN?
THEY'RE DONE.
NO.
LEAVE THE COCHRANE FAMILY ALONE.
THE END